ATLANTIC DISASTER

ATLANTIC DISASTER
The *Titanic* and Other Victims of the North Atlantic

RICHARD GARRETT

Time present and time past
Are both perhaps present in time future
And time future contained in time past.
If all time is eternally present
All time is unredeemable.

T.S. ELIOT, 'Burnt Norton', *Four Quartets*

BUCHAN & ENRIGHT, PUBLISHERS
LONDON

First published in 1986 by
Buchan & Enright, Publishers, Limited
53 Fleet Street, London EC4Y 1BE

British Library Cataloguing in Publication Data

Garrett, Richard
    Atlantic disasters: the *Titantic* and other victims of the
    North Atlantic.
    1. Disasters — North Atlantic Ocean — History —
    19th century   2. Disasters — North Atlantic
    Ocean — History — 20th century
    I. Title
    909'.09163'1   G525

ISBN 0-907675-57-3

Typeset in Great Britain by Leaper & Gard Ltd
Printed in Great Britain by
Biddles Ltd, Guildford

—For Anthony—

Contents

List of Illustrations

Ships' positions near the *Titanic*, 14–15 April 1912

Californian 00.15, 15 April
Samson
Frankfurt 09.40, 15 April
Titanic Foundered 02.20, 15 April
Mount Temple 22.25, 14 April
Carpathia 22.45, 14 April
Birma 23.55, 14 April

EDINBURGH
SHANNON
PLYMOUTH
PARIS
MADRID
LAJES
X

Greenland Current
Denmark Strait
1956
1919
1812

Oceanic Shetland Is
North Sea
British Isles
Belfast
Cobh Liverpool
Stat. Charlie
Air India 747 Fastnet Lusitania Falmouth
Volturno Suevic Cherbourg

MAIN SHIPPING LANES

EUROPE
Mediterranean Sea

Azores
Lakonia
OCEAN
Madeira
AFRICA
Canary Is

42°N
41°N
60 N
45 N
30 N
51°W   50°W   49°W
30°W   15°W   0°

Introduction

I am never quite certain why a book such as this should have an introduction. Is it that the author feels a need to explain why he wrote it? If this is the case, it would surely be better addressed to the publisher than to the public. Or is it, in the event of its being read in a shop, a suggestion that here is something worthy of being bought? But that, I have always imagined, is the job of the blurb on the jacket. It can put the case more briefly and more trenchantly. Or, again, is it to provide a background against which to set the narrative? To entrust it with such a responsibility is dangerous. Some people, admittedly, like to start at the very beginning and to study these preambles before getting down to the book itself. Others look at them as a kind of afterthought — having, one must suppose, enjoyed the work and wishing to be sure they haven't missed anything. The majority, however, do not read introductions at all.

Thus this is no place in which to print any facts that are essential to the story. The chances are that only a minority will discover them.

For what it may be worth, the idea for this particular project occurred to me during a conversation, when somebody wondered whether a disaster on the scale of the *Titanic* could happen nowadays. In theory, of course, it could. The unsinkable ship has still not been built; and, as the number of tankers and other bulk carriers lost at sea over the past dozen or so years shows, there are still captains (mostly employed by 'flag of convenience' firms) who, uncertain of their surroundings,

1

nevertheless blunder on until they eventually come to grief.

On the other hand, it is equally safe to say that, should such a disaster occur, there would be far fewer casualties. So far as the North Atlantic is concerned, the advances made in the field of search-and-rescue have, indeed, been remarkable. It is just as well; for, despite the fact that the world's population of passenger liners has diminished so considerably, the rage of the old ocean has not. Nor has there been a decline in the output of icebergs that drift down from the arctic regions, aimlessly and yet potentially deadly.

This, perhaps, is one reason why the fascination about the *Titanic* persists — and why, indeed, the discovery of the liner's remains at the beginning of September 1985 should have aroused such considerable excitement. During the Second World War, a well-placed shell from Germany's super-battleship *Bismarck* exploded in the magazine of HMS *Hood* and caused the death of 1,413 officers and ratings. In the case of the White Star liner, a chance encounter with a large slab of frozen water killed 1,490 people. Proportionately, of course, these figures are less impressive. Seven hundred and twelve survived the *Titanic* disaster; only three of the *Hood*'s complement were rescued. Nevertheless, there is something about this comparison that appeals to the darker side of one's imagination. The warship was destroyed by intent; the ocean greyhound by chance — or by accident, it doesn't much matter. It is not surprising that there have been innumerable attempts, not very successful, to turn the latter's sinking into a symbol of something.

But the scene is almost as dramatic as the ship. More vessels have been sunk in the North Atlantic, and more lives lost, than in any other of the seven seas. There may, conceivably, be more disagreeable tracts of ocean, but they are not populated by so many ships; they are not thoroughfares for trade between the world's most technically highly developed continents. Indeed, during both world wars (and never mind Jutland) the decisive naval battles were fought between submarines and surface ships in the deep waters of the Atlantic.

Several excellent books have been written about the *Titanic* and her encounter with the iceberg that came out of the night and then stole away back into the darkness. They go into immense detail; but, strangely perhaps, none has yet put the event into its historical context. Once you attempt to do this, you find yourself wandering off in several directions. It is, after all, necessary to study the development of steam navigation across the Atlantic — and, indeed, of navigation itself. In the day of the *Titanic*, it depended upon the very inexact science of dead reckoning — assisted by an occasional opportunity to obtain a more precise position by taking a star sight. Nowadays, there are radar, satellites, and a great deal of other very advanced technology available to the master mariner. But this is far from the end of it. To see the whole picture one must venture into the birthplace of icebergs — ideally to discover whence came the *Titanic*'s destroyer. And, above all things, it has been necessary to study other disasters.

This does not presume to be a work of scholarship, and consequently there is no bibliography. Some books have done no more than provide material for a paragraph here, a sentence there. *The Times Atlas of the Oceans* has been invaluable in this respect and also Jay Robert Nash's *Darkest Hours*. To anyone who has not yet read them, and wishes to study a particular subject or event in greater detail, I can recommend:

A Night to Remember by Walter Lord (Longman, Green & Co., 1956; reprinted in an illustrated edition by Penguin Books in 1978) — probably the best known of all the books about the *Titanic*. It was filmed in 1958 with the late Kenneth More as Second Officer Lightoller. *The Maiden Voyage* by Geoffrey Marcus (Manor Books, 1974; published in paperback by New English Library in 1976) — the most comprehensive account of the disaster, and as readable as Mr Lord's book. *The Titanic* by Wyn Craig Wade (Weidenfeld & Nicolson, 1980) — excellent on the American inquiry and on the press coverage in the United States. *The Sinking of the Titanic and Great Sea Disasters* edited by Logan Marshal and published in 1912 — a fascinating curiosity, if you can find a copy. It is lavishly illustrated and must be one of the earlier examples of an instant book (but the other 'great sea disasters' seem to have been mislaid by Mr Marshal). *Fourteen Minutes* by James Croall (Michael Joseph, 1978) — the sorry story of the *Empress of Ireland* which, when she sank in 1914, accounted for 1,024 lives; but which has never been described as the end of any epoch. *Collision Course* by Alvin Moscow (Longman, Green & Co., 1959) — the story of the *Andrea Doria/Stockholm* collision. *Lusitania* by Colin Simpson (Longman, 1972) — the original exposé of a probably scandalous business upon which all subsequent revelations must have been based. *Fire at Sea* by Thomas Gallagher — the disgraceful story of the *Morro Castle* in flames, which reads almost like a thriller, and, as a thriller should, takes the reader by surprise before it ends. *Some Ship Disasters and their Causes* by K.C. Barnaby — a virtual encyclopedia of maritime misfortune and folly written by an authority on naval architecture. *Adventure Unlimited* by Harold Waters (Hutchinson, 1956) — Mr Waters's account of his career in the United States Coast Guard; recommended for those who enjoy jolly good yarns. *The North Atlantic Run* by John Maxtone-Graham (also entitled *The Only Way to Cross*; Cassell, 1972) — a beautifully told history of it by an old Atlantic hand, albeit as a passenger. *The Liners* by Terry Coleman (Allan Lane, 1976) — a nicely illustrated history combining all the essential information with some fascinating asides for good measure (particularly good in its account of the legends that grew up about the *Titanic*). *Ocean Liners* by Robert Wall (Collins, 1978) — an informative text in a wonderfully well-designed volume: certainly the best illustrated work on the subject. The pictures are tremendous. *The Water Jump* by David Beaty (Secker & Warburg, 1976) — essential reading for anyone interested in man's attempts to conquer the Atlantic by air.

I have not included biographies of Guglielmo Marconi or Admiral Robert Fitzroy, of which there are several — nor one or two more technical works which have been essential to my understanding of modern navigational aids, but which would have little appeal to the general reader.

It is, perhaps, a small list, but much of the research has been done from newspaper accounts, old magazines, other books not mentioned here, records of courts of inquiry, and in interviews. I must especially thank:

Members of the United States Coast Guard; the Canadian Coast Guard; the International Ice Patrol; HM Coastguard (Department of Transport); Ministry of Defence (Air); the Passenger Shipping Association; Shell Tankers; Gdynia America Shipping Lines (London) Ltd; Polish Ocean Lines; the

Meteorological Office; Den Kongelige Grønlandske Handel; the International Maritime Organization; British Telecom; the Tudor House Museum, Southampton; the London Library; the National Maritime Museum; the Department of Transport Marine Library; Department of the US Air Force, Head-quarters Space Command; the Scott Polar Research Institute; and Lloyds Register of Shipping. Also Lieutenant-Colonel George Styles, GC for his account of the *QE2* bomb hoax; Miss Helen West for recollections of her late grandfather — who survived the *Titanic* disaster; Captain Telesfor Bielicz — master of the *Stefan Batory*; Mr Frank O' Shanohun; Mr Charles Haas, President of the Titanic Historical Society; Toby Buchan who helped to germinate the idea and then com-missioned the book; Dominique Enright who edited the manuscript so meticulously and sympathetically; and Mrs Betty Jenner who typed it.

There are, I dare say, mistakes and for these I am sorry. As I have said, this does not presume to be a definitive account of the subject. It is no more than an attempt to hold the reader's interest with the story of the never-ending war of Man versus the North Atlantic. The fact that the ghost of the *Titanic* tends to overshadow everything else is inevitable. That was the most appalling, saddest, story of them all.

Finally, when I was working on this book, the remains of the liner were discovered by the robot submarine *Argo*, developed by the American Oceanographic Institution for the United States Office of Naval Research, and, in this case, operated by the Woods Hole Oceanographic Institute of Massachusetts. This is referred to in 'Afterword'; but, at the time, there were doubts about who owned the wreck. Was it, for example, the property of the Crown? If this were so, and if one or another of the proposed salvage attempts succeeded, whatever came to the surface would be seized by the Government. During the last week of November 1985, the matter was resolved by the Admiralty Court in London. No, it seemed, the Government would have no such entitlement. This was immediately taken as a sign that nothing but the ocean and the obviously infirm condition of the ship were likely to impede those who planned to raise her.

However, a number of voices were raised in protest. Mr

Haas summed up the views of many when he said, 'Those who lost relatives on the *Titanic* feel strongly that the ship should be left alone. It would be like disturbing a cemetery. If it is not the literal resting place of 1,500 souls, then it is the symbolic resting place.'

Dr Robert Ballard, the senior marine scientist at the Woods Hole Oceanographic Institute, took a very similar view. Whatever the aspiring salvage experts may claim, it seems impossible that the White Star liner is in any state to be lifted through two and a half miles of water. On the other hand, it would not be impossible to pillage the wreck and, later, to sell off the items (or fragments) as souvenirs. Any such idea seems to me deplorable. This, surely, is a mass grave. To loot it for squalid commercial purposes would be an act of profanity. For God's sake give the ocean best; and let the dead sleep on undisturbed.

—1—

The Liner's Story

The quartermaster in the wheelhouse at first mistook the berg for a windjammer with all her sails set; and then realized his mistake. Hs estimated its height as 100 feet. The captain and first officer were sure they saw 'a small black mass, not rising very high out of the water' — though, to others such as the quartermaster, it appeared much larger. No two accounts of the impact were precisely the same. One passenger likened the sound to that of 'tearing a long strip of calico'. A party of men in the smoking room caught a brief glimpse of the iceberg. One of them made a joke about going out on deck, and topping up his glass of Scotch with ice. The chairman of the liner's owners was aware that his ship had struck something, but he wasn't sure what. Perhaps his vagueness was understandable; he had been asleep at the time. The second officer, also aroused from slumber, described 'a sudden, vibrating, jar'. A famous banker, one of an investment of millionaires on board, was advised to put on his life-jacket. The precaution, he sharply retorted, was unnecessary. The *Titanic*, as everyone knew, was unsinkable.

But the unsinkable sank. The process did, admittedly, take the better part of three hours — plenty of time for everyone to escape the consequences in a well-ordered ship adequately provided with lifeboats. But, in this respect at least, the *Titanic* was neither well-ordered nor sufficiently equipped. In any case,

7

to deserve the adjective 'unsinkable', a damaged ship should remain afloat for rather longer than three hours.

The White Star Line never advertised the *Titanic* as having this impossible property. Her master, Captain Edward J. Smith, had inspired the concept of unsinkability some years earlier, when he assumed command of the recently commissioned *Adriatic*. A reporter had questioned him on the possibility of its foundering in really bad weather. Rather pompously, and obviously without giving the matter sufficient thought, he replied, 'Modern shipbuilding has gone beyond that.' It is easy to excuse this as the unguarded reply of a man with many other things on his mind. Nevertheless, if such was the case, Captain Smith should have dodged the question — or at least qualified his answer. After all, storm and tempest are not the only hazards a ship encounters. Collision, fire, going aground — there are several others. In any case, modern shipbuilding had not progressed in this respect since the day when, fifty-two years earlier, Brunel's *Great Eastern* had departed on her maiden voyage to New York. Indeed, if the construction of the *Titanic* were to be compared to that of the *Great Eastern*, it had gone backwards.

But Captain Smith did not actually *use* the word 'unsinkable'; he merely implied it. The first occasion on which it was attributed to the *Titanic* was in a souvenir supplement produced by the magazine *Shipping World*. But, to give him his due, the writer qualified it with 'practically'. The popular press, less scrupulously concerned with accuracy, ignored this reservation, and raptured about the sheer indestructibility of what — for the time being — was the world's largest ship.

Thus the *Titanic*'s bubble reputation spread, and the White Star Line, no doubt grateful for this gratuitous piece of public relations, did nothing to deny it. It was, after all, the greatest compliment anyone could pay a ship — and the most silly. But, then, the White Star Line was in the throes of hubris. It is a state of mind that, as every well-informed ancient Athenian knew, carries a penalty clause.

When the *Titanic* cast off from the quayside at Southampton on 10 April 1912, steamships had been running regular passenger and freight services across the North Atlantic for all of eighty years. In 1819 the *Savannah*, which had been built for nothing more ambitious than the United States coastal trade, and in which the 90-hp steam-engine had been added as an afterthought, crossed from Savannah, Georgia, to Liverpool, Lancashire, in 27 days and 11 hours. She admittedly made the greater part of the voyage under canvas (only six days with assistance from her engines: for the rest of the trip, her paddle-wheels were unshipped to improve her sailing qualities), and there were no passengers on board. Indeed, the reason for the trip was that her owners were hoping to sell her. (There were no takers: Tsar Alexander I expressed interest, but offered no cash.) Still, steam had played a modest part in her achievement. Symbolically, her captain was afterwards presented with an inscribed silver kettle.

Had he been alive at the time, the *Savannah*'s achievement would have delighted a Philadelphia engineer named John Fitch. In 1787 Mr Fitch built a somewhat rudimentary steamship, propelled by a strange arrangement of vertical paddles, that plied for hire on the Delaware. But this far-sighted American realized that there were greater things to come. In a letter to a friend — requesting a loan of £50 — he wrote: 'This, sir, whether I bring it to perfection or not, will be the mode of crossing the Atlantic, in time, for packets and armed vessels.' Later, he told two visitors, 'Well, gentlemen, although I shall not live to see the time, you will, when steamboats will be preferred to all other means of conveyance, especially for passengers.' His audience was not convinced. Afterwards, one was heard to remark to the other, 'Poor fellow — what a pity he is crazy!'

In August 1833 the 800-ton *Royal William* did rather better. With eight passengers on board, she sailed from Quebec, stopped at Picton, Nova Scotia, to take on coal, and was sighted off Cowes on the Isle of Wight three weeks later. But, then, she had a 200-hp engine. It is, perhaps, significant that the *Royal William*'s owners were a firm named the Quebec and Halifax Steam Navigation Company. One of the directors was a Nova Scotian business man named Samuel Cunard.

Five years later, a race (if such it could be called) took place between two steamers making the journey from east to west. They were unevenly matched. One, the *Sirius*, had been built for trade across the Irish Sea. The other, the *Great Western*, was considerably more advanced in concept, capacity, and power. Her creator, Isambard Kingdom Brunel, had designed her specifically for the North Atlantic — with the idea of extending his other masterpiece, the Great Western Railway, from its terminus at Bristol all the way to New York.

Sirius weighed in at about 700 tons; the *Great Western*, at 1,340 tons. Despite the fact that *Sirius* was carrying 40 passengers in addition to her crew of 35, her accommodation was as basic as might have been expected of a cross-channel steamer. The *Great Western*, on the other hand, gave intimations of greater luxuries to come.

From a betting point of view, *Great Western* had to be accounted the favourite — not only for making the fastest passage, but also as the ship most likely actually to reach New York. Nevertheless, on the eve of departure, the odds suddenly tilted in favour of the smaller vessel.

The *Great Western* slipped her moorings in the Thames three days after the *Sirius* had departed. However, her master, Lieutenant James Hosken, RN, knew that his rival intended to replenish his supply of coal at Cork. This diversion, he considered, would give him ample time in which to overtake the smaller ship and, indeed, to gain a substantial lead.

It might have done, had it not been for one of those strokes of misfortune that bedevilled Brunel's shipbuilding endeavours. The *Great Western* was off Leigh in the Thames estuary when fire broke out in the foreward stoke-hold and engine-room. Captain Christopher Claxton, a director of the line, was standing in the boiler-room, discussing the situation with the chief engineer, when a figure tumbled down on to him and knocked him over. It had, apparently, fallen through the hatchway, eighteen feet above, and now lay in an insensible heap in the bilge.

Claxton dragged the man to a place that seemed to be more safe, and called for a rope. As the victim was hauled up, Claxton was able to make out his identity. It was none other than Brunel himself. It transpired that he had been on his way down to the boiler-room, when a partially burned rung of the ladder gave way. If Claxton hadn't broken his fall, it would almost certainly have been the end of Brunel — and, indeed, of any originality in shipbuilding concept for at least a couple of decades.

Happily, neither the injuries of Brunel nor those of his ship turned out to be serious. The blaze had been started by some lagging and red lead that were too close to the steamer's funnel. It set fire to the wooden deck beams and to the underside of the planking supported by them. Hosken's reaction to the apparent emergency had been to run the ship on to a mud bank off Canvey Island. Here, Brunel was taken ashore by boat, and the damage was made good. The *Great Western* floated off on the evening tide. A week later, she docked at Bristol.

Originally, 57 passengers had booked accommodation in her at 35 guineas a head. Unfortunately, reports of the ship's apparent tendency to auto-ignite (exaggerated, naturally) had arrived ahead of her, and fifty people promptly cancelled their passages. When, on 8 April, she headed down the Severn on her way to the ocean, there were no more than seven lonely souls to fill her echoing halls and listen attentively to the thump of her paddle-wheels.

The *Sirius* had been faring better, though her master, Lieutenant Roberts, RN, had not been without worries. As the little steamer rounded the south-eastern corner of Ireland she ran into strong headwinds approaching storm force. The sea seemed to be so large, the ship so small, and the gale so furious, that a wet, sick and thoroughly miserable deputation of crew and passengers approached Roberts. This, the ringleader explained, was far from what had been in their minds when they agreed to cross the ocean. Would Lieutenant Roberts, as a man of compassion, kindly put back to Cork and release them from the ordeal?

History is niggardly in its portrait of Roberts. He was, we must assume, an able commander: a man who, when the occasion required it, could assume a stern posture. He assumed it now to such good effect that the rebels, thoroughly chastened, returned to their quarters, mutely accepting the doom that appeared inevitable.

Lieutenant Roberts, assisted by his unquiet crew and accompanied by his anxious passengers (who were fervently praying that God would, indeed, bless this ship and all who sailed in her) battled on against the equinoctial westerlies. After 3,000 miles, supplies of coal ran short. The story goes that, to complete the voyage, it was necessary to burn the panelling in the cabin, all the furniture, and one child's doll. In fact, this is to do Roberts and his engineer less than justice. One or two unimportant items on the cargo manifest were thrown overboard to lighten the ship. Apart from that, prudent management brought *Sirius* safely to New York with 15 tons of fuel remaining in her bunkers.

She docked on the morning of 23 April. The crossing had taken 19 days. That afternoon, the *Great Western* arrived. It was 15 days and five hours since she had left Bristol, and she still had 200 tons of coal to spare. What was more, she caught people's attention. As a reporter on the *Morning Herald* (later renamed the *New York Herald*) described her, she 'looked black and blackguard ... rakish, cool, reckless, fierce, and forbidding in sombre colours to an extreme'. Perhaps he had forgotten that he was writing about a passenger ship and not a man-of-war. Nevertheless, words such as these caught the popular imagination. When she went back to Bristol, she had 58 passengers abroad and completed the passage in a day over two weeks. The *Sirius* returned to less arduous duties, trading between London and St Petersburg. The *Great Western* remained in business upon the ocean for which she had been built.

Later that year, two more steamships made the crossing, and gave the final proof that steam navigation across the North Atlantic was not merely possible, it was to be recommended for its speed. Admittedly, a sailing packet named the *Andrew Jackson* had once accomplished the crossing in 14 days, but this feat was greatly assisted by the weather. As everyone knew, the voyage was a freak and nobody but a fool would trust the wind. As they were to discover, machinery, too, was sometimes unreliable, but, on the whole, it was the more constant ally.

Although she was larger and more elegantly appointed than other steamers, the *Great Western* was Brunel's only essay in conventional ship design. She had a wooden hull, and she was driven by paddle-wheels — just like all her contempories. Once she had proved herself, and was plying regularly between

Britain and North America, her designer anticipated future technology by rather more years than were commercially comfortable.

The events of 1838 had been noticed with interest by that enterprising Canadian, Samuel Cunard. Shrewd business man that he was, it quickly became clear to him that running a steamship service across the North Atlantic could be profitable only if it were subsidized. In effect, the subsidy would be payable for carrying the mails. The contract was put out for tender from time to time by the British government, but the conditions, imposed by the Admiralty, stipulated that the Royal Navy must be represented by an officer on board; that, in time of war, the vessels must be handed over to the government for use as troopships; and that they must have wooden hulls. In this last respect, the Admiralty was restraining the innovative ideas of shipowners by applying the very restrictions that hampered the development of its warships.

Among the early opponents of steam navigation was a talkative theorist named Dr Dionysius Lardner. Since his doctorate, conferred upon him at Trinity College, Dublin, was in divinity, he might have been better preoccupied if he had applied himself to spiritual matters. But Dr Lardner was fascinated by anything to do with science or engineering. Mainly, he seems to have dedicated himself to the proposition that anything intended to be progressive wouldn't work.

In this respect, he had a good deal in common with certain senior British Army officers who, at about the time of the *Titanic* disaster, were busy explaining why aeroplanes would never replace the cavalry for purposes of reconnaissance.

Lack of knowledge never deterred Dr Lardner from expressing an opinion. Surprisingly, there were many learned men — even members of the British Association — who took him seriously. When, for example, Dr Lardner asserted that, if the brakes of a train failed on a downward gradient in a tunnel, the train would gather momentum and emerge from the darkness at 120 mph, the sages nodded their heads and muttered 'just so' (or something rather like that).

Dr Lardner, as this may suggest, had a talent for making far-fetched assumptions without any data to support them. Having issued his warning about railway trains and tunnels, he

applied himself to steam-propelled vessels as conveyances
across the North Atlantic. Despite the evidence of the *Royal
William*, he dismissed such undertakings as impossible. His
argument hinged on the question of fuel. To make the crossing, he told the British Association in 1836, a ship would have
to carry a great deal more than her own weight in coal. 'I
think,' he said, 'it would be a waste of time, under all circumstances, to say much more to convince you of the unexpediency
of attempting a direct voyage to New York.'

Since all the statistics he mentioned were products of his
imagination rather than of practical experience, it may seem
surprising that his address was rewarded by an enthusiastic
round of applause. Fortunately, there were engineers such as
Brunel, who recognized Dr Lardner for the crank he was, and
who paid no attention to his utterances.

There is no knowing whether the British Admiralty had
studied the opinions of this pseudo-scientific cleric. Nevertheless, they tended to take the view that technical developments
were dangerous and could, conceivably, set mankind on yet
another road to disaster.

Not without reason, they pointed out that, if Britannia were
to rule the world's waves with steamships, coaling stations
would have to be established in unacceptably far-flung places.
Quite sensibly, Their Lordships directed their collective finger
at paddle-wheels, and made much of their vulnerability to
hostile shot and shell. There was, of course, an alternative
method of propulsion: the screw. But, in spite of sufficient
evidence to the contrary, they made it plain that, in their
opinion, a screw-driven ship would not be sufficiently
manoeuvrable.

Steam-engines, they concluded, might serve a useful
purpose when entering or leaving harbour. Once the warship
was clear of the bar, however, the driving force would still have
to be the combination of the wind and sails.

As for hulls, the very idea of building them from iron and
inserting steam-engines was described by one very senior
officer as 'scientific bosh'. Funnily enough, the public — or
most of it — agreed with him. Victories such as Trafalgar had
been won by ships built of oak — and, if we are to believe the
song, manned by sailors with hearts constructed from the same

timber. The admirals and the less articulate men in the streets became almost maudlin in their regard for the 'old wooden-walls', and hotly denied the suitability of any other substance for warship construction. Somehow what should have been a subject for serious technical debate had become a matter of national honour.

There were people, however, who were prepared to contest these prejudices. One of them was John Laird, the son of a Scotsman who, in 1810, had established a boiler factory at Birkenhead on the western bank of the River Mersey. It was obvious that the skills required to fashion iron plates into boilers could be adapted without much difficulty to building hulls for ships. Thus, if the idea of iron ships ever became acceptable, the pickings for the Birkenhead works would be substantial.

Inevitably, the effect of an iron hull on the vessel's compass had to be identified and overcome. To begin with, it was alarming, and there were certainly several wrecks that could be attributed to this cause. The trouble was that, whilst the subsequent investigations made the reasons for these disasters clear, they did nothing to suggest how this state of affairs could be overcome.

Eventually, in 1838, John Laird was confronted with the probability that all his arguments might be reduced to nothing, and that the Admiralty — and the underwriters, come to that — would never heed him. In a mood verging on despair, he invited the Astronomer Royal, Professor Sir George Airy, to carry out tests on his latest vessel, a small enough steamer, but the largest iron ship of her day, the *Rainbow*.

Airy's research produced the breakthrough. Since an iron ship was iron all over, the effect on the compass was not the same as that of a movable iron object on a wooden ship. The metal certainly pulled the compass off course, but the mis-direction created by it was constant. If you discovered what it was, you could make allowances and correct it. Indeed, there was no reason why navigation should not become more, rather than less, accurate.

It was not until the 1850s that the Admiralty finally withdrew its objections to iron ships, and not until 1859 that Lloyds at last issued specifications for them. Nevertheless, there had been some progress. In 1839 the East India Company, breaking all the rules, had ordered four gunboats to be built of iron. On their completion, they were diverted to China to fight in the Opium Wars. One of them, the *Nemesis*, was so effective that the Chinese dubbed her the 'Devil Ship' and offered $50,000 to anyone who could deliver her into their hands.

One year after the *Nemesis* and her companions had been laid down, the Admiralty quietly contradicted itself by agreeing to the construction of the first iron ship ever to be placed at the British government's disposal. But this was only a 113-foot-long packet boat named the *Dover* and intended for short voyages across the English Channel. When, a few years later, Their Lordships appeared to have become more daring, and actually ordered five iron frigates, public outcry and argument among themselves caused a sudden reconsideration of the matter. The vessels were stripped of their guns and converted into troopships.

In February 1852 one of them — HMS *Birkenhead* — struck a submerged rock while carrying soldiers and their families to the Kaffir War in South Africa. The effect of the iron hull upon her compass was inevitably regarded as the cause. The issue was made more emotive by the fact that 454 of the 638 on board her were drowned. It does not seem to have occurred to anybody that her captain might have got it wrong.

Back in 1838, when the *Great Western* was racing the *Sirius* across the Atlantic, the British government had invited tenders for the carriage of mail to North America. That enterprising Nova Scotian, Samuel Cunard, had no ships of his own, but this did not deter him from making a bid. If he was successful, he promised, he would build three vessels, keeping strictly to the rules and guaranteeing reliability. To the dismay of the other contenders, he was given the contract — which, in effect, provided him with an annual subsidy of £55,000. When, shortly afterwards, it was decided that a fourth ship would be necessary, it was raised to £81,000.

Thus the British and North American Royal Mail Steam Packet Company (soon and sensibly shortened to Cunard Line) came into being; and thus four paddle-steamers, with wooden hulls and a sufficient spread of sail came to be built. The first to be completed was the 1,156-ton *Britannia*. Appropriately, she made her first departure from Liverpool on 4 July 1840 (American Independence Day). Twelve days later,she docked at Halifax; two days after that, she arrived at Boston.

Britannia was not a comfortable ship. Dickens, who made the crossing with his wife, described his cabin as an 'utterly impractical, thoroughly hopeless and profoundly preposterous box'. 'Nothing smaller for sleeping in was ever made except coffins,' he added. Just the same, the *Britannia* did all that Samuel Cunard and the British government required of her; and so, when they came into service, did her sisters.

Meanwhile, in New York, an entrepreneur named Edward Knight Collins was running a firm of sailing packets named the Dramatic Line. Provided the United States government would give him a subsidy, he saw no reason why Cunard's dominance of the North Atlantic should go unchallenged. What was more, he had carefully observed the *Britannia* and the others, and he knew how to wean away their passenger trade. The Cunarders had clipper bows, which looked very pretty, but caused them to ship a lot of water. He would build his steamers with straight stems. The Cunarders were cramped; his would be at least twice the size. The facilities in the Cunarders were limited; his would be equipped with such luxuries as barbers' shops, steam heating, ice rooms, smoking rooms and even bathrooms. They would also be more technically advanced. For example, *Atlantic* — the first of his new fleet — was to become the first steamer to be equipped with an engine-room telegraph. Hitherto, all instructions from the bridge to the engine-room had been conveyed by means of voice pipes.

He might have gone all the way and stipulated iron for the building of their hulls. Unfortunately, as yet there was no yard in the United States capable of constructing iron ships, and he certainly had no intention of taking his order elsewhere.

Uncle Sam obligingly contributed to his enterprise — to the tune of one million dollars (then £100,000) a year — upon the condition that, in wartime, the ships should be employed as armed cruisers. In 1850 the first four paddle-steamers — *Atlantic*, *Pacific*, *Arctic* and *Baltic* — made their débuts, and quickly demonstrated that they were not only more comfortable, but also faster than Cunard's steamers. With speeds of up to 12 knots, it was not long before they cut the time of the crossing to just over nine days.

Naturally, the transatlantic travelling public found them more agreeable than the more rudimentary Cunarders: after twenty-eight round trips, Collins could boast of having accommodated 4,306 passengers — Cunard, over the same period, had carried only 2,969. Even so, despite the federal subsidy, Collins was losing a lot of money. As if this was not enough, nemesis was devising an even unkinder cut. It happened in 1854, when the *Arctic* was homeward-bound from Liverpool to New York.

The ship was 60 miles from Cape Race, steaming at 12 knots, when she ran into thick fog. The passengers were sitting down to lunch, when they experienced what one of them described as 'a violent shock'. It had been caused by collision with a much smaller, iron-hulled, screw-driven, French ship named the *Vesta*.

No doubt the *Arctic*'s master, Captain Luce, should have reduced speed — especially since, according to one account, he had experienced an extraordinary presentiment of disaster before leaving Liverpool. Inevitably a bad dream came into it and a general state of apparent depression. But this may be apocryphal. People rather liked the notion of presentiments and dire forebodings in those days. Luce, who has been described as 'sensitive' and 'melancholy', was a natural subject for such speculation. However, whatever came into his mind on the eve of departure does not seem to have inspired him to act with prudence. As the *Liverpool Albion* observed afterwards, the *Arctic* was a 'sacrifice offered to the great Moloch of the day — speed. Ninety-nine out of every 100 casualties are more or less attributable to the go-ahead principle.'

At first it seemed as if the French ship was doomed. Captain Luce, presumably not yet aware of his own plight, sent a boat to her with the first officer in charge. Some of the *Vesta*'s passengers and crew jumped into it, and this was unfortunate. For, on the way back, the officer misjudged things: the *Arctic*, still forging ahead, cut the small craft in two and all its occupants perished.

The French ship's master now began to lighten ship. The

cargo and all the passengers' luggage were flung into the sea, and anything else that could be moved was shifted aft to raise the level of the bows. For a few moments, it seemed as if the small steamer were bound to sink. But then, miraculously, she recovered.

Improbably, the *Vesta* survived. Some days later, with her bows 'completely battered to pieces' (one observer's description) she arrived at St John's, Newfoundland. Feelings among her crew and passengers were still running high against Captain Luce and his ship. According to the *Vesta*'s master, Captain Duchesne, the *Arctic* had been travelling dangerously fast; she had rammed his ship (which seems unlikely, since the *Vesta* ran head-on into the *Arctic*'s side); and had then, without the smallest compassion for those in peril on this particular part of the sea, hurried on his way.

In fact, Captain Luce now made another mistake. Underestimating the severity of the damage to his vessel, he decided that his best course was to make for home as quickly as possible — still without reducing speed.

The fog had now been joined by a deadly accomplice: a near gale-force wind. Struggling against high seas, squeezing power from her engines, the battered *Arctic* did her best to fight her way to safety. But the damage was too great. After 15 miles, the boiler-room became flooded and the furnaces were extinguished. At last, Captain Luce had to face the truth that he had avoided for so long. His ship was mortally wounded. Four hours after the collision, she sank.

From time almost immemorial, the precedence for abandoning ship had been clearly established. Once selected crew members had taken charge of the boats, any women and children should be the first to depart from the wreck — followed by the male passengers, followed by the crew and then, finally, by the captain. In the case of the *Arctic*, the rules were forgotten, and panic prevailed.

The liner's supply of lifeboats had already been diminished by heavy seas crashing on to her deck. Most of those that remained were taken over by the crew. One, with a capacity for 50, remained lashed uselessly to the deck for want of sufficient men to launch it. Another, with Edward Collins's wife and two children among the occupants, fell into the sea when the tackle

gave way. The only survivor was a woman, who was grabbed
by a sailor leaning over the bulkhead above. The pandemonium grew worse. Pistol shots were heard as one officer
tried to produce order from the rabble that had once been a
disciplined ship's company. They seem to have had little effect.
However, the chief engineer did manage to pack a number of
women and children into one boat — only to find that it had
neither food nor a compass on board.

Among the 249 who drowned was the new French Ambas-
sador to Washington, and a man who, furiously treading water,
was heard to offer £30,000 to anyone who would snatch him
from the sea. The crew of one boat did try to oblige, but he was
dead before they reached him.

Captain Luce was the last to leave, accompanied by his
handicapped son who, ironically, had made the voyage for the
sake of his health. The boy was killed when part of a paddle-
box structure fell on him. Luce, amazingly, was able to cling to
the wreckage for two days, and was rescued by the Cunarder
Cambria.

Only two of the boats — a total of 42 people — reached the
coast. One survivor described the experience as 'forty-six hours
of intense agony of mind and body'. Still, as he agreed, he had
much to be thankful for. His only injury was a sprained ankle
incurred by jumping into the boat. Another was more eloquent.
'How,' he asked a reporter, 'shall I describe to you what
followed? Men jumping into the water and sinking beside us
while we would not let any more into the boat, 25 already
being in it. Most of them were good seamen and to whom,
under God's direction, we owe our safety.'

This was, perhaps, putting it rather kindly. The *New York
Express* summed up the crew more harshly. 'Ah what a manly
spectacle that must have been!' it sneered.

Hardy, rough-handed, broad-shouldered, strong-framed
men — accustomed to a business, too, the constant hazard
of which, one would naturally think, deadens everything like
personal fear — men like these treacherously deserting
feeble and delicate women, and shutting their eyes to cries
from little children that should have touched hearts
adamant! It is enough to make us all ashamed of humanity

and envy the better nature of the beasts of the field. Not one women saved! — not one child!

Anyone who has tried it may have found shutting the eyes an ineffective way of ignoring sound, but never mind — the writer made his point.

Once the news of the *Arctic*'s fate was received, there was no shortage of well-meaning suggestions. 'A Constant Reader' living in Torrington, Devon, addressed a letter to *The Times*, discussing the 'feasibility of a steam whistle being constantly used on board during dense fogs'. Fog bells were used, but their sound was 'faint compared to the shrill scream of a whistle'. Somebody else urged that captains should be 'compelled at least once a week to launch all [their] boats, the same as if the ship was in distress'.

One correspondent argued that the *Arctic* would not have sunk had she been built of oak instead of pine. This may have been true. Pine is certainly less robust than oak; but, since there was an abundance of such timber in North America, it was cheaper. United States shipbuilders partially overcame the shortcoming by designing clipper ships. They were faster (hence 'clipper' — they sailed at a good clip and thus clipped time off the voyage) and also handled better. The latter characteristics, it was assumed, made them better able to stay out of trouble. Strangely, nobody used the liner's fate to argue the cause of the iron ship. Nor did anyone remark on the fact that, although there were 391 people on board, there was sufficient lifeboat capacity for only 150. In other words, 241 were sentenced to death — no matter how impeccable the crew's behaviour might have been.

Samuel Cunard, the Canadian who gave Britain mercantile supremacy over the North Atlantic, was a realist. Isambard Brunel was a romantic — though he'd probably have denied it. Cunard built the kind of ships that were known to be possible within the bounds of contemporary knowledge, and which would be suitable contenders for whatever subsidies the British Government might care to contribute. Brunel, an engineer rather than a business man, designed the vessels he believed to be right — hoping, no doubt, that the Admiralty would eventu-

ally catch up with him. He was, of course, responsible to his
fellow directors of the Great Western Steamship Company.
But, whatever may have been their personal misgivings about
his visionary attitude, he usually managed to win their support.

Brunel thought big. The *Great Western,* conventional though
her wooden hull and paddle-wheel may have been, was larger
than anything that had yet been seen on the Atlantic. For his
next project — and it is worth remembering that he was
working on it some while before the Admiralty had so much as
agreed to the construction of a tiny iron-hulled cross-Channel
packet — Brunel took several long strides into the future. He
devised an iron ship, one-third longer than the largest ship of
the line in the Royal Navy, registering 2,936 tons, and
propelled by a screw. She was to be named the *Great Britain.*

When she was launched in 1843, the Prince Consort
indicated his approval of Brunel's enterprise by attending the
ceremony. His wife's senior naval officers were less impressed.
Seven years later, in 1850, they were still of the opinion that an
iron ship should not be allowed to carry the Royal Mail across
the oceans. Cunard had no need to worry: his subsidy was not
in peril. Indeed, it was not until 1856 that he built his first iron
ship, the *Persia,* and until some while after that, that he
abandoned the paddle-wheel in favour of the screw (the *Persia*
and her sister, the *Scotia* — completed in 1862 — were the
Cunard Line's last paddlers). By this time, both iron hulls and
screw propulsion had become respectable.

The *Great Britain* set off on her maiden voyage to New York
on 26 July 1846. She took 14 days and 21 hours to make the
passage, which was regarded as disappointing. On her arrival,
the *New York Herald* described her as 'a monster of the deep'.
It may have been intended as a compliment; but it could, one
feels, have been better put. Given a following wind, she was
able to cover 287 miles a day with all her sails set. Using her
engines only, the distance was 160 miles.

But speed was never the prime accomplishment of Brunel's
ships. Luxury was, and so was their strength. Applying the
knowledge of bridges he had amassed when constructing the
Great Western Railway, he fitted the *Great Britain* with longitudinal bulkheads along the length of her hull, which were able
to withstand considerable stresses. Furthermore, and nobody

had done this before, he used transverse watertight bulkheads to divide the ship into six compartments. Without a doubt, this newcomer to the Atlantic was the strongest, safest, ship of her time.

This was proved beyond any doubt — and the argument in favour of iron ships greatly advanced — in the following year. The *Great Britain* left Liverpool on her second passage to New York on 9 September. Her route lay to the south of the Calf of Man, then round the top of Northern Ireland and so into the Atlantic. Her captain — John Hosken, who had already completed sixty-four Atlantic crossings as master of the *Great Western* — made one of the few mistakes of his career. The truth of the matter, and as he admitted afterwards, was that he lost his way. Instead of steaming up the North Channel towards the ocean, the *Great Britain* ran aground in Dundrum Bay near Newcastle in County Down.

As one of the passengers wrote to the *Illustrated London News*:

> We have indeed been in fearful peril ... All was confusion; men and women rushed from their berths, some threw themselves into the arms of complete strangers. Mr ____'s first words to me were 'I think there will be no loss of life but the ship is gone.'
>
> What fearful words on such a dark night. Oh, I cannot tell you the anguish of that night!

And so on.

In fact, Mr ____ was correct about there being no loss of life, but he was wrong about the ship. She was far from gone. For eleven months, she lay there until, at last, she was towed off into deeper waters. Ironically, the vessel that performed the task was the iron frigate-turned-trooper, *Birkenhead,* so soon to be lost with such a sorrowful toll of lives off south-east Africa.

When the *Great Britain*'s hull was examined, the surveyors discovered that it was perfectly sound and that none of the frames had been strained. Had she been a wooden ship, she would have long been reduced to a mass of rotting timber.

In spite of this proof of iron's superiority to wood in matters of large ship construction, there could still be no hope of a government subsidy. In any case, the strength of the Great Western Steamship Company's fleet was now down to one — and she, whilst her fabric remained sound, required costly repairs before she would be able to sail again. Such had been the strain on the firm's resources by the *Great Britain*'s eleven-month-long sojourn on an Irish beach, that the *Great Western* had to be sold to the Royal Mail Steam Packet Company. There was nothing that could be done: the *Great Britain*, too, would have to go. She was bought by a firm with offices in Liverpool and Bristol. Her new owners re-engined and re-rigged her. For the next twenty-three years, she behaved faultlessly trading to and from Australia. As L.T.C. Rolt observed in his biography, *Isambard Kingdom Brunel*, '... the performance of the *Great Western* and the *Great Britain* on the high seas very probably advanced the progress of ocean steam navigation by a quarter of a century.'

For those who enjoy identifying the beginnings and ends of epochs, the year 1856 deserves attention. In the latter instance, however, the occasion called for mourning rather than rejoicing. The wooden-hulled Collins liner *Pacific* and Cunard's first essay in iron, the *Persia*, sailed from Liverpool within a few days of each other. Both, we have to assume, steamed into an icefield half-way or more across the Atlantic. The *Persia* certainly did. After five days at sea and travelling at 11 knots, she struck a berg on her starboard side. Sixteen feet of plating were torn away, and the paddle-box was damaged. Although down by the head, she completed her voyage. The *Pacific* was never heard of again. It seems certain that what had been no more than a wound in the side of the Cunarder was a fatal thrust to the *Pacific*. The case for iron ships could rest.

As for Edward Collins, this final arrow of outrageous fortune killed his business. The federal subsidy was withdrawn. He was forced to sell off his remaining ships to pay his debts. It would be some considerable time before liners flying the Stars and Stripes again achieved eminence on the North Atlantic.

Evidence of the epoch that was beginning could be seen beside the River Thames at Millbank. Her owners, the Great

Ship Company, intended to call her the *Leviathan*. Her designer, Brunel, said they could 'call her Tom Thumb so far as I'm concerned'. In the end, she was named the *Great Eastern*.

In *The Liners*, Terry Coleman remarked that 'The *Great Eastern* was genius, which did not work. The Cunarders were talent, and did.' One might have thought that the economic disappointment produced by the *Great Britain* going aground would have blunted Brunel's enthusiasm for designing ships. He could even have considered retirement: he had, goodness knows, achieved enough. But his restless intelligence, his creative energy, were far from spent. It was almost as if the building of the *Great Western* and *Great Britain* had been warming-up exercises for the greatest feat of all.

The discovery of gold in Australia in 1851 had increased considerably the demand for passages to that country. In that year, a company named the Eastern Steam Navigation Company was established to exploit this trade — only to see, in the following year, the government renew the P & O line's mail contract. It was not, perhaps, the best of auspices.

Nevertheless, Brunel undoubtedly had the new company in mind when making notes for another ship. The interest was mutual and, now that the Great Western Steamship Company had been wound up, he was free to accept the appointment of Engineer.

Foremost in his mind was the matter of coal. He intended to build a vessel that could travel all the way to Australia without the need to refuel on the way. A large ship, a *very* large ship, could, he believed, accomplish this. Once in motion, moreover, it would be more easily propelled than a smaller steamer — one of say, between 2,000 and 3,000 tons. As a result, it would be faster and considerably more economical.

Such thoughts prompted him to recommend that, instead of investing in a fleet of smaller vessels, the Eastern Steam Navigation Company should stake everything on one huge steamer — the like of which had never been seen before, and would not be seen again for the next thirty years.

Any naval architect who glanced at his calculations would have thought either that Brunel was going out of his mind, or else that he was playing with abstractions. Whatever was built

would have had to register at least 20,000 tons. The diameter
of the screw would have to be 25-foot, but even this was not
enough. The engineers of the day were incapable of putting
together units that could generate enough power to propel such
a huge hull sufficiently fast, no matter whether a screw or a
pair of paddle-wheels were used. Consequently, unable to
demand the impossible, Brunel decided to employ both. Inevitably, of course, there would have to be two engine-rooms, one
for each system.

So far as the hull was concerned, he used the technology he
had applied with such good effect to the *Great Britain.* Two
longitudinal bulkheads, 36 feet apart, ran along the length —
criss-crossed by watertight bulkheads dividing the ship into ten
compartments. On this occasion, however, he went a stage
further by providing (and this was the first time that any ship
had been so constructed) a cellular double bottom and an inner
skin that extended 35 feet above the keel plate.

To steer such a monster without assistance would be a
Herculean task and so (another innovation) he proposed to
introduce a steam-driven steering engine. Accommodation was
provided for 4,000 in conditions that put to shame even the
high standards of his previous ships. Finally, since there were
no facilities in Australia large enough to dock such a giant, two
steam-launches should be carried for the embarkation and
disembarkation of passengers.

For want of a government subsidy, the Eastern Steam
Navigation Company went into liquidation before the *Great
Eastern* had been completed. Rather than see the giant steamship auctioned off, a new enterprise, named the Great Ship
Company, was formed. Brunel remained as Engineer. But he
was now confronted with what General Wolfe, faced with the
problem of taking Quebec, described as 'a choice of difficulties'. His health was failing. The task of getting the big ship
from her berth on the Millbank mud and into the Thames
turned out to be more difficult than anyone had foreseen; and,
now, economies had to be made.

The idea of steam-driven steering had to be abandoned —
with the result that, in bad weather, it required ten men to
operate the helm. The steam launches for transferring passengers from ship to shore were scrapped, and so was the

notion of using the great steamer on the Australian run. She would have to be employed on the North Atlantic. This was an economic disaster. On the former route, the only competition would have been clipper ships. She'd almost certainly have halved the time for the journey; she might, quite probably, have established a monopoly in the emigrant trade. By contrast, commercial conditions on the Atlantic were as competitive as they had ever been.

In August 1858 this ill-starred steamer was ready for her trials. Brunel made a final tour of inspection. Afterwards, he went home and, that afternoon, collapsed from a stroke. As she headed down the Channel at 13 knots, his ship seemed to be faring better. But then, off Hastings, the explosion occurred.

As *The Times* put it, 'the forward part of the deck appeared to spring like a mine, blowing the funnel up into the air. There was a confused roar amid which came the awful crash of timber and iron mingled together in a frightful uproar, and all was hidden in a rush of steam.' The cause of the trouble was an arrangement of stopcocks used for pressure-testing the boilers. They ought to have been removed; somebody forgot. To make things worse, the stopcocks serving the paddle-engines were actually closed.

One fireman, who jumped overboard, was mangled to death by the paddle-wheel. Three more died that day, and two more the next. Fifteen men in the paddle engine-room were injured. To this sombre list, one more casualty can be added. Brunel died a week afterwards — his death no doubt hastened by the stresses and frustrations the *Great Eastern* had inflicted upon him.

The *Great Eastern* had been designed to trade with Australia, and Brunel had always said that she would not be suitable for the Atlantic. Her 800 cabins could not unreasonably have been described as 'staterooms'. Each was double the size of anything else available at the time, and each included hot and cold running water, a dressing table, a rocking chair, and a bath among its amenities. The trouble was that, with so many shipping lines competing on the North Atlantic run, there were not enough people to fill them.

On her maiden voyage to New York in June 1860 she carried no more than 38 passengers. The one occasion when she was filled to anything like her capacity occurred in the following year, when the War Office chartered her. Irish Seinn Feiners in America were known to be planning armed raids on Canada. The garrison at Quebec needed reinforcements. On board her were 2,144 soldiers, 437 women and children, and 122 horses. The passage took eight and a half days. On the return trip, she carried 500 passengers and the company's directors could congratulate themselves on a profit of £10,000. But such good times never happened again: there were no more War Office charters.

The *Great Eastern* was immensely strong. When, in 1862, she ran on to an uncharted reef at the approaches to New York, a diver afterwards reported a hole 85 feet by 4 feet in her outer hull. The inner skin, however, was undamaged. The repairs took four months to complete. Not the least of reasons was that there was only one dry dock large enough to accommodate her bulk, and that was at Milford Haven in Wales. Rather than risk a return passage in this condition (it should, in fact, have been possible), her master insisted that the work be done on the spot. Consequently, a good deal of ingenious, but none the less laborious, improvisation was required.

On the other hand, her handling in a high sea was rather less than good. She rolled heavily, and — without the steam-steering engine that Brunel had deemed necessary — she was extremely difficult to navigate. In 1861, on passage to New York, she steamed into a gale. Her paddle-wheels were put out of action; her steering shaft was damaged; and her sails were torn to shreds. For three days and nights, she lay inert on the storm-racked ocean. Finally, she limped back to Cork.

The triumph of the *Great Eastern* was that of laying the first transatlantic cable. The tragedy was that she was a freak. She was a dream that went wrong: a ship that belonged more to the world of Barnum than to the realms of commercial common sense ruled by such men as Samuel Cunard — indeed, much of the income she generated was to come from sightseers who paid to see round her. To compound the tragedy, while the *Great Eastern* was under construction, another project that was to have a profound effect on the shipping world was going forward. On 17 November 1869 the Suez Canal was opened. The great ship was too broad to use it; any time that her speed might have saved would be forfeited by the need to go round the Cape of Good Hope, while smaller ships, such as those used by P & O, could now take a short cut. This might have been dismissed as bad luck — but, since a report handed over to the British government in 1830 convincingly demonstrated that building such a canal was feasible, it would surely have been prudent to consider it as a possibility for the future.*

Brunel may have thought that the world was ready for her, but the world was not. Before being consigned to the breakers, the *Great Eastern* spent her last days as a kind of floating exhibition hall on the Mersey. But even this venture failed. The local authorities refused to grant her owners a licence to sell liquor. Without the incentive of a well-stocked bar, thirsty Merseysiders preferred to remain on shore.

It was not until 1899 that a bigger ship was brought into service: the White Star's *Oceanic.* By then, however, immensity was no longer remarkable. *The Great Eastern* was revolutionary; the *Oceanic* was evolutionary.

In 1871 an earlier liner named *Oceanic* had come into service. Like her later namesake, she was owned by the White Star Line — or, as it was called at the time, the Oceanic Steam Navigation Company. The firm's founder, Thomas Ismay, had, like Brunel in the case of the *Great Eastern,* originally envisaged the Australian trade as his objective. Ismay, too, had strong and decidedly progressive ideas about the kind of ships he wished to build. The Belfast shipbuilders Harland & Wolff, with which he had close connections (Harland & Wolff built all the White Star ships), convinced him that such vessels were better suited to the North Atlantic.

The earlier *Oceanic* was the company's first steamship, and she had all manner of improvements. The first-class accommodation, for example, was situated where it should always have been: amidships. The wooden bulkheads were replaced by teak

---

*On the other hand, a similar remark might be made concerning the Channel Tunnel. A study made in 1865 showed that it was feasible and, ever since, it has been on the cards. Nevertheless, this threat or promise (according to how you view the project) has done nothing to hinder the development of ferries employed on the Dover Strait.

and iron railings; there were skylights, deckhouses, bathrooms
with fresh-water and salt-water taps, electric bells to summon
the stewards, and a smoking room. Ismay took over Collins's
custom of giving all his ships names ending with 'ic'. He also
adopted that unhappy shipowner's concern to make the
passenger's lot more agreeable.

It is one of history's ironies that, whilst the Stars and Stripes
was not to be seen on the staff of an Atlantic liner for many
years after the demise of the Collins Line, the most powerful
figure in the world of transatlantic shipping was an American
banker: John Pierpont Morgan. He owned a succession of
steam yachts, each named *Corsair* to draw attention to his
assertion that he was descended from the pirate, Henry
Morgan. He also owned a sailing yacht, the *Columbia*, which
twice beat Sir Thomas Lipton's *Shamrock* in the contest for the
America's Cup. When a friend asked him how much money
was needed to own such vessels, he tartly replied, 'Anyone who
has to ask how much it costs to run a yacht cannot afford to
keep one.'

As well as what one might call his personal fleet — and he
used his first *Corsair* (purchased in 1882) to carry him up the
Hudson River on his daily journey from his home on Rhode
Island to his office on Wall Street — he owned a very considerable slice of the world's shipping. In 1912 the extent of his
holdings was estimated at 126 vessels with a gross tonnage
totalling 1,000,140. He owned the White Star Line, the Red
Star Line, Atlantic Transport, the Leyland, and the Dominion
Lines. He had reached what might be loosely called an understanding with those formidable German companies, the
Hamburg-Amerika Line and Norddeutscher Lloyd (mercantile
echoes of the Kaiser's passion for building dreadnoughts).
Indeed, the only transatlantic companies that eluded him were
Cunard and the French Compagnie Générale Transatlantique,
and that certainly was not for want of trying by the monopoly-
minded Mr Morgan.

When pounds of flesh were being dished out, J. Pierpont M.
could invariably be found at the front of the queue. What's
more, he could be relied upon to weigh his portion to make
sure that it was no less than a pound. Nevertheless, he was
compelled to allow the companies in which he had such a

sizeable investment (the holding company, International Mercantile Marine was valued at £25 million) a surprising amount of autonomy. Nor was even his agile mind able to dodge restrictions imposed by the governments of the nations in which his shipping companies had originated. For instance, when he helped himself to a controlling amount of White Star shares, it was on the strict understanding that the vessels should continue to sail under the British flag and be crewed by British seamen. The reason was not difficult to deduce: come war, and the White Star ships could be taken over by the Royal Navy. Even so, while the United States made little apparent impact on the Atlantic's passenger trade, it was actually the one and true owner of very nearly the lot — simply through Mr Morgan's considerable spread of funds.

The Cunard Line had resisted Morgan's blandishments on the insistence of the British Admiralty. Nobody was in any doubt that the crack German liners had been built with wartime uses in mind, and it seemed only proper that the UK should have vessels that, whilst peacefully plying for commercial gain in times that were not troubled, could assume the role either of armed merchant cruiser or else of troopship, in times that were.

By the 1880s — the precise date of its origin is unknown, and so is its originator — a somewhat nebulous distinction had been conferred upon whichever ship made the fastest North Atlantic crossing. It was known as the 'Blue Riband' — a name that seems to have been inspired by the Order of the Garter's insignia. Make of that what you will: it is difficult to make anything at all, except an inference that it had a British connection. Only one of its several holders ever actually flew a blue ribbon from her mast — the French Line's (formerly Compagnie Générale Transatlantique) *Normandie*. Nor, until 1933 — when a British MP, Harold Hales, handsomely paid for an ornate trophy — was there any award for the winner.

Nevertheless, to hold the Blue Riband conferred status. At the beginning of the twentieth century it was securely in German hands. The Hamburg-Amerika Line's *Deutschland* wrested the title from her compatriot *Kaiser Wilhelm der Grosse* in 1900, and there seemed to be no reason why this state of affairs should not continue. There were certainly no British contenders to dispute it.

From the point of view of the British public, it seemed wrong that, while Britannia might be ruling some of the waves, she was certainly not ruling those that wrinkled the surface of the North Atlantic. If something were to be done about it, Cunard was the company most likely to succeed — though the cost would be enormous and no plan was worth consideration without the promise of a state subsidy.

The Admiralty, quite properly, concerned itself with the realities of armed combat rather than the romance of a race for a trophy that did not exist. If the German ships had been built with a wartime role in mind, there was no reason why Britain, too, should not construct crack liners that could be converted into armed merchant cruisers — indeed, there was every reason why it should. The negotiations between the government and Cunard took place in 1903. When they were concluded, the Admiralty had agreed to contribute to the cost of two new liners — to the extent of more than £2 million, plus an annual subsidy of £75,000, and plus the assurance of the mail contract.

In return for this munificence, whatever was built must be capable of steaming at 24½ knots in moderate weather, and be able to carry a dozen 6-inch guns. The ships were to be built to Admiralty specifications, and Cunard would have to yield to the Admiralty on all matters of design and construction. Cunard, for his part, agreed that the company would never pass out of British hands — no matter how tempting offers from the likes of J.P. Morgan might be. Should war ever break out, its entire fleet would be placed at the nation's disposal.

The first of the sisters, the *Lusitania* was ready for service in the summer of 1907. The second, the *Mauretania*, followed in November. The former was built at the Clydebank yard of John Brown and Company; the latter, on Tyneside at Swan, Hunter and Wigham Richardson.

Cunard was determined to create the most sumptuous accommodation that had ever been experienced, and it was not without reason that one reporter described the *Lusitania* as 'a floating palace'. Another used the phrase 'ocean greyhound', which was also appropriate. The *Mauretania*, almost identical to her sister, was the fastest ship on the North Atlantic for twenty-nine years. She did, however, show that the notion of wartime employment as an armed merchant cruiser was ill-founded. She consumed too much coal and her design precluded an essential of such vessels: armour. Apart from an appearance as a trooper at the Dardanelles, she spent most of the First World War safely berthed at Liverpool.

Building a luxury liner can, perhaps, be compared to erecting a five-star hotel in an area that is prone to earth-quakes. Far more important than the replica Adam fireplaces, the Italian walnut panelling in the smoking room, and all the other frills and fancies, is the basic requirement that, no matter what the punishment inflicted from outside sources, the ship shall remain afloat.

The *Lusitania* and her sister were fitted with eleven water-tight compartments created by ten transverse bulkheads with watertight doors. In addition to this, two longitudinal bulkheads extended down the length of the ship, one on either side of the boiler- and engine-rooms. However, to make the voyage to New York, 6,600 tons of coal would be required; partly for want of anywhere else to store it, and partly because the Admiralty had used this method ever since 1858, it was accommodated in the space between the longitudinal bulk-heads and the outside skin of the hull.

In theory, this was no doubt an excellent idea. It assumed that the coal would absorb the force of any shot that pene-trated the hull and would, therefore, protect the boilers. Unfortunately, it overlooked three factors. One was that coal absorbs water. Any inrush of sea would saturate the fuel, add substantially to its weight, and, consequently, cause the ship to list dangerously. The second was that the creators of this concept seem to have overlooked the law of diminishing returns. Towards the end of a long voyage the contents of the bunkers would be severely depleted, and thus there would be less coal to absorb whatever shock there was.

Finally, bulkheads though they were, they were certainly not watertight. There had to be a number of openings through which stokers would shovel coal for the furnaces. As Colin Simpson wrote in what is certainly the definitive book about the *Lusitania,* 'Anyone who has ever drawn coal from a

domestic coal bunker will know the difficulty of closing the
hatch, as the weight of coal inside, plus the accumulation of
dust and fine scraps of coal precludes an easy or efficient
closure.'

Exactly. It required a torpedo to demonstrate these weak-
nesses, though it is an interesting speculation to swap ships and
to put the *Lusitania* in the place of the *Titanic* when she hit the
iceberg. In theory, since the *Titanic* was not fitted with longitudinal bulkheads, the *Lusitania* should have been safer. In
practice, one feels that she might not have fared very much
better. The management of White Star and Harland & Wolff
were certainly of this opinion. Longitudinal bulkheads, their
counsel insisted at the Board of Trade Inquiry, had been
deliberately omitted. Filled with water on one or the other side,
the list would have been so great that the lifeboats could not
have been launched.

Thomas Ismay, founder of the White Star line, died in 1900
and was succeeded as chairman by his son, Bruce Ismay.
Whilst Morgan and his fellow directors of the International
Mercantile Marine Co. doubtless kept sharp eyes on the value
of their investment, they left the handling of White Star in
Ismay's hands. It was probably sensible. Morgan's practical
experience of shipping was confined to matters concerning his
tribe of steam yachts, *Corsairs* I, II, III and IV. Furthermore,
there was the British government's insistence that the firm's
ships must remain under the British flag and be manned by
British crews. American interference was unlikely to be toler-
ated.

Harland & Wolff, which had built the first White Star liner
in 1872, remained in favour and continued to enjoy the
monopoly of the White Star orders. Indeed, Bruce Ismay and
Lord Pirrie, the builders' chairman, were close friends.

One evening in 1907, the Ismays were dining with the
Pirries at the latters' house in Belgrave Square, London. After
the meal, and no doubt with the *Lusitania* and *Mauretania* well
to the front in their minds, they quite casually roughed out a
plan for three transatlantic giants that would eclipse the
Cunarders. They would not be the fastest things on the North
Atlantic — despite the fact that the *Teutonic* had briefly held

the Blue Riband in 1889, speed had never been White Star's first consideration. They would, on the other hand, be by far the most luxurious. Significantly, when more detailed discussions were held with Alexander Carlisle, Harland & Wolff's general manager, between four and five hours were devoted to matters of décor; no more than five or ten minutes to lifeboat capacity, the regulations of which had remained unchanged for years in spite of the fact that ships had grown very much larger. As a result no more boats were required by law for a ship registering 50,000 tons than for one of, say, 15,000 tons. To do him credit, Mr Carlisle obviously had misgivings about this, though they cannot have been very acute: the addition of four more than the stipulated number seems to have been sufficient to satisfy them. In hard statistics, this meant that, in the event of an emergency, and with the ship filled to capacity, twenty boats (able to accommodate a total of 1,178) would be at the disposal of 3,547 people. The question that anyone with imagination must surely have asked, was who should play the part of God? Who should sit in judgement, and select the living from the soon-to-be-dead? The captain?

Clearly, the lesson afforded by the fate of Collins liner *Arctic* in 1854 had not been properly learned. Indeed, if those concerned with the design of this ocean-going trio of titans paid any attention to history, their studies seem to have been incomplete. Did they, for example, consider the case of the Guion Line's *Arizona* in 1879? Did they note that, enveloped in the fog that hangs shroudlike over the Newfoundland Grand Banks, she had struck a 60-foot-high iceberg head-on, crushed her bows to pieces, and yet been able to travel stern-first to St John's? Did they read that the collision bulkhead up front had contained the damage — to such an extent that it was possible to fit a temporary wooden bow, and then to make the crossing to Liverpool in a mere six days, 17 hours and 13 minutes?

Yes, they probably did. But this information, taken alone, was dangerous. As any soldier knows, defence is something that must be all-round, and many a battle has been lost because the commander did not protect his flanks. They should also have studied the case of another liner — the *Oregon*, which had been owned by the Guion Line and then sold to Cunard. On 11 March 1886, she was off Fire Island on her approach to New

York, when a schooner rammed her amidships. The 824
passengers and crew were all taken off safely by the Norddeutscher Lloyd ship *Fulda*, but the *Oregon* sank. When the
German company was invited to make a claim for compensation for the time and trouble taken, the directors cabled,
'Highly gratified having been instrumental in saving so many
lives. No claim.' All of which illustrates one of the nicer aspects
of human nature. More germane to the future of shipbuilding,
however, was one of the court of inquiry's findings. A 'prime
factor' responsible for the *Oregon*'s loss, it noted, was the
failure of watertight bunker hatches to close.

It was an observation which, coupled with the fact that a
mere schooner could dispatch a large liner by striking her in a
sensitive area, should have been pondered over by the
designers of both the *Lusitania* and the Ismay-Pirrie trio —
which were now to be named *Olympic, Titanic* and *Britannic*.
(It has been suggested that the third vessel was originally to be
called the *Gigantic*, but this is almost certainly apocryphal.)

The *Lusitania*'s designers tried to guard her flanks, but
failed, those responsible for the *Titanic* and her sisters more or
less ignored them. They concentrated their defences on transverse bulkheads running the width of the ship, with coal stored
between them. This suggests that they paid too much attention
to the good fortune that attended the *Arizona*, to the exclusion
of almost everything else. The ships had, admittedly, sixteen
allegedly watertight compartments; they could, it was said,
remain afloat when two of them were flooded. It did not seem
to occur to anyone that more than two might fall to the enemy
— or that an iceberg might (in the words of a shipping expert)
'slice the *Titanic* down the side like a bloody great tin-opener'.
Nor did they consider the possibility that unless, as the regulations require today, the bulkheads extended upwards to a
continuous deck, the inrush of sea-water might overwhelm one
compartment, pour over the top, and flood the one next door.

Perhaps the truth of the matter was stated by Lord Mersey,
head of the Board of Trade Inquiry into her loss. 'I suppose,'
he conjectured, 'it is impossible to make a ship unsinkable and
at the same time a commercial success? You can, of course,
conceive an iron box riveted so that nobody can get into it, but
that would not do as a ship.'

Nevertheless, the *Titanic* might have survived if, on sighting the iceberg, the officer of the watch had not, as it were, tried to swerve in order to avoid it. By swinging round, her flank was exposed and this was her weakest point. If you had to hit an iceberg, history may have suggested, the only thing to do was to clout the damn thing head-on . . . and then pray hard.

The Iceberg's Story

The iceberg came out of the night. Once its task had been accomplished, it disappeared back into the night. There was no moon. A few days after the disaster, a passenger in the German liner *Prinz Adalbert* may have photographed it. The evidence for his claim was what appeared to be a length of red paint running along the waterline. Since the picture provides nothing against which to measure its scale, it is difficult to estimate its size. Nor, being a black-and-white snapshot, does it give any idea of the berg's colour. It looks like a small, grey, volcanic island, rising to a sharp pinnacle in the centre with, at one end, a kind of prow not unlike the rams once used on warships. At the other, it is sheer and flat — as if a portion has been broken off. A knife-edged ridge progresses along its spine: gentle at first, and then very steeply as it rises to the climactic peak. A mountaineer might find it an interesting challenge. It doesn't require very much imagination to describe its appearance as 'cruel'. It looks as if it might have killed a liner — even an immensity such as the *Titanic*.

The ship died in three hours. The iceberg survived for longer; but it, too, was nearing the end of its life. It had travelled from its birthplace in western Greenland, and endured the hazards that hinder the passage of bergs round Baffin Bay and southwards down the Davis Strait. Now, in the

38

warmer waters of the Gulf Stream, it would be gently but remorselessly melted away. It had nearly reached the end of its journey to extinction. Indeed, if the evidence of the liner's second officer, Charles Lightoller, is to be believed, it had quite recently turned over. But this can only be conjecture. It seems doubtful whether Mr Lightoller had more than a very brief glimpse of it.

It could be argued, and many have done so, that the *Titanic* was not really destroyed by the iceberg, but by carelessness born of custom and complacency. But, even so, the berg was the instrument: a weapon as effective as a torpedo, but as simple in its design as the liner was sophisticated. The ship had been constructed by Harland & Wolff of Belfast, builders to White Star ever since Thomas H. Ismay had taken over a financially destitute line of clippers and nursed it into the age of steam. The iceberg was a product of nature: created without cost, but alarming in its capacity for destruction.

For many years, Liverpool had been the port of departure for shipping on passage across the North Atlantic. In 1907, however, White Star had moved its base to Southampton. Not only was it nearer to London; it also enjoyed the rare distinction of having four high tides in every 24 hours. The advantages of this for large ships with deep drafts were considerable.

On the morning of Wednesday, 10 April 1912, the *Titanic* slipped her moorings and headed down Southampton Water towards Calshot. As she departed, Captain Smith made his first mistake. He underestimated the immense surge of water created by the propellers of such a large and powerful ship. As a result, the liner *New York* was torn from her berth, flung helplessly into the channel and narrowly missed colliding with the giant. It was, some people remarked, a bad omen.

The departure of the iceberg was less spectacular and it had occurred months, even years, earlier. There was nothing extraordinary about the fact that, at 11.40 p.m. (ship's time) on the night of Sunday, 14 April 1912, the *Titanic* should be approaching the Grand Banks off Newfoundland and had reached latitude 41°46'N longitude 50°14'W. Such was her course, and this was the point in the ocean where her master had intended her to be at 11.40 p.m. The fact that the iceberg

— this particular iceberg — happened to be there too is more singular. Of the two journeys that led to this meeting place, the berg's had been by far the more eventful. Good fortune is not something that can be attributed to small floating islands of ice. Nevertheless, something of the kind was needed for it to have survived the obstacles of its passage and to have come this far south.

Where, then, did it originate? The answer is from somewhere on the west coast of Greenland. If one excludes Australia, this is the largest island in the world. Its coastline extends for 24,295 miles, which is very nearly the girth of the globe at the equator. Originally, it was a depression surrounded by mountains. It may even once have been green and pleasant, though its name was created as a kind of public relations device to encourage settlers.

About 2,500 years ago, it began to snow. Since 'thaw' is a word virtually unknown in these latitudes, each year's fall survived, and increased the weight imposed on previous deposits. As time went by, the growing pressure compacted the snow into ice. Nowadays, something like 90 per cent of all land ice in the northern hemisphere lies on the Greenland ice-cap. According to one estimate, it is something like six and a quarter miles deep. Another, more moderate and probably more realistic view, suggests two miles — and then only in places. Whichever the case, the seas and oceans of the world would rise by twenty feet if this frigid mass were ever to melt.

The pressure, which transformed snowflakes into ice, squeezed the lower levels down into the valleys that cut through the mountains. In a more moderate climate, the process would have created rivers. Up here, where 80 per cent of the land lies within the Arctic Circle, glaciers were formed. Like rivers, but less perceptibly, they move. They creep towards the sea — although one source (Richard Brown's *Voyage of the Iceberg*) has credited the massive Disko glacier with a speed of 65 feet a day.

As the Greenland glaciers emerge from the land, they become like tongues extended into the sea. As more and more ice is added, the weight becomes so considerable that they snap their tethers to the shore and float away. The process is quaintly known as 'calving' — a term originally used by whalers.

The total iceberg production of Greenland is thought to be between 12,000 and 15,000 a year, of which 7,500 emanate from the west coast. On average, about 400 of them drift sufficiently far south to menace transatlantic shipping — though numbers in this instance do not mean a great deal. As the case of the *Titanic* so sadly showed, one is sufficient to account for a ship.

For the fanciful, this breaking of the link with land might seem to be an act of liberation: the occasion when it becomes possible for an iceberg to travel inconsequently over the sea until the time when, if it ventures too far south, the warmer air and water cause it to melt. In fact, a berg is always in thrall to something: to the wind, to the currents, to other icebergs, to beaches upon which it may become stranded, or to inlets in which it may be trapped. Those that are calved on the east coast of Greenland drift southwards, pass round Cape Farewell — the extreme tip of the island — and then change course to the north. Once they have entered the Davis Strait, the majority melt. None of them reach the Grand Banks, though they are nonetheless a hazard to vessels from Europe engaged in the Greenland trade.

Icebergs produced on the west coast have longer lives and journey farther. In 1978, eleven bergs from this side of the island were fitted with transponders (a radio device that not only transmits a signal, but also enables its source to be identified). With the help of two satellite systems — Nibus G and Tiron N: the latter is nowadays known as NOAA 7 and 8, and is used for weather forecasting — their drift was charted northwards up the eastern side of Baffin Bay, around the top to Lancaster Sound, and thence in a southerly direction towards and eventually down the Davis Strait. Since the current is narrow and flows at its fastest along the edge of the continental slope, they tended to hug the coast. Most of them made excursions into Lancaster Sound before resuming their trek. Some never got farther than this.

One of the purposes of the exercise was to discover how long it took the surviving bergs to reach the shipping lanes. The most rapid rate of drift was about 12 kilometres a day, though there were many interruptions. On some occasions, they ran aground; on others, they were hemmed in by a mass of ice.

Some disappeared completely from the trace — no doubt having rolled over as icebergs are apt to do despite their misleading suggestions of stability. In popular belief, nine-tenths of a berg's volume lies under the water. In fact, this idea is not entirely accurate. According to a member of the Scott Polar Research Institute, 'The ratio ranges from 7:1 to 5:1 on average, but it varies because the difference in density between the ice above water and below it is not consistent. Features such as the shape of the iceberg and the number of times it has rolled over also add to the confusion. So it appears that, once again, a simple question has no simple answer.'

In one or two instances the transponders packed up.

At the end of the investigation, the conclusion was that it could take something in the order of three years for a berg to reach the area of the Grand Banks. It also became clear how very difficult it is, in spite of modern technology, to keep track of individuals. An official at the Meteorological Office in Bracknell, England, recalls an earlier attempt to maintain such contact:

> This berg was well beyond the limits where you'd normally find one. Initially, a United States Coast Guard cutter was told to stay with it. Then they tried the experiment of dropping darts fitted with radio transponders, so they stuck into the ice. But that didn't work. Then they tried ringing the berg with Carley floats equipped with transponders — they tied them to the berg with ropes. So they were merrily tracking the iceberg until they sent an aeroplane up to have a look at it and see if it was still as big as ever, and it wasn't there. Eventually, they discovered that it had moved 20 miles away. It had turned turtle and gone under water. That sometimes happens: they become unstable. The waves, the swell, and the wash cut away the water line, and they topple over.

In theory, it would nowadays be possible to identify with tolerable accuracy the birthplace of a berg such as the *Titanic*'s killer — provided anyone were able to monitor its progress after it had sunk the liner and knew its height at the moment of calving. To have a record of both would, of course, be as far beyond the question now as it was then. However: the overall dimension from bottom to top of a berg at the moment of its release from the land is an indication of the depth of the valley occupied by its parent glacier. Icebergs have been variously described as white, green, blue, brown and black in colour — observations that may be interesting, but which have little relevance to the present case. But there is one factor common to many of them: within their composition, there are veins of soil. When a berg melts, these fragments of earth fall to the seabed. If they can be retrieved, it is not beyond the powers of geology to identify the place whence they came.

But, even if somebody had been able to track the *Titanic*'s berg throughout most of its life — to have observed its dissolution, and then to have dived to the ocean's floor in search of a scattering of gravel — it would have served little purpose. Those responsible for investigating the disaster were concerned to discover why it had occurred, and, if it could be done, to make sure that such a calamity should not occur again. Tracing the life and times of the instrument of death might have made a paragraph or two in the newspapers; it might have been of some academic interest; but it would have had no practical use.

The iceberg that sank the *Titanic* is invested with an image that is evil. Black should have been its colour; a creature of the night, calved in some dark infernal land far away in the north and launched upon its dreadful mission by the devil's admiral or else by nemesis. One experiences, perhaps, a feeling of surprise that a passenger in another ship should have been able to take its photograph (assuming that this really was the berg in question). As an instrument of fate intended to puncture man's self-esteem, there is something allegoric about it. It should have vanished once its purpose was accomplished. A dramatist, or a writer of legends, would have invested it with mystery, a ghostlike quality, conceivably. But such is not the case.

It has been generally assumed that the birthplace of the *Titanic*'s iceberg was the Disko glacier, very roughly half-way up the west coast of Greenland at approximately 70°N 54'W. The evidence for this may seem to be flimsy: it is based on the fact that, of all the glaciers on this side of the island, the Disko is by far the most prolific. Statistically, then, the odds are weighed in its favour. There is also, it must be admitted, a certain fascination about the idea: a kind of irony not unlike the notion of describing the origination of an iceberg as 'calving'. Just as a berg has little in common with a whale — and none with a mild and rather useful domestic animal — so is the area around Disko an unlikely source for the killer of nearly 1,500 people. For it is not at all sinister. In winter, there are, admittedly, clusters of icebergs on the frozen sea off-shore — for all the world like small ranges of uncommonly steep mountains. On a fine day in summer, however, small bergs float placidly on surprisingly blue water.

Disko itself, which stands to seaward of the glacier, is Greenland's largest island. From 1924 until 1972, when the settlement was closed down, 0.6 million tons of coal were mined from it. Nowadays, it is a place of small importance, though, now and again, parties of naturalists travel to God-havn at its southern end. In 1982, they observed fulmars, the Lapland bunting and the redpoll. They also identified the island's only apparent social problem. A species of bumblebee known as *Bombus Polaris* was threatened by an intruder named *Bombus Hyperboreus* — a parasite that occupies the nests of the less aggressive and gradually usurps them. With so little vege-tation, it may seem surprising that bumblebees can survive at all — though, it seems they do not employ workers such as those in more temperate zones do. The queen and her children, very wisely no doubt, remain at home. This, of course, begs other questions, and suggests that there is more work to be done by those robust investigators of nature who venture to Godhavn.

On the mainland, and quite near the glacier, there is a small town named Jakobshavn. There are some large warehouses that were erected when the coal-mining industry was flourish-ing. A rather elegant little wooden church satisfies the needs of the faithful. Outside, a huge anchor from some ancient sailing ship is mounted on a stone plinth. But the most imposing building is now a museum. It was here, in this two-storey house painted a pleasant shade of dark red, that the explorer Knud Rasmussen was born in 1879.

It may, indeed, seem strange that the destroyer of Britain's largest liner, the agent of fate that accounted for so many lives, may have originated in the midst of such surroundings. The coal deposits on the island would have been sufficient to fuel a fleet of ships throughout their lives — and then more fleets. In the church so close to the glacier, men and women sing hymns. On the island, bumblebees come out of hibernation in summer, in much the manner of bumblebees in New England or in a Surrey garden. Instruments of death should be wrought in ungodly places. The pastor of Jakobshavn, familiar though he must be with the Disko glacier, would certainly not so describe his parish.

Whilst the glacier is no doubt the manufactory of potential disaster, and its production capacity is infinite, Jakobshavn's most famous son, Knud Rasmussen was more helpful. He, more than anyone, produced the true definition of Greenland. Admittedly an American, Robert E. Peary, made the discovery that it is an island. But, as Rasmussen found out, Peary committed one or two errors. He mistook a deep fjord for a bay, and he recorded a cliff on what he believed to be the coast, but which was, in fact, a hundred miles inland. As the result of Rasmussen's more accurate observations, the United States government withdrew Peary's maps of northern Greenland in 1915.

Among Rasmussen's several other accomplishments was that of establishing a trading base for the Eskimos at Thule — about 657 miles to the north of Disko — in 1910. As early as *c.*300 BC, the Greek navigator Pytheas (who was also a leading Athenian magistrate) came across an island wrapped in mist, a place of sparse vegetation and where only a few human beings lived. The Greek word *thule* (afterwards adopted by the Romans) applied to the most northerly land in the world. This, Pytheas decided, had to be it, and so *thule* became Thule. The Shetlands, Iceland, Norway and even Greenland have been mooted as its possible location. However, since the journey involved only six days' sailing up the coast of Britain, and since Pytheas then went on to discover what we know to be the Baltic, Shetland seems to be the most likely possibility — and Greenland the least likely. Whether this served any great geographical purpose may seem to be doubtful. But when Virgil added the adjective *ultima,* lexicographers benefited. A glance at *The Concise Oxford Dictionary* shows *ultima Thule* defined as 'Faraway unknown region', which is no doubt how Pytheas would have described it.

Rasmussen's Thule was far beyond the limits of the intrepid Greek's exploration. It might, indeed, have seemed to be the edge of the world: the last stop, very nearly, before the traveller reaches the northward conclusion at the Pole. In 1951, the Eskimo settlement, with its 130 inhabitants, was moved seventy miles even farther north. The object was to clear the ground for building a base for the USAF's Strategic Air Command. No less than $370 million was spent on five hundred buildings, spread over 338,000 acres and provided with the last word in electronic equipment. In 1960, it was converted into the world's first Ballistic Missile Early Warning System, which gave United States citizens a few minutes to run for cover before the advent of Doomsday. It is now part of a network using radar and optical sensors that makes 20,000 observations every day, and keeps track of more than five thousand objects in space. In addition to this, there is the electro-optical Deep Space Surveillance system, which is really a collection of television cameras mounted on deep-space telescopes and connected to a computer. It is the northern extremity of the USAF's Space Command — or, as it calls itself (and Mr Reagan must surely have approved: he might even have thought of it) 'Guardians of the High Frontier'.

One doubts whether a posting to Thule would be the first choice of many people. On 22 November each year, the sun sets and remains out of sight until 22 February, or thereabouts. Although the temperature can be as high as 63°F in summer, it is commonly −44°F in winter. The second highest wind ever endured on the face of the earth was recorded there on 8 March 1972: at its height, it was blowing at 207 mph.

Nevertheless, somebody has to be there. If one understands it correctly, the apparatus at Thule helps to prevent collisions in the way-out-yonder of the heavens, and it enables Space Command to respond (a spokesman's words) 'to shuttle contingencies — such as an unscheduled landing at one of the worldwide recovery bases'. It also assists in 'developing Air Force space doctrine and strategy' and 'promoting a compre-hensive documentation of the Soviet space threat'. More to the point so far as this book is concerned is that the harbour is used by ships of the United States Coast Guard. It was from here, in August 1969, that the USCG *Southwind* set out to make a survey of bergs and glaciers between Kap York and Upernavik — an area that includes Melville Bugt, which shares with the Disko glacier the distinction of being the prime producer of icebergs.

If the results of these and other observations were compared with the iceberg population of the South Atlantic, they would show a considerable difference in size. In the latter case, the bergs are seldom a result of the calving process, but of seismic disturbances within the Antarctic ice-cap. As a consequence, they are very much larger. Between 1890 and 1915, a record was kept of the bigger bergs sighted in the general area of the North Atlantic approaching the Grand Banks from the east. No more than ten of them exceeded 500 feet in height; only one was judged to be 1,000 feet. None of their lengths could be measured in miles.

Down in the South Atlantic, on the other hand, over a period of thirty-two years, twenty-four bergs were seen to be 1,000 or more feet in height — the tallest was a massive 1,700 feet. One was reported by the steamer *Strathdon* as 40 miles long; but the largest was a monster encountered earlier in 1854. Shaped like a hook, the longer shank stretched for 60 miles; the shorter for 40 miles. However, even this is small when set beside the current entry in the *Guinness Book of Records*. Observed by the USS *Glacier* to the west of Scott Island in the South Pacific on 12 November 1956, it occupied a staggering 12,000 square miles (208 miles long and 60 miles wide). In this respect, the northern hemisphere receives no mention at all in the Guinness book.

Within the *Titanic*, providing the sea was calm, it was easy to forget that you were not on land. The Café Parisien was adorned with trellis-work and ivy: the cuisine was as good as that of any hotel ashore. A private stretch of the promenade deck, accessible only to those who had paid the top prices (a suite cost anything from £400 to £870 for a one-way passage), was decorated in a style more recently known as 'Stockbrokers' Tudor'. The public rooms were adorned in extravagantly good taste: there was a gymnasium, a Turkish bath, a swimming pool, a hairdresser's shop, and other comforts galore. Even the steerage-class passengers — for so long the under-privileged and often under-nourished travellers of the seas — enjoyed accommodation very much more agreeable than anything previous generations had experienced.

But a ship is a ship no matter what else she pretends to be. One of the most important requirements of sound navigation is the ability to observe. This responsibility was invested in the two look-outs up in the crow's nest. It has to be assumed that their eyesight was adequate for the task: neither of them had undergone a test to make sure. Nor were they provided with binoculars. There had been a pair when the ship arrived at Southampton from her builders' yard at Belfast. Then — strangely, it may seem — they were removed.

Readers of Mr David Hughes's enlightening *But for Bunter* (Heinemann, 1985) may recall that the Fat Owl of the Remove is reputed to have embarked on the *Titanic* at Southampton and to have been thrown off at Cherbourg. This was just as well for Bunter — though, if this tale is to be believed, it would have been better had he never been allowed near the ship in the first place. Somewhere off the Isle of Wight, he came across what we must assume to have been the vessel's only pair of binoculars lying on a lifeboat cover. He picked them up to take what should have been a last look at the Old Country — and then, as two officers approached, threw them overboard in panic. Since Mr Hughes's account is clearly a work of fiction, this explanation cannot be taken too seriously. But, for want of any other option, it seems as good a reason as any for this curious oversight.

At the inquiry into the disaster, one of the men complained about this, and remarked how much better the situation had been in an earlier White Star liner, the *Oceanic*. The explorer Sir Ernest Shackleton, who was called as an expert witness, disputed this. 'I do not believe in any look-out man having glasses at all,' he said. 'I only believe in the officer using them, and then only when something has been reported in a certain quarter or a certain place on the bow.' His argument was that a watchful pair of eyes could take in the entire horizon; binoculars, on the other hand, localized the vision. Lord

Mersey, President of the Inquiry, agreed with him. 'The judgement,' he said, 'is that binoculars are not desirable in the crow's nest.' When making his recommendations, however, he did concede that 'every man taking a look-out in such ships shall undergo a sight test at reasonable intervals'.

Captain Smith had given instructions that, despite the warnings received from other ships, the *Titanic* should reduce her speed of 22 knots only if the visibility on this unusually clear night were to be deteriorate. One question that vexed the Board of Trade Inquiry was whether it had done so. According to the look-outs — Reginald Lee and Frederick Fleet (both had survived) — a mist had formed. Lee recalled his companion remarking, 'Well, if we can see through that, we'll be lucky.' Fleet did not remember saying this, though he was fairly sure that the sharp-edged night had lost something of its definition fifteen minutes before the moment of impact. On the other hand, Charles Lightoller, the only senior officer to come through the disaster, refused to be deflected from his insistence that there had been no mist. Even when he was reminded that it can often be more easily seen from somewhere higher up than the bridge — the crow's nest, for example — he would not be budged. The firmness of his denial is, perhaps, surprising. Not only was he resting in his cabin at the time: it is common knowledge that, when the water is colder than the air (to quote Commander S.T.S. Lecky, RNR, FRAS, FRGS, the author of a definitive work on navigation first published in 1881), some fogs 'have a tendency to lie in a thin stratum, which extends but 30 or 40 feet above the surface. In such cases it is quite possible to see over it by ascending to the masthead, from which position we may discern land, icebergs, or the masts of other vessels, when they are quite concealed to those on deck.'

A drop in the sea temperature is not necessarily a warning of bergs in the vicinity, but a drop in air temperature is. Lecky says that it may fall by 10° or even 12°, and there is plenty of evidence that, before the collision, it had become noticeably colder on the *Titanic*'s decks. Another warning is (Lecky tells us) 'a sort of whiteness or halo, known as "ice blink"'. There is no suggestion that Lee, or his friend Fleet, observed this phenomenon, though the question arises of whether they might have done — had they been given binoculars.

One must, then, allow the berg credit for providing some warning of its presence — despite Lightoller's suggestion that it had probably capsized. 'That', he told the inquiry, 'would leave most of it that had been below the water above it, and practically all black ice, or it must have been a berg broken from a glacier with its blue side towards us.' This means very little, since all bergs in this area had, and still have, broken from glaciers at the start of their lives. However, let him continue: 'Had it been a normal iceberg with three white sides, we could easily have made it out one-and-a-half to two miles away.'

Were they, then, confronted with some sort of freak; and, if this was the case, would that extra distance have been suffi-cient to save the ship? The first officer, William Murdoch, was on duty. When he received the look-outs' report of the iceberg, he ordered a sudden change of course, and rang down 'full astern' to the engine-room. If we disregard the first instruction, which was probably unwise, would putting the engines suddenly into reverse have halted the liner in time to avoid a head-on collision?

The former master of the *Mauretania*, Captain John Pritchard, stated that he could have stopped his own ship in three-quarters of a mile when she was travelling at 26 knots — five knots faster than the *Titanic*. We have to accept Captain Pritchard's word for this, though it seems unlikely. A modern supertanker requires all of seven miles in which to be brought to a standstill. With their finer lines and much higher speeds, one would have expected ships such as the *Mauretania* and the *Titanic* to have needed an even greater distance. Nor does evidence produced by the *Titanic*'s sister, the *Olympic*, seem to support him. Steaming at 18 knots in an Irish lough (three knots slower than the *Titanic*) her engines were suddenly put into reverse. Within three minutes all the way had gone off her — though there is no telling how far she travelled in this time. The members of the inquiry team had to be content with the information that, within 15 seconds of the instruction being given, she had travelled 1,000 yards (or just under three-quarters of a mile). Since the berg created no counter velocity — it was only ambling through the night — the extra distance might just have sufficed. But, it would have been a near-run thing: two miles would have been better than one and a half, and anything would have been an improvement on 100 yards or so.

But then, had she struck the berg head-on, and had her collision bulkhead held, she would probably have survived in any case.

The first ice warning from another ship — which, admittedly, was 48 hours out of date — arrived at 9 a.m. (all the times mentioned here are those of the *Titanic*'s clocks) on the 14th from the *Caronia*. Its text was: 'Captain, Titanic — westbound steamers report bergs, growlers and field ice in 42°N to 51°W, 12 April.' By this time, the *Titanic* was sufficiently far to the west and to the south of the area for the message to be disregarded. However, a signal received at 1.42 p.m. on the 14th from the *Baltic* deserved closer attention. It read: 'Greek steamer Athenai reports passing icebergs and large quantities of field ice today in lat. 41°51'N 49°52'. Also German tanker Deutschland Stettin-Philadelphia short of coal and out of control 40°42'N 55°11'W wishes to be reported to New York and other steamers.' Again, the liner was clear of the area in question — and, indeed, some way removed from the stricken tanker. Nevertheless, the message should have been pinned up on a board in the chartroom. Instead, when Captain Smith handed it to his chairman, Bruce Ismay, the latter put it into his pocket. That afternoon, he showed it to a couple of ladies, using it to illustrate his hypothesis that they might witness icebergs during the evening.

Other warnings were received. At 1.45 p.m., the *Amerika* reported bergs to the south of the *Titanic*'s course. At 7.30 p.m. a message was intercepted from the Leyland liner *Californian* to the *Antillian* advising of 'three large bergs to the south of us'. At 9.40 p.m. from the *Mesaba*: 'Ice-report in lat. 42°N to 41°25'N long. 49° to 50°30'W. Saw much heavy pack-ice and a great number large icebergs. Also field ice. Weather good, clear.' This never reached Captain Smith let alone Bruce Ismay's pocket. The wireless operator replied with a curt 'thanks' and put the message to one side. During the previous night, a transformer in his set had failed and he had been busy repairing it. He was now trying to catch up with the mass of telegrams that first-class passengers insisted were urgent.

Later, the east-bound *Rappahannock* out of Halifax on
course for Europe, warned that she had 'just passed through
heavy field ice and several icebergs'. Again the *Titanic*'s
acknowledgement was no more than perfunctory; and when, at
11 p.m., the Leyland liner *Californian*, now hove-to on the
edge of the *Rappahannock*'s 'heavy icefield', issued yet
another warning, her well-meaning wireless operator was
actually told to 'shut up'!

Inevitably, there have been speculations about whether the
Titanic would have escaped destruction had she been equipped
with radar. It is a fantasy about as sensible as suggesting that,
if the French had been armed with machine-guns, they might
have done better at Agincourt. Nevertheless, let us examine it.
According to an official at the Meteorological Office:

> Ice is still a serious hazard around the Grand Banks. You get
> so much fog. The trouble with radar is that, if the berg is a
> big one, it will detect it. But if it's what we call a 'bergy bit',
> which is an old piece of weathered glacier ice, the response
> of sea waves is very much the same, so it's very difficult to
> determine which is ice and which is water. The probability is
> that the bergy bits can do as much damage as the big
> icebergs.

At the inquiry, Lightoller described the sea as 'smooth as the
top of a table or a floor'. Under these circumstances, there
would have been no waves to misguide the observer. The berg,
no matter what its size, would have shown up — assuming
that, in the euphoria caused by such amazingly calm and clear
conditions, anyone had taken the trouble to consult the radar
screen.

If the helmsman's estimate of an iceberg 100 feet high was
correct, the danger would have been foreseen in plenty of time.
But, if we accept the captain's and first officer's description of
something 'not very high out of the water', the situation might
still have been critical.

On 10 August 1979 the MV *Reynolds* was on passage
through the Davis Strait from Rouen to Churchill, Manitoba.
At approximately noon GMT, she was approaching the
Hudson Strait. There was patchy fog and a number of icebergs
were known to be in the vicinity. At 1 p.m., the first echoes

appeared on the radar screen. During the next twenty-four hours, many more blips were observed — on several occasions, as many as twenty at a time. The largest seen by the crew was 1,094 yards long by 109.4 yards wide and about 98.46 feet high. The big bergs showed up clearly on the plot at a range of 12 miles. Smaller ones became apparent at six miles, and even growlers and bergy bits produced echoes — though, in these instances, they were only one or two miles from the ship.

Twenty-hour hours later, once the *Reynolds* had entered Hudson Strait, the sightings ceased. According to her master, Captain J.K. Cooper, 'Most of the icebergs were weathered, had sharp edges and were dark blue in colour around the water-line.'

So far as the *Titanic* is concerned, the most this achieves is to confirm what we already know: that she was in much the same situation as that of a partially blind man running down a crowded street at the speed of a marathon competitor on top of his form. However, the experience of the *Reynolds* should also be compared, and more properly so, with that of the 7,261-ton Yugoslavian freighter *Kastela*. On 3 August 1963, she was on passage through the Hudson Strait bound for the UK, when she struck a berg and sank. There is no record of any survivors. The difference between the *Kastela* and the *Reynolds* is that, while the latter was equipped with radar, the former had only a radio direction finder and an echo sounder.

At the *Titanic* inquiry, no fewer than five master mariners were prepared to testify that, provided the weather was clear, they would proceed through an ice-cluttered sea without reducing speed. They might (though they didn't) have mentioned how many ships had got away with it — and, possibly, how many had survived collisions with bergs. The 8,400-ton *City of Rome*, an elegant ship built for the Inman Line, had struck one and survived. The *Columbia*, the *Persia*, the *Arizona* — all of them had been equally fortunate. Nevertheless, in the days before radio, nobody knew what had happened to vessels that disappeared. Towards the end of the nineteenth century, the *Naronic*, travelling from Liverpool to New York, went missing in the vicinity of the Grand Banks. Presumed cause of disaster: impact with an iceberg. The *Allegheny*, the *Huronian*,

and the *State of Georgia* — all three vanished from the surface
of the ocean. Again the presumed cause of disaster was an
iceberg.

But there were many other vessels known to be lost by these
deadly collisions. In a list compiled by the *Polar Record*, no
fewer than fifty-nine ships were mentioned as iceberg victims
during the final decade of the last century. In 1899 alone,
seven were either sunk or damaged beyond repair. Add to these
the number lost in the first twelve years of the twentieth
century — making a total of twenty-two years before the
Titanic incident — and the figure becomes 102.

No doubt those distinguished liner captains who gave
evidence at the *Titanic* inquiry knew their business — though
their apparent determination to stick to the schedule, ice or no
ice, appears strangely irresponsible. The case of the Collins
liner *Pacific* and the Cunarder *Persia* should have served as a
sufficient illustration.

In 1851 the *Pacific* had established herself as the fastest
vessel on the North Atlantic when she accomplished the
crossing in just over nine days. Such evidence that there is
suggests that her master was determined to hang on to his
record — just as the captain of the *Persia*, the latest addition to
the Cunard fleet, was out to beat it. The two ships sailed from
Liverpool within days of each other in January 1856. The
weather was bad, and there were rumours of ice. It was a time
for prudence to prevail over ambition.

On 23 January the *Pacific* slipped away from the quayside at
Liverpool. She crossed the bar at the mouth of the Mersey, and
that was the last anyone saw of her. A few days later, the *Persia*
followed. After about five days at sea, she ran into an icefield
and struck one of the bergs. She was out of action for 36 hours
while repairs were carried out, and one or two members of her
crew suffered frostbite. But she reached New York, which was
more than the *Pacific* did.

It was eventually assumed that the *Pacific* died the death
that the *Persia* so mercifully escaped, but it took a long time for
her owners and the relatives of those on board to accept the
probability. Forty-two days after her departure, when there
was still no news, people continued to propound theories that
might encourage hope. One idea was that she had become

hemmed in by ice and was unable to move. Everything would be all right when the weather turned warmer. Another posed the proposition that she had been damaged by a berg off the Grand Banks. According to this school of thought, her machinery had been disabled and she had been compelled to depend upon her sails. If this were so, her captain might have taken advantage of the strong westerlies and, instead of heading for the nearest land (Nova Scotia), have put back across the Atlantic on course for Ireland.

There was a precedent for such an action. In 1851, the engines of another Collins liner, the *Atlantic*, had broken down. Unable to make any progress against the headwinds, her captain had gone about. Her canvas, described by *The Times* as 'scanty and insufficient at all times', was torn to shreds, and for several days she was virtually a hulk drifting helplessly away from the shipping lanes. Nevertheless, she reached Cork, repairs were made, and she resumed her passage. She arrived in New York 49 days later.

If something very similar had happened to the *Pacific*, the public was assured, there was no cause for alarm. The experience would undoubtedly be uncomfortable, but there was sufficient food on board to last for three months.

But no trace of the *Pacific* was every discovered. The ship was insured for $600,000; her cargo for $1,400,000, but this was of no help to her owners. The company's financial affairs were already in a chaotic state; the loss of the *Pacific* was the last straw. The US government withdrew its subsidy and the firm went into liquidation.

Inevitably, the tragedy attracted a great deal of comment. A correspondent in *The Times*, who signed himself 'The Dove from the Ark', suggested that all ships should be compelled to take a complement of carrier pigeons with them. If a vessel was in difficulty, the birds should be released — taking with them such basic details as the latitude and longitude, and any other pertinent information that could be crammed on to a small piece of paper. *The Times* itself, no doubt indebted to a traveller in the *Persia* for its insight on the prevailing conditions, condemned the folly of 'rushing, amid the densest fog and at full speed, through thronging ice islands'. As it quite rightly pointed out, a diversion, which need have added no more than ten or fifteen hours to her voyage, would probably have saved the ship. But there was the *Persia* hot on her tail. The *Pacific* had hurried heedlessly on until she was ice-locked. An attempt to push through to clear water probably caused the fatal damage.

There was also the matter of her hull. The *Persia*'s was constructed from iron and she had survived her wound. The *Pacific*'s was wooden and, even though it was sheathed in copper, it was more vulnerable. It was something to think about, but even good fortune such as attended the *Persia* could not be counted upon. That March, owners of United States mail steamers announced that, after 1 August, none of their vessels would cross the Grand Banks north of latitude 43°N.

In their assumption that the best way in which to avoid collision with a berg was to avoid anywhere in which these menaces might be found, the owners were obviously correct. However, their decision demonstrated how much they still had to learn about the seasonal habits of icebergs. Spring is the most dangerous time of all in the neighbourhood of the Grand Banks; and, when the *Titanic* foundered in April 1912, her position was 1.14° south of the prescribed limit. But, then, the ice drifted unusually far south that year.

On 6 February 1856, a fortnight after the *Pacific* had sailed, the *Atlantic* — she of the 1851 ordeal — departed from Liverpool, and it is from one of her passengers that we receive the best picture of the conditions that faced the *Persia* and the *Pacific*. The liner was not far out into the Atlantic when the fog first appeared: so thick that 'you couldn't see the length of the ship'. This was joined by gales and, three days later, by ice. The captain, who had crossed the Atlantic 243 times, said that he had never known such weather (had he forgotten 1851; or was even that preferable to his present problem?).

The ice, the same passenger recalled, was 'increasing to such an extent we could only feel our way ... fog, fog, fog! Nothing but fog and ice!'

At seven in the morning a day or so later, it briefly lifted. 'The atmosphere as far as the eye could reach was clear, the sun shone brightly on a continuous chain of icebergs above 100 feet high, intermingled with fields of ice. Chain after chain burst into sight and the sight was awfully impressive. Then the fog returned.'

Wisely, the *Atlantic*'s captain did what the *Pacific*'s should have done. He turned his ship round, steamed back in the direction of the UK for the remainder of the day and then, during the night, took a southerly course. Next morning, he resumed his passage to New York. The voyage from start to finish took 18 days.

Although icebergs from the east coast of Greenland generally end their lives by melting at the entrance to the Davis Strait, it should not be imagined that they pose no hazard to shipping. Their toll may not have been so large as those that find their way to area of the Grand Banks, but fewer vessels pass this way. In 1888, a former whaler named *Castor* was bought by the Danish government and modified for the Denmark-Greenland ferry service. On her second voyage in her new role, she vanished somewhere near Cape Farewell. Twenty-five lives were lost. The mystery of her disappearance has never been explained, though it is fair to assume that an iceberg was the cause. In 1927 the chartered steamer *Hugo* was lost in the same region again probably after hitting a berg.

In January 1959 the 2,800-ton motor vessel *Hans Hedtoft* came into service as flagship of the Royal Greenland Trade Department's fleet. Her specifications exceeded the most demanding requirements of any insurance syndicate. Her hull was divided into seven watertight compartments. She had a double steel bottom; her bows and stern were strongly reinforced; and she was equipped with the most modern navigational aids — including radar.

The *Hans Hedtoft*'s master, fifty-eight-year-old Captain Poul Ludvig Rasmussen, was a veteran of the Denmark-Greenland route. He had joined the company in 1935 as a mate. In 1949, he had been given his first command. Between them, the ship and the man could be regarded as a match for anything the sea, the ice and the weather, might devise.

Late on the evening of 29 January, the *Hans Hedtoft* sailed from Godthåb, the capital of Greenland. She called at Julianehåb on the extreme south-west corner of the island and, at 15 minutes past midnight, set off on her journey to

Denmark. High winds were blowing; the sea was unusually rough even for this unquiet corner of the ocean; and there were a great many icebergs about. The voyage should have taken her between six and seven days, but she never got beyond a point 37 miles south of Cape Farewell.

The first intimation that the *Hans Hedtoft* might be in trouble came in a radio signal. It said, briefly, 'Collision with iceberg.' This was followed, shortly afterwards, with 'Filling fast'; and, finally, by 'Taking a lot of water in the engine-room'.

Her distress signal was picked up at 2.10 p.m. GMT by the USCG cutter *Campbell*, which was on station at 56°30′N 51°W — about 280 miles to the south-west of the *Hans Hedtoft*'s reported position. The *Campbell* set off at once; aircraft from Greenland, Canada, and Iceland joined in the search for the stricken ship. None of them found any trace of her. Her crew of forty, and her fifty-five passengers — among them a member of the Danish parliament, six children, and several civil servants returning to Copenhagen — were all lost.

Nobody was blamed for the disaster. As a member of the Royal Greenland Trade Department said, 'it was deemed to have been an unforeseen contingency'. The assumption was that, in trying to avoid collision with a berg, the impact took place aft and the sea broke through into the main engine-room and into the auxiliary engine-room. This, however, is specu-lation: no more detailed information than the reference to 'taking a lot of water in the engine-room' was received.

Afterwards, an ice reconnaissance service was established. It is based on the airfield at Narssarssuaq in southern Greenland, and covers the area around Cape Farewell — on the east coast to a point as far north as Angmagssalik, about one-quarter of the way up. Furthermore, it became the Royal Greenland Trading Department's policy to carry no passengers on these voyages between 1 December and 28 February. There have been no subsequent disasters.

The case of the *Hans Hedtoft* had certain features in common with those of the *Titanic*, which foundered about 600 miles to the south. Both ships were making their maiden voyages. Both ships were commanded by captains of consider-able experience. And both ships seem to have been hit in the engine-room while turning in an attempt to avoid collision.

In April 1912, the Cunarder *Mauretania* was following the *Titanic* across the Atlantic, a day or two behind her. The news of the disaster reached the ship when she was about half-way across the ocean. The casualties were reported as 1,500 (actually, they were 1,490). Distress and shock at this appalling toll were universal — and there were doubtless some who reflected that there but for the grace of God went them, and those who wondered whether God's grace had expired and there was time for them to go as well. At least one passenger, a doctor named Samuel Eyde, was determined that something must be done to prevent a recurrence. He discussed the matter with the *Mauretania*'s captain and with some of his companions. On 18 April, he collected the ideas together and wrote a memorandum. The gist of it was that an international ice patrol should be established. Not long after he landed, he presented the document to US Senator William Smith of Michigan. As he pointed out:

> The information that great steamers receive today regarding the location of icebergs depends entirely upon reports given by ships that occasionally have seen them and by observations of low temperatures in the water that follows them. [Lecky would not have agreed with this second statement.]
>
> The movement of icebergs depends largely on the winds and currents, so that a ship getting a report of an iceberg never knows the exact position of it after a time. A ship of the size of 25,000 tons [the *Titanic* was 46,328 tons] striking an iceberg in foggy weather, even at low speed, would go down if, as in the case of the *Titanic*, the ice was low enough to permit her to ride over it. [This can only have been an assumption: Dr Eyde wrote this paper a mere four days after the disaster, while still at sea, and before the details were generally known. However, in general, it was fair comment.]
>
> That kind of information of the whereabouts of icebergs is insufficient to prevent disasters. To have full security for such calamities it is recommended that special ships be sent out. There must be a regular fully organized guard service.

Greatly to its credit, the American government acted quickly. For the remainder of 1912 two US Navy cruisers were detailed to patrol the area in which icebergs were liable to be encountered. In 1913 the responsibility was assumed by the Treasury Department, which handed over the work to the US Revenue Cutter Service (later called the United States Coast Guard). The cutters *Seneca* and *Miami* were employed. In the same year, the British government became involved to the extent of chartering the steam-trawler *Scotia*. She was suitably fitted out and dispatched to make ice and weather observations off the coast of Newfoundland. The Board of Trade paid some of the cost; the rest was contributed by steamship companies that ran services across the Atlantic.

Between them, the American and British authorities had created the nucleus of the International Ice Patrol. Nowadays, the patrol is run by the United States Coast Guard's Research and Development Centre at Groton, Connecticut. It is no doubt significant that, since its inception, no passenger ship has been lost by impact with ice in the North Atlantic. However, the *Titanic*'s much maligned British Board of Trade Inquiry should also take a little of the credit. It concluded 'that the loss of the said ship was due to collision with an iceberg, brought about by the excessive speed at which the ship was being navigated'. Its recommendations included the suggestion that 'instruction should be given in all Steamship Companies' Regulations that when ice is reported in or near the track of the ship, the ship should proceed in the dark hours at a moderate speed or alter her course so as to go well clear of the danger zone.'

Captain Edward J. Smith was, perhaps, a martyr to the cause of sticking to the schedule at all costs — or of bashing-on-regardless. Unhappily, his martyrdom was shared by 1,489 others.

The Captain's Story

If Sherlock Holmes had been invited to investigate the case of the *Titanic*, he might well have recalled one of his observations made when looking for the missing race horse, Silver Blaze. As noted afterwards by the zealous Watson, the conversation went as follows:

> *Watson*: Is there any point to which you wish to draw my attention?
> *Holmes*: To the curious incident of the dog in the night-time.
> *Watson*: The dog did nothing in the night-time.
> *Holmes*: That was the curious incident.

Substitute the word 'captain' for 'dog', and you identify one of the several puzzles that are contained in the *Titanic* mystery. Captain E.J. Smith, a master mariner of considerable experience, did not receive all the warnings of icebergs that reached the liner's wireless operators. Nevertheless, he had sufficient information to know of the perils that lay in the liner's path. Presumably, as a conscientious sailor, he paid attention to it, though his reaction seems to have been strangely casual.

There was, for example, the signal received from the *Baltic* at about lunchtime. Instead of posting it on the board in the chartroom, he allowed his employer, Bruce Ismay, to slip it into his pocket. It was not until six hours later, in the smoking room before dinner, that he realized his mistake and asked for it back. Nor does anyone appear to have been made responsible for marking the positions of the known icebergs on a chart. At the British inquiry, the fourth officer, Joseph Boxhall, said that he could recall only plotting bergs to the north of the liner's track. It was not, he explained, really his duty: 'I just seemed to be the one that he told to do it each time.'

Whose duty was it then? And why, with so much evidence of danger to come, did Captain Smith not double the look-outs by placing a couple of men up front in the bows? And why, oh why, did he not order a reduction in speed? The *Titanic* was not trying to capture the Blue Riband on this her maiden voyage. Fastest passages had never been the policy of the White Star Line, which preferred to entrust its reputation to luxury and reliability. In any case, very prudently, the attitude of the engineers had not been that required of aspiring record-breakers. By bringing more and then more boilers into operation, the ship's speed had been gradually built up. Now, approaching the area of maximum hazard, she was steaming at $22^{1}/_{2}$ knots — faster than at any other time on the voyage.

The luckless Ismay, target for the public wrath, has been accused of goading his captain on: a figure rather like the white rabbit in *Alice in Wonderland* who, constantly looking at his watch, kept muttering, 'Oh dear! Oh dear! I shall be too late.' This is nonsense. Ismay is known to have told the chief engineer that the Wednesday morning, rather than the Tuesday night, should be the time to arrive in New York.

Indeed, the problem with some owners in the preceding years had mostly been that they restrained their captains rather than egged them on. Samuel Cunard, for instance, had always insisted on a policy of caution. In his instructions to Captain Judkins, master of the *Britannia,* he stressed that, 'In navigating of our vessels we have great confidence in the ability of our captains, but in the matter of fog, the best officers become infatuated and often attempt to push through when prudence would indicate patience.' Judkins, no doubt aware that, at sea, the skipper is next to God and that the Almighty takes precedence over the owner, usually had other ideas. When the going was hazardous, he tended to keep the engines at full speed — in the belief that, the faster you travel, 'the sooner you are out of it'.

Throughout the voyage, Ismay never once visited the bridge, and the fact that the *Titanic* was now steaming at almost maximum speed had nothing to do with him. It was part of a carefully worked-out plan to bring the new machinery quite gently up to its full performance. Unhappily, Smith did nothing to modify the programme.

At the British inquiry, no fewer than five master mariners were prepared to testify that, in clear weather — and this night was unusually clear — their attitudes would have been the same as Smith's: to hold course and not reduce speed. Ismay himself admitted that he had not expected Smith to slow down the liner (though this is not to suggest that he tried to force this view on the captain). When he was asked whether, in view of the certainty of ice ahead, it was not a strange attitude, the White Star chairman had nothing to say. In an apparent attempt to be helpful, but deftly laying a trap, the Attorney-General suggested, 'I presume the man would be anxious to get through the ice region. He would not want to slow down on the chance of a fog coming on.'

Ismay side-stepped it, though his distinguished inquisitor may have been interpreting 'the man's' intentions correctly. The area of the Grand Banks is notorious for fog brought about by the conjunction of the warm Gulf Stream and the cold Labrador current. It is more than a possibility; it is a probability — and such nights as that of 14/15 April 1912, are rare. That, perhaps, is the sorrow of it. Had the visibility been less good, Smith would have been compelled to be more prudent.

Captain S.G.S. McNeil, one-time commander of Cunard's *Mauretania*, recalls an occasion in 1914 when, commanding the *Ascania* and outward bound from the St Lawrence for England, he suspected the presence of ice to the east. 'A few minutes after passing Belle Isle,' he wrote, 'a dense fog came down ... After running a mile to the east of the island, I stopped the engines. The tide was setting east and when, two hours later, the fog lifted, there, two hundred yards ahead of us, was an iceberg as big as the White House.'

This, of course, was after the event. Among the items put into the *Titanic*'s chart room at Southampton, however, was Part I of *The United States Pilot (East Coast)* compiled by the Hydrographic Department of the Admiralty. Within its contents was the following passage:

One of the chief dangers in crossing the Atlantic lies in the probability of encountering masses of ice, both in the form of bergs and of extensive fields of solid compact ice released at the breaking up of winter in the Arctic regions, and drifted down by the Labrador Current across their direct route.

Such conditions were most likely to be encountered 'Between April and August, both months inclusive — although bergs are seen at all seasons, north of 43′N.' 'It is', the book warned,

impossible to give . . . any distinct idea of where ice may be expected, and no rule can be laid down to ensure safe navigation, as its position and the quantity met with differs so greatly in different seasons. Everything must depend upon the vigilance, caution and skill with which a vessel is navigated when crossing the dangerous ice-bearing regions of the Atlantic Ocean.

In 1984 an official of the Meteorological Office put it more succinctly when he said: 'Passenger vessels should not enter International Ice Patrol "danger" areas otherwise their insurance is invalid!' But times, thankfully, have changed.

On the night in question, when 'vigilance, caution and skill' were most needed, Captain Smith was not navigating at all. He was being sociable to the passengers. Before dinner he was in the smoking room, chatting with Ismay; then was at a meal specially arranged in his honour by one of the millionaires on board. At nine o'clock, he made a brief visit to the bridge, where he remarked upon the fall in temperature to the first officer, William Murdoch. This, surely, should have given him cause for thought; but no. He then went to his cabin. Throughout the most dangerous hours of the trip, the ship was virtually under the command of Mr Murdoch. It was an awesome responsibility.

And so it was Murdoch who, at 11.40 p.m. received from the crow's nest the report that an iceberg lay ahead. It was he who ordered the engines to go full astern; and he who, instinctively trying to avoid a collision, made the fatal decision of ordering the helmsman to go 'hard-a-starboard' (which, if his manoeuvre had worked, would have been followed by 'hard-a-port', as he attempted to bring the liner round the iceberg without touching it). It was Murdoch, too, who caused the watertight doors to be closed; and Murdoch who, no doubt tormented by his one mistake, shot himself just before the liner sank.

Smith might have argued that, in mingling with the first-class passengers, he had been doing nothing less than his duty. Brunel had seen the problem when the *Great Eastern* was being built in 1855. In his *Memorandum on the Management of the Great Ship*, he wrote:

> The Commander's attention must be devoted exclusively to the general management of the whole system under his control, and his attention must not be diverted by frivolous pursuits and unimportant occupations. I believe that even in the present large steamers much advantage would result from relieving the captain from all care of passengers and cargo; but in our case, where we may have to provide for thousands instead of hundreds, the present system of a captain dining at table and associating with the passengers would be impracticable, even if it were desirable ... still less would he have his mind occupied with the troublesome and frivolous concerns of a vast hotel, nor should he be hampered by the necessity of attending to the hours and forms of a large society.

As was so often the case, Brunel was years ahead of his time. One result of the *Titanic* disaster was the creation of a new appointment on most of the large, 'express', ships: that of staff captain. Captain McNeil was the first to undertake this task on behalf of Cunard, in the *Mauretania.* As he wrote: 'With a staff-captain under him, the captain would be free to devote his time and thoughts entirely to the navigation of the ship; and he would know that as the staff-captain's duties were solely of a disciplinary nature, the standard of efficiency on board would be constantly improving.'

One of Captain McNeil's earlier, and less pleasant experiences on the *Mauretania* was that of overcoming a lunatic who was thought to have a revolver in his pocket. It turned out to be nothing more lethal than a tobacco pipe, but the incident was an unnerving game of bluff and counter-bluff.

Some captains took more readily to the social duties than others. Cunard's Captain William Turner (known as 'Bowler Bill' for his habit of always wearing a bowler hat when not on the bridge) disliked them intensely. He referred to passengers as 'a lot of bloody monkeys' and ate most of his meals in the wheelhouse. Captain E.J. Smith (nearly always referred to as 'EJ') was less reclusive. Like most of his contemporaries, he had served his apprenticeship in sail, and his first command had been a square-rigger. He joined White Star in 1887 as fourth officer in the *Celtic*. In 1912, he had been commodore of the line for several years and, as such, was in charge of newcomers to the company's fleet on their maiden voyages. It was during his previous command — the *Olympic*, which had been completed nearly a year earlier than her more exotic sister — that, in September 1911, he was involved in the only accident of his career so far. The weather was perfect: the *Olympic* was coming up the Solent, when the cruiser HMS *Hawke* charged into her side. The court of inquiry put the blame on suction created by the liner, and unaccountably ignored the fact that, a few seconds before the collision, *Hawke*'s steering gear had jammed.

Smith was short, rather plump, and his chin was decorated with a superb beard. Nobody seems to be sure of his age in April 1912. Fifty-nine had been one guess; sixty, sixty-two and sixty-three have also been mentioned: it may be best to settle for the early sixties. His home was a large house on the New Forest side of Southampton. He was married, and had a daughter. The *Titanic* would have been his last command, for he was due to retire.

The fact that it was an unguarded remark of his that led to the use of that pernicious word 'unsinkable' may seem strange. Captain Smith was not given to making extravagant statements. He once told a newsman in New York that he was 'Not very good material for a story'; and, on another occasion, 'One might think that a captain taken from a small ship and put on a big one might feel the transition. Not at all. The skippers of big vessels have grown up to them, year after year, through all these years. First there was the sailing vessel and then what we would now call small ships — they were big in days gone by — and finally the giants today.'

As a captain he was demanding, though his crews liked him and admired his ship-handling. Passengers enjoyed his company; he was good with children. Altogether, you might say, E.J. Smith was a very model of a model master mariner. By all that was reasonable, he should have brought his career to a triumphal conclusion with the command of the *Titanic*. He would have come ashore to enjoy a comfortable retirement in that large house on the edge of Southampton and, just possibly, have been rewarded for his services to steam navigation with a knighthood. But then everything went most terribly wrong.

The object of an inquiry is to discover the truth, and the truth of that April night was that Smith blundered. His liner stampeded, half-blind, into the jaws of death while the captain exchanged small talk with her passengers. In the end, however, he did the correct thing. He died. For a man to have survived, as Ismay found to his cost, was dishonourable. The American inquiry, headed by the eloquent Senator William Alden Smith of Michigan, gave his seafaring namesake his due for shedding his mortal coil. 'Captain Smith,' said Senator Smith, 'knew the sea and his clear eye and steady hand had often guided his ship through dangerous paths. For forty years, storms sought in vain to vex him or menace his craft ... Each new advancing type of ship built by his company was handed over to him as a reward for faithful services and as evidence of confidence in his skill. Strong of limb, intent of purpose, pure in character, dauntless as a sailor should be, he walked the deck of this majestic structure as master of her keel.'

Captain Smith's 'indifference to danger', the Senator continued, 'was one of the direct and contributing causes of this unnecessary tragedy, while his own willingness to die was the expiating evidence of his fitness to live.'

It was all very nice, and you had to read the small print to gather that the tragedy was 'unnecessary'; that, under similar circumstances, 'other and less pretentious vessels doubled their look-outs or stopped their engines'; and so on and so forth. But Smith had been all right in the end: he died like a man. Unfortunately, a great many other men, whose professions did not require them to be 'dauntless', died, too.

At the British inquiry, Lord Mersey was more restrained. From him there was no eulogy — though he did remark that 'I am told . . . that it is not the practice to find negligence against a dead man. He has no opportunity of giving any explanation.' And: 'The parties and the court have always been very tender to the good name and the honour of a dead man.' Had Smith survived, the parties and the court would doubtless have been a great deal less 'tender', and he would obviously have shared the abuse that was heaped upon Ismay and Captain Stanley Lord of the *Californian* (patience: he'll be appearing in a minute or two). Perhaps it was as well that he perished, for the shame would have broken the old man's heart.

Die he certainly did — despite the assertion of another sea-captain that he sighted him in a Baltimore street seven days after the disaster. Nor was he 'Whispering' Smith, the down-and-out in Columbus, Ohio, who, just before his death some while after the disaster, announced that he had been the *Titanic*'s commander. Contrary to a story telegraphed by Reuters in error and printed in the *Daily Mirror*, he did not shoot himself — that was the luckless Murdoch's act of despair. He is reputed to have yelled 'Be British!' through a megaphone shortly before the liner sank. Considering the number of Americans and European emigrants on board, such an exhortation would have been downright stupid. But this seems unlikely: it was related by a naval officer at a memorial service to him.

Nevertheless, the 'be British' bit caught the mood of the day — at any rate in the United Kingdom. The hero who met his doom with dignity, if not with relish, was still in vogue. In some respects the public attitude to the captain was not unlike that accorded to General Gordon, who had died an equally point-less death at Khartoum twenty-seven years earlier. Indeed, the whole business of the *Titanic* became invested with a kind of spurious nobility — to such an extent that Bernard Shaw felt compelled to comment that, 'The effect on me was one of profound disgust, almost of national dishonour. Am I mad?'

Mr Shaw was by no means 'mad'.

Captain Smith was seen helping a child into a lifeboat. He was observed swimming beside a boat and, seeing that it was full, heard to say 'God bless you' before vanishing into the dark. He was glimpsed on a wing of the bridge, gallantly going down with his ship. And so on. Whatever the circumstances, he was one of the tragic 1,490.

Captain Turner, master of the *Lusitania* when she was torpedoed in May 1915, did survive — not only death, but also the calumny that the First Lord of the Admiralty (Churchill) and the First Sea Lord (Fisher) tried to heap upon him. Fisher, in a note that bordered on the insane, described him as 'a scoundrel' and hinted that he had 'been bribed'. One thousand one hundred and ninety-eight people were drowned on this occasion; but, despite monumental chaos after the missile exploded, Lord Mersey (who was in charge of this inquiry, too) found no fault with him. But this was the result of enemy action. There had been nothing that, under the circumstances, Turner could have done to prevent the disaster. Moreover, the Admiralty had been unusually inept — not only in failing to provide the liner with an escort, but also in making no effort to mount a rescue operation. Lieutenant-Commander Walther Schweiger of the German submarine U20 may have been the first choice as villain — though, had people realized it, there were other, lesser, knaves nearer home.

If the ocean can be regarded as a stage, there were four captains playing in the drama that, on that April night in 1912, came to its conclusion with the inevitability of a Greek tragedy. Smith it was that died; Captain Arthur Rostron of the Cunarder *Carpathia* covered himself with glory; Captain Lord of the *Californian* was branded as a kind of traitor; and the master of a Norwegian sealer named the *Samson* slunk away like a thief in the night. The last simile is not altogether inappropriate for, wrongly as it happened, this man, Henrik Naess, believed himself to be breaking the law. In fact, he was doing nothing more heinous than going about his business on a Sunday.

As the inquiries on both sides of the Atlantic were to reveal, there was some confusion about the disposition of shipping in

the vicinity of the *Titanic*. The one element that can be placed
with any certainty is the Cunarder *Carpathia*, commanded by
Captain Arthur Rostron and on passage from New York to the
Mediterranean. She was 58 miles to the south of the stricken
liner, when, at 12.35 a.m., her wireless officer picked up the
first distress signal. Captain Rostron immediately changed
course and, ordering his engineers to squeeze the maximum
power from the boilers, made haste to the rescue. At about
2.40 a.m., a look-out spotted a green flare lit by Fourth Officer
Boxhall in Number 2 boat. By this time, the sea was littered
with icebergs.

The *Carpathia*'s errand of mercy put a singular strain on
both the ship and her master. The liner, which had never been
conceived as one of the ocean's 'greyhounds', accomplished
speeds of which neither her crew nor her builders imagined her
capable. When she entered the icefield, having completed just
over half her journey, her course had to be changed almost
minute by minute as she negotiated a path between the far too
abundant hazards. Her performance might, perhaps, have
been compared to that of a middle-aged lady executing a long
and complex slalom; but execute it she did. Although Rostron's
career at sea stretched back for twenty-seven years, he had
been in command of a Cunarder for little more than a year,
and of the *Carpathia* for a paltry two months. But, as this
obstacle course across 58 miles of ice-strewn North Atlantic
demonstrated so well, he was a superb seaman. (Later he
commanded the *Mauretania* and, later still, the *Berengaria*. He
became Commodore of the Cunard Fleet and received a
knighthood.)

At five minutes past four, just as the first glimmers of
daylight were illuminating the eastern sky, Boxhall's boat was
sighted. There were others scattered over an area of four or
five miles, and it was not until eight o'clock that they had all
been accounted for. All told, the *Carpathia*'s crew rescued 712
people — one of whom died shortly afterwards. Then, his
business accomplished, Captain Rostron set course for New
York. The journey to the Mediterranean would have to come
later.

But the *Carpathia* was not the nearest vessel to the *Titanic*.
Everyone concerned with the matter — from the crew mem-

bers and passengers that survived, to the members of the inquiry teams — knew that there had been one other a great deal closer. What none of them knew, and which didn't become apparent until several years later, was that, in fact, there were two. The lights of both were probably visible from the liner, but when there are two where only one is believed to be, and when the unknown factor suddenly decides to darken ship and make a rapid departure, there is bound to be confusion. What is more, either vessel could have done so much to reduce the toll of casualties, and the captain of neither seems to have realized that there was any such task to be performed.

The Leyland (another member of the J.P. Morgan conglomerate) liner *Californian* had sailed from London on 5 April. She registered 6,223 tons gross; her maximum speed was between $12\frac{1}{2}$ and 13 knots. Although she had accommodation for 47 passengers, she was carrying only freight on this voyage. One has to assume that, with so many faster and more comfortable alternatives available, the *Californian* did not rate high when it came to choosing a vessel for the Atlantic crossing.

Her master, Captain Stanley Lord, was a tall man, inclined to stoop, and not normally very communicative. He may — though there is no evidence to support it — have shared the scepticism with which some master mariners still regarded the value of wireless. If this is so, he must have been of an uncommonly reactionary disposition. It had now been in use for more than twelve years, and it had shown its value as a means of saving lives at sea on several occasions. Nevertheless, Captain Lord seems either to have been careless, or unaware of the correct procedure, on one occasion this trip; while on another, had it occurred to him that wireless should be used, the affair of the *Titanic* might have had a very different conclusion.

At 7.30 on the evening of 14 April three large bergs were sighted to the south of the *Californian*'s position. On his master's instructions, the liner's only wireless operator, a youngster straight from training school named Cyril Evans, transmitted this information to the *Antillian*, which was known to be in the vicinity: '6.30 p.m., 42°3'N 49°9'W. Three large bergs five miles to southward of us. Regards, Lord.' He also offered it to the *Titanic*, but that ship's operator replied: 'It is all right. I heard you sending it to the *Antillian*, and I have got it.'

The *Californian* continued on her course of S89°W until 10.20 p.m. By this time, the sea had become cluttered with bergs in a field that extended so far as the eye could see (which, since it was dark, was not very far). At this point, Lord prudently shut off his engines and decided to wait until first light before going any further. His position — which, he insisted, had been determined by dead reckoning and after-wards confirmed by celestial observations — was, he stated, 42°5′N 57°7′W. In other words, it was about 19 miles north-by-east of the point at which the *Titanic* later collided with the berg.*

It may seem reasonable to assume that a man of Captain Lord's experience would not have been mistaken. Neverthe-less, on two occasions at the British inquiry, the Wreck Commissioner, Lord Mersey, remarked that 'I am satisfied that this position is not accurate.' Surprisingly, he estimated that the distance was only five miles — or, at the most, between eight and ten.

Later, at about 11.00 p.m., Evans tried to contact the *Titanic* again. On this occasion, the message was: 'We are stopped and surrounded by ice.' At the time, the big liner's operators were talking to the coastal station at Cape Race. Since the *Californian* was so much closer, the strength of her transmissions drowned the ship-to-shore conversation, and young Mr Evans was told to 'keep out' — which is precisely what he did. It doesn't appear to have occurred to him — or to Captain Lord — that the purport of his message was a great deal more important than anything the *Titanic* might have to say to Cape Race, or Cape Race to the *Titanic*. Had it done so, Evans should have prefixed his signal with the letters MSM, or 'Master Service Message'. The *Titanic*'s man would then have been bound to listen, traffic or no traffic with Cape Race.

Half an hour later, presumably with his captain's permis-

---

*The discovery of the *Titanic*'s remains in 1985 suggested that the *Californian* was indeed closer to the sinking liner than Lord claimed. But, at this distance in time, nothing can be said for certain.

sion, Cyril Evans decided that it had been a long day and that the time had come to turn in. Apart from a brief interruption from the third officer, Charles Groves, at 12.15 a.m., he abandoned himself to sweet slumber until the ship shook herself and became fully awake at about four o'clock. That visit from Groves might still have saved the situation, but it was only a social call. Evans was drowsy and paid little attention. He may have seen Groves, who was interested in wireless, put on the earphones. He may have heard him mutter something about not hearing anything. But he certainly did not think to tell Groves that nothing could be heard. A gadget in the set known as a 'magnet detector' was worked by clockwork — Cyril Evans, believing his duties to have been done for that night, had not wound it up.

The question must be asked as to why Captain Lord allowed his young wireless operator to sleep on undisturbed — and why, indeed, was Lord himself so ready to get his head down and, once asleep, so determined to remain so. As we shall see, even the report of rockets exploding in the sky produced no more than a drowsy response. He knew very well that something was happening not very far away: some mystery was occurring to which he could think of no solution. The whole matter might have been resolved had Evans been instructed to bestir himself, wind up his magnetic detector, and to listen carefully for anything that might supply a clue to the strange enigma of the lights in the night.

But Evans was allowed to sleep on. The cries for help, that he would inevitably have heard, went unheeded. The *Carpathia* heard them. The *Olympic*, travelling to Southampton heard them. Other ships heard them. But the two vessels able to render more or less instant assistance did not. The *Californian* had become, so to say, deaf. The Norwegian sealer *Samson* was always in this situation, for there was no wireless installed aboard.

Third Officer Charles Groves was on watch when the first lights were sighted at eleven o'clock. They were, he decided, those of a steamer approaching from the east. He told Lord, who asked Evans what vessels were known to be in the vicinity. He was informed: 'I think the *Titanic* is near us.' This prompted the instruction: 'You had better advise the *Titanic* we are stopped and surrounded with ice.' *He did not tell him to use the letters MSM, and so the warning was never received.*

The evidence given by Lord and his officers at the inquiry might have been more convincing had they been in agreement about what happened that night. As things were, they were a jumble of opinions and contradictions — even regarding the location of Lord himself at times. Was he, for example, on the bridge — as he claimed to have been — or was he resting fully dressed on a bunk in the chart room? Did he see what was to be seen, or did he depend on information spoken down a voice-pipe by the officer of the watch — or else brought to him by an apprentice? There was certainly a ship not very far away, and it seems to be true that, at 11.40 (the time the *Titanic* hit the berg) the stranger's lights went out. Groves could be sure of this time, if of nothing else, because, at 11.40 p.m., one bell was sounded to rouse the middle watch.

But the *Titanic*'s lights did not go out at the moment of impact: they remained on until almost the very last moment. So were these the lights of some other vessel: the mysterious intruder that is now known to have gone dark and to have crept away? Lord might, perhaps, have been excused if he mistook them for the *Titanic*'s; for whilst he knew that the one was not far away, he had no knowledge of the other.

It should have been remarkably difficult to confuse the two ships in the vicinity: the largest liner in the world and a quite small vessel of 506 tons — the great lady and the drab no more than about one-tenth of her size. But there was no certainty aboard the *Californian* about what sort or size of ship it was. Lord was initially of the opinion that it was not big enough to be the *Titanic*: indeed, it seems to have occurred to him at one point that it was not a ship at all, and that their imaginations were being misled by a star. Later, he said, 'That does not look like a passenger steamer'; and later still he decided that it was a medium-sized steamship — 'something like ourselves'.

There was one man on board the *Californian*, however, who was in little doubt about the nature of the ship. This was assistant donkeyman Ernest Gill (a very junior engineer whose duties were concerned with the auxiliary machinery). In return for $500, Mr Gill swore an affidavit on the invitation of the Boston *American*. In his statement, he said: 'She looked as if she might be a big German.' The identity, admittedly, was wrong, but he was on the correct lines. He also recalled over-hearing the second officer ask 'Why in the devil they didn't wake the wireless man up' — which must have been something that every thinking man on board (with the exception of Captain Lord and the peacefully dreaming Evans) must have been wondering.

At the British inquiry, Mr Gill stuck to his guns. 'It could not have been anything but a passenger boat,' he said. 'It was too large.' This, of course, amounted to a modification of his opinion as expressed in the Boston *American*. To be large enough to serve as a 'passenger boat' did not necessarily imply largeness on the scale of the *Titanic* or 'a big German'. The *Californian*, when anyone chose to pay for a passage in her, became a passenger boat, and Lord himself had concluded that such was roughly the size.

However, despite his apparent lack of awareness that Cyril Evans might have some useful role to play in this matter, Captain Lord did decide that his ship and the other ship might engage themselves in conversation — though by signal lamp. Time and again questions were flashed into the night sky, and time and again they went unanswered. If, as Lord had calcu-lated, the two ships were 19 miles apart, the signals could very well not have been seen, in spite of the good visibility. And nor, very likely, was anybody on board the *Titanic* alert for such flickering messages. Communications were in the hands of the two wireless operators: everyone else was either concerned with the proposition of saving his or her own life, or else with helping others to save theirs.

Captain Smith himself was particularly concerned with the problem of suppressing panic — as well he might have been. On 4 July 1898 a French liner named the *Bourgogne* had collided with a British sailing ship off Sable Island, Nova Scotia. The *Bourgogne* sank within a few minutes of the impact; but, within those minutes, all hell was let loose. Italian steerage passengers, nearly all of them men, fought with knives and fists to secure places in the boats. The officers tried to bring about order, but nothing could quieten these fear-crazed emigrants. Of the 600 people on board, 571 perished. Some of them, beyond reasonable doubt, were murdered.

Smith obviously knew about this — just as he knew that he had insufficient boats to accommodate more than a small proportion of those in his ship. The possibility of some occurrence very similar to that which attended the *Bourgogne* must have been well to the front in his mind. He was certainly not scanning the horizon in the hope of seeing flashing lights.

There are those who condemn Captain Lord of the *Californian* and those who rush to his defence. It is, however, difficult to understand his attitude to the matter of the rockets. The *Californian*'s lights could be seen from the *Titanic*. Indeed, in Smith's mind, she was near enough for the lifeboats to be able to ferry batches of survivors across and then to return for more. When she made no answer to the wireless operator's distress signals, it seemed necessary to catch her attention by visual means. This required more than flashing lights, informative though they might have been: rockets were what were needed.

At 12.30, Gill, the observant assistant donkeyman, who was doubtless enjoying a quiet cigarette on deck before retiring, saw the first two rockets — or so he said. At 1.10 a.m. the second officer, Herbert Stone, reported to Lord down the voice-pipe that he had seen five white rockets. The captain asked, 'Are they company signals?' Stone said that he didn't know, but 'they appear to be white rockets'. Lord instructed him to 'go on Morsing'.

Now this is curious. Company signals were arrangements of coloured lights that, in the dark, enabled one ship to identify itself to another. For all the elements in such a display of pyrotechnics to have been white would have indeed been rare. Furthermore, if Lord really did believe them to be company signals, why did he not get somebody to look them up and have the mysterious neighbour identified? Why, too, did he not reply by identifying his own ship?

But if they were *not* company signals (a probability that must have suggested itself) what *did* he think they were? That they were signs of revelry by night: a party in which somebody had decided to let off fireworks?

The last rocket erupted in the sky at 1.40 a.m. Almost simultaneously, Stone remarked to James Gibson, an apprentice who was sharing the watch with him, 'Look at her now. She looks very queer out of the water. Her lights look queer.' He was also heard to mutter, 'A ship is not going to fire rockets at sea for nothing;' which was certainly very true. Nevertheless, another twenty minutes went by before he told Captain Lord about this. The message was taken to the chart room by Gibson. Lord asked him whether these rockets had also been white. Again, at 2.40 a.m., he inquired whether Second Officer Stone was certain all the rockets had been white. He was assured that they were. Then, for some strange reason apparently satisfied, the gallant captain went to sleep. But, by this time, the ship — whatever she was — had vanished: 'a gradual disappearance,' Stone recalled, 'which would have been perfectly natural with a ship steaming away from us.'

At the American inquiry, Lord stated that he had been told only twice about the rockets, and that, on the second occasion, he was half-asleep. His statements to newspapermen who interviewed him in Boston contained no reference to rockets at all; indeed, to the New York *World*, he went so far as to say that 'no message of distress or any signal was received or sighted'. How could they have been when the wireless was shut down and its operator was tucked up in his bunk; or when Lord himself was too far removed on the wrong side of sleep to pay much attention to the second account of the visual signals?

Lord Mersey, at the British inquiry, pointed out 'contradictions and inconsistencies in the story as told by various witnesses [in the *Californian*]'.

But the truth is plain. The *Titanic* collided with the berg at 11.40. The vessel seen by the *Californian*, stopped at this time. The rockets sent by the *Titanic* were distress signals. The number sent up by the *Titanic* was about eight. The *Californian* saw eight. The time over which the rockets from the *Titanic* were sent up was from about 12.45 to 1.45 o'clock. It was about this time the *Californian* saw the rockets. At 2.40, Mr Stone called to the master that the ship from which he had seen the rockets had disappeared. At 2.20, the *Titanic* had foundered. It was suggested that the rockets seen by the *Californian* were from some other ship — not the *Titanic*. But no other ship to fit this theory has ever been heard of.

When she first saw the rockets, the *Californian* could have pushed through the ice to the open water without any serious risk, and so have come to the assistance of the *Titanic*. Had she done so, she might have saved many if not all the lives that were lost.

But would this have happened? Captain Lord had told Lord Mersey and his colleagues 'that, to have ventured through the ice on such an errand would be most dangerous. I do not think we should have got there before the *Carpathia* did.' This, of course, begs the uncomfortable question of whether Lord failed to read the rockets as distress signals because he did not wish them to be. His employers were satisfied with his conduct; but, then, he had done nothing to jeopardize his ship, which was their ship. Few other people were able to take such a charitable view. For Lord, unlike Rostron, there was no applause.

As Lord Mersey said, there was 'no other ship to fit [the] theory' of the rockets. Just so. But, for some of the time, there *was* another vessel present — and, almost certainly, even closer to the *Titanic* than the *Californian*. She was a wooden ship of 506 tons with eight small boats on board. Her name was *Samson* and her master was a Norwegian named Henrik Naess. Captain Naess's income, as those of his crew, was generated from profits made by killing seals.

It is hard to make Captain Naess out. He was either equipped with too much imagination, or else with too little. A seal hunter was not too fussy about what he killed. For example, seal pups are so small and slender that they have negative buoyancy when dead. Out of every three shot, somebody had worked out, two sank and their corpses were never recovered.

There are all sorts of good reasons for not killing young seals. In the present instance, we must confine ourselves to economics. With such a high rate of loss, the practice was wasteful. They would, if left alone, grow up until they were big enough to be shootable — and indeed, with a bit of luck, produce more little seals that would grow up, etcetera.

For reasons such as these, an international treaty had been signed in 1911, banning the slaughter of seal pups in the

Pacific. Strangely, the rule did not apply to the Atlantic (too much political clout from Canada and the Danes who owned Greenland?); so, keep to the Atlantic, and you could massacre as many of the little creatures as you liked. There was only one stipulation: some countries (Norway, for instance) insisted that there should be no such shooting on a Sunday. Anyone caught breaking this law had to pay a by no means exorbitant fine.

Captain Naess knew about the treaty, but he didn't know enough about it. It hadn't penetrated his mind that the regulations applied only to the Pacific. He believed that the Atlantic, too, was out of bounds if you wanted to bag a few baby seals.

But this did not deter him. Captain Naess was his own man, and if he felt like killing three pups to be the richer by one, he intended to do so. That April, he'd been operating to the north of Iceland; then, at about the time when the *Titanic* was setting off from Southampton, he moved to the Grand Banks.

On the night of 14/15 April, his ship was drifting amid the ice when, from the east, a giant steamer appeared. When she was no more than a mile or so away — five at the most — she suddenly stopped. Not very long afterwards, a small fleet of rockets streaked into the sky.

The *Samson* had no wireless: even if there had been a set on board, it seems unlikely that Captain Naess would have made much sense of its utterances — though he might have made something out of CQD, a signal devised by Marconi meaning 'All Stations — Urgent!' (Soon to be replaced by SOS, since most people interpreted it as 'Come Quick — Danger'.) Since there was no moon that night, he was unable to make out the big ship's appearance, and, as people are apt to do when they are breaking the law (or think they're breaking it), he came to the wrong conclusion. The way he saw things, this was a battleship dispatched by one of the great powers to enforce the don't-kill-seal-pups rule — and here was he, Henrick Naess, breaking said rule, or having broken it, or about to break it: it all amounted to the same thing.

If Captain Lord was unable, or unwilling, to understand the meaning of the rockets, Captain Naess was in no such dilemma. They were clearly a signal to heave-to and await a boarding party that would probably be armed to the proverbial teeth. There was only one thing to do: put out the lights immediately, start up the engines, and get away from this particular patch of sea as quickly as the *Samson*'s not very powerful engine could push her. He set a course for Iceland and chugged away into the darkness. On arrival at Reykjavik, he naturally heard about the *Titanic* disaster, and the truth about the ship that failed to pass in the night dawned upon him. To give him his due, he immediately went to the Norwegian consul's office, where he is reputed to have said, 'If we had known, what might we not have done?'

Clearly, Captain Naess would have made a useful witness at the inquiries on both sides of the Atlantic. Whilst the addition of the *Samson*'s lights to the picture — and their sudden extinction — might not have added much to the story, it could have taken some of the heat off Captain Lord. But, for reasons unknown, the Norwegian consul kept the information to himself. It was not until many years later that the truth emerged and the final piece was inserted into the *Titanic* jigsaw puzzle. But, by then, it was too late to avail the disgraced Lord.

The unfortunate Captain Smith blundered, no matter what his apologists may say or have said. Such things had happened before; and, whatever epoch the sinking of the *Titanic* was supposed to be the end of, it was certainly not that of human error. Indeed, this weakness, this misjudgement of a situation, has been one of the sea's most staunch allies in its war against those who venture upon it. The amazing thing, perhaps, is that, in the history of passenger carrying, there have been so few disasters: more than sufficient, perhaps, but still by no means prodigious. Smith's trouble may have been that his luck ran out. The survival of the other master mariners who testified at the British inquiry can, perhaps, be accounted for by the fact that theirs did not.

Captain James Williams, commander of the 3,707-ton White Star liner *Atlantic*, which was written off with 637 victims on the night of 1 April 1873, cannot be excused as unlucky. He escaped with his life; and, although the inquiry suspended his master's ticket for two years, the owners were quick to re-employ him once the period had expired. Considering the size of the casualty list, the penalty must have seemed small — especially since, in one respect if not in another,

Williams must have been guilty of considerable negligence.

But just as Lord had his defenders, so had Williams. Even as recently as 1977, when I included an account of the *Atlantic* affair in a book, I was severely taken to task by one critic. It can hardly be described as an argument, since the reviewer always has the last word. The rub of the matter was coal. Had the White Star Line been too niggardly in its supply? Had Captain Williams miscalculated his stock? Or had he driven his ship too hard, and used up too much?

If, as the critic insisted, Williams was to be excused, the shipping company was obviously to blame. If (as I believe) he had got his sums wrong, this was his first error on this voyage — and it was by no means the last. The time taken to cross the Atlantic (after eleven days at sea, the coast of North America was still 460 miles away) certainly does not suggest excessive speed even if one allows for the continual bad weather. Perhaps Captain Williams had studied carefully his owners' insistence that 'No supposed gain of expedition or saving of time on the voyage, is to be purchased at the risk of an accident.' Or, in a letter on his appointment as commander of the *Atlantic* one voyage previously:

> We invite you to dismiss from your mind all idea of competitive passage with other vessels, the advantage of success in which is merely transient, concentrating your whole attention upon a cautious, prudent, and ever watchful system of navigation, which shall lose time or suffer any other temporary inconveniences rather than run the slightest risk that can be avoided.

It was an instruction that, nineteen years later, Captain Smith of the *Titanic* might well have pondered upon.

The *Atlantic* sailed from Liverpool on 20 March 1873, on passage to New York with 1,038 people on board and 1,836 tons of cargo. There were 967 tons of coal in her bunkers which, or so one might have thought, would have been more than sufficient. The liner's consumption, taken over an average of eighteen voyages across the Atlantic, had been 744 tons a trip. The most she had ever used had been 896 tons, and this had been under conditions far worse than those of the present voyage.

Nevertheless, after eleven days at sea, Captain Williams (supported, one must assume, by his chief engineer) conceived the idea that supplies were running short and that only 100 tons remained. He ordered a reduction of speed to seven knots and a change of course to Halifax, Nova Scotia.

Coal, then, was at the heart of the matter. If Williams had not succumbed to these misgivings, the *Atlantic* would have continued her voyage to New York and would doubtless have arrived there safely. Halifax was another matter: despite his long and so far faultless career on the North Atlantic, forty-three-year-old James Williams had never visited the port. Even more to the point was that fact that he was entirely unfamiliar with the Nova Scotian coastline.

Under these circumstances, one might have imagined that Captain Williams would have remained on the bridge all night. At midnight, he unaccountably ordered the speed to be increased to 12 knots. He also instructed the officer of the watch to maintain the present course until 3 a.m. Then he retired to the chart room, where he gave an interview lasting twenty minutes to a writer from the American magazine *Cosmopolitan.* After that, he went to bed. He slept so soundly that, when his steward tried to wake him at 2.15, he never stirred. The steward was a former Cunard hand, and he later said that, in all his long experience, this was the first occasion on which he had known a captain to sleep when his ship was approaching a hazardous coast.

Had he understood the situation better, Captain Williams would have rested less peacefully. His second officer had already confused one lightship with another. What he assumed to be the Sambro light at the approach to Halifax harbour, was really the light marking Peggy's Point — a dangerous reef some distance to the south-west. Since the former was white and the latter was red, this error may suggest carelessness. As if to compound this mistake, an unsuspected current — between 50 and 60 miles wide and travelling at four knots — had pulled the *Atlantic* off course. Unknown to everyone on board, she was no longer heading in the direction of Halifax, but blundering towards a collection of rocks off Meagher Island, about 30 miles to the west.

At 3 o'clock one of the passengers heard the look-out call,

'All's well.' About twenty minutes later, another sailor cried, 'Breakers ahead!' After that, all was very far from well. The passenger glimpsed the rock when it was about 300 yards away. 'I thought at first it was an iceberg,' he recalled. 'Then the ship commenced to heave and plunge, and after three or four plunges, she settled and the water seemed to be rushing in.'

The steerage passengers were trapped below decks: none of them had a chance. When a boat on the port side was lowered with 40 people on board, the *Atlantic*, which had now snapped into two pieces, keeled over, and the craft was thrown into the sea. Everyone on board was drowned. Immediately afterwards, all the remaining lifeboats on this side were swept away by a large wave.

Meanwhile, distress rockets had been sent up, though — to begin with — nobody seemed to heed them. Williams, so rudely snatched from sleep, was now on deck and showing a great deal of courage. He ordered all the survivors to take to the rigging. Soon afterwards, when the purser had frozen to death while clinging on to a length of rope, he encouraged them to move about as much as they could. When, at last, some local fishermen arrived on the scene, he called down an offer of $500 for every boatload rescued. On shore, where the local citizens were now thronging the clifftop, somebody had removed the blackboard from a school. On it, he had chalked: CHEER UP, THE BOATS ARE COMING TO YOUR ASSISTANCE.

There were not many heroes that night, but Third Officer Cornelius Brady was unquestionably one of them: without his courage, many more would have died. Somehow, this sturdy officer managed to swim the 150 yards that separated the fragmented ship from the shore. He took with him a rope. Once he had secured it, and with the help of two seamen, three more lines were stretched across. Fifty people reached safety by traversing them; though several (the chief steward among them) were drowned in the attempt.

Mr Brady's task was far from done. He walked quickly to a habitation named Prospect and mobilized the fishermen. Then he trudged on to Halifax, where he arrived at about midnight. He informed the shipping companies of the disaster, and they responded quickly. The Cunarder *Delta*, the Dominion Line's

Lady Head, and a tug named the *Goliath* were all ordered to quit their berths and to steam as quickly as they could to the region of Meagher. Brady's task was done. He could check in at an hotel where, after a substantial meal, he went to bed.

Afterwards, there were a lot of unpleasant questions to be answered. Why, for example, were there no women and children among the survivors? Was it true that the crew had behaved badly throughout the trip — and that, at the time of the disaster, many of them had been guilty of panic? Was it true that, once the situation had become stable, several of them had robbed and mutilated the corpses? (No, said White Star officials: it was the work of eight stowaways who were known to have been on board.) Was it true that the officers had spent too much time enjoying themselves with the passengers, and too little attending to their duties? And why had not Captain Williams been on the bridge?

There was, of course, also that matter of the coal. In the opinion of the inquiry's members, there had not been sufficient — a verdict that produced a host of legal arguments.

No matter what social encumbrances there were to distract a master before the *Titanic*'s loss helped to create the position of staff captain, a captain's first responsibility was the safety of his ship and of those who sailed in her. When conditions were dangerous, his place was on the bridge — something one might have expected such veterans of the North Atlantic as E.J. Smith and James Williams to have realized. Years later, another White Star captain, Bertram Hayes (he was then commodore of the fleet) spent 69 hours on end in the *Majestic*'s wheelhouse as the giant liner groped through fog. Hayes expected to endure such marathons of vigilance: a special chair was installed on the bridge for his exclusive use. It was known as 'the captain's fog chair'.

But even conscientiousness such as this was not proof against misjudgements in navigation, and other people's mistakes. In 1875, the German liner *Schiller, en route* from New York to Plymouth and Hamburg, was approaching the English Channel in thick fog and heavy seas. Unknown to her master, an Englishman named Thomas, she was eight miles off course. Thomas had done all the right things such as reducing speed and doubling the look-outs, but such precautions could not save her from her fate. She ran on to a reef near the Scilly Islands. Of the 372 people on board, only 43 survived. Captain Thomas was among the casualties.

Also in 1875, the Norddeutscher Lloyd's *Deutschland* was outward bound from Bremerhaven for New York via Southampton. Nobody could have accused her master, Captain Edouard Brickenstein, of neglecting his duty. The wind was approaching gale force; there were sudden flurries of snow; and he had been on the bridge all night. Unfortunately, he had miscalculated. He reckoned that he was only 140 miles from the port of departure when, in fact, the distance was 170 miles. This mistake meant that he was very much closer than he thought to a sandbank off the Essex coast. Nevertheless, he was travelling at reduced speed and, when he saw a light marking the hazard, he signalled 'full astern' to the engineers. This should have averted the disaster, but then a sudden giant wave seemed to take hold of the *Deutschland* and hurl her on to the bank. One hundred and fifty-seven were drowned; 155 were saved. Captain Brickenstein was among the latter.

In 1914, the Canadian Pacific liner, *Empress of Ireland*, was proceeding down the Saint Lawrence on her way to Liverpool. A Norwegian coal-carrier named the *Storstad* was approaching her, when a bank of fog blotted everything out. The *Empress of Ireland*'s captain, Henry Kendall (it was he who, when commanding the *Montrose* in 1910, identified Dr Crippen among the passengers, and sent the wireless message that led to the murderer's arrest), was on the bridge. The *Storstad*'s master, Thomas Andersen, was tucked up in bed with his wife.

The first mate, Alfred Toftenes, should have called him when the fog came down, but he may have been too preoccupied. When Andersen did come on deck, it was because he had experienced a sudden feeling of anxiety. But, by then, it was too late.

In each ship, the men on watch could hear the other vessel's whistle, but it was hard to tell from which direction the sounds came. Toftenes stopped the *Storstad*'s engines for a minute or two: then he decided on a change of course to compensate for the current. He found that he no longer had any steerage way, and put them to slow ahead. The collier swung round and, very soon afterwards, smashed into the CPR liner's side. The *Storstad* was an exceptionally strongly built vessel with her bow reinforced against ice. Such a blow was almost bound to be lethal, though Kendall clung on to one hope. Shouting through a megaphone, he urged Andersen to 'Keep going ahead on your engines.' His idea was that the *Storstad's* further intrusion might plug the hole — at any rate until he could abandon ship.

Either Andersen never heard the words, or else he misunderstood them. At any rate, he backed away into the swirling mist. The *Empress of Ireland* sank fourteen minutes later. Since it was now just after 1.30 in the morning, most of the liner's passengers and many of her crew were in their cabins. There was hardly any time for them to get up on deck; and, in any case, the ship was listing so severely that it was impossible to lower any of the ample number of lifeboats (at least one lesson had been learned from the *Titanic*). As a result, 1,024 died; 458 (including Captain Kendall) were rescued by the *Storstad's* boats.

Who was to blame? According to the British inquiry, Kendall should have given the *Storstad* a wider berth, and the *Storstad* had too much way on her. That business of putting the wheel hard over was a fatal mistake, and Toftenes should have called his captain when the fog came down. The Norwegian inquiry decided otherwise: Andersen and his crew were absolved from all blame. The investigators agreed with Andersen's assertion that the liner had been travelling too quickly. The legal wrangles continued for several years, but Andersen resumed command of his ship once it had been repaired. Kendall spent most of his subsequent career as CPR's marine superintendent at various ports.

And then, on 7 May 1915, the *Lusitania* was torpedoed within sight of the Irish coast. In a period of just over three years, three passenger liners on the North Atlantic run had been lost — and, with them, 3,712 lives. This, in itself, was bad enough, but the really terrifying thing was that two of the ships and 2,222 of the casualties were dispatched *after* the sinking of the *Titanic*. Captain Kendall may have misjudged the situation, but he certainly could not have been accused of neglect. Captain Turner of the *Lusitania* had no means of knowing that the U20 was in the immediate vicinity and that its command-

ing officer was regarding his ship maliciously through a periscope. Indeed, even if he had been aware of it, it seems unlikely
that he could have done very much.

The *Titanic* had been wickedly short of lifeboats, though by
no means all of them were filled to capacity and some were not
used at all. Nevertheless, at the inquiry, Lord Mersey very
rightly recommended that lifeboat and raft accommodation
should no longer be based on a ship's tonnage but on the
number of persons carried. In the case of the *Empress of Ireland*
and that of the *Lusitania,* there was no such shortage. The
tragedy in these cases (and in that of the *Titanic,* too) was one
of crowd control. To have sufficient boats was not enough. A
mass of frightened people, some of them reluctant to leave a
doomed ship in the illogical belief that it was safer on board
than in the sea below, had to be turned into a disciplined unit
that would know where to go, do the correct thing when it got
there, and to be reassured.

A captain's duty is to command. In an emergency, he must
control the actions of everybody on board. He cannot do this
unless he is able to communicate. It need not have posed many
problems in a small liner such as the *Atlantic.* In the much
larger vessels, however, it was impossible. Ideally, Lord
Mersey's suggestions after the *Titanic* inquiry would have
included the installation of public address systems. The fact
that they did not was not an oversight on the part of Mersey:
such things had not yet been invented. According to *The Shell
Book of Firsts,* the first was used in 1913, when the Governor
of Oklahoma City addressed 345 people in a Tulsa hotel. It was
not, however, until some years later, that it occurred to anyone
that such systems might be advantageously used in big ships.

One of the less practical though certainly imaginative ideas
that followed the *Titanic*'s sinking was that of fitting self-
contained, detachable, stern sections to ships. The theory was
that, if the rest of a vessel was badly damaged, everyone on
board would retreat to this sanctuary, which would then, as it
were, be cast off. Apart from the engineering problems
involved, by no means the least difficulty would surely have
been getting them there. The crew might have managed it,
given enough time. But as the *Empress of Ireland* demonstrated,
time is sometimes in very short supply.

The Passengers' Story

In its advertisements for the *Titanic* and her slightly smaller (by about 1,000 tons) sister, the *Olympic,* the White Star Line really took off. The shipping company was not content to stick to the facts, impressive though they might be. There had to be some greater significance. The two ships, readers of newspapers and magazines were told, stood 'for the pre-eminence of the Anglo-Saxon race in command of the seas'. They contributed to 'the movement of the British and American people towards international and universal peace'; and they were 'eloquent testimonies to the progress of mankind and the conquest of mind over matter'. No doubt the writer of these high-flown phrases was to regret the last remark. So far as the *Titanic* was concerned, matter, in the form of an iceberg, made a very fair job of conquering mind — as personified by the White Star management and the shipbuilding resources of Harland & Wolff.

To experience such 'progress of mankind' at its ultimate, you had to be rich. As one effusion explained, it could cost over £850 to travel 'in a palace of delight'. But what, it asked, 'is £850 to an American millionaire?' What, indeed! Nowadays, a voyage to New York in May, travelling in the *QE2* and availing yourself of the most luxurious accommodation, would set you back a paltry £3,550. It may sound a lot; but, when you allow for inflation, it seems quite reasonable compared to that charged by this previous 'palace of delight'.

One has to assume that it did not amount to very much, for several had booked passages for the *Titanic*'s maiden voyage. George Widener's father, for example, claimed to be the richest man in Philadelphia, and he probably was. The money had come from improving the city's transportation by introducing streetcars. Colonel J.J. Astor was able to console those less affluent than himself with the words 'A man who has a million dollars is as well off as if he were rich.' 'Rich', in Astor's case, added up to about $150 million, none of which had been earned by the sweat of his handsome brow. The fortune had been amassed by his ancestors' shrewd investment of fur trade profits into real estate. Isador Straus, who was returning with Mrs Straus from a holiday in the South of France, had started in quite a small way with a ceramics business. But then he co-founded that famous New York emporium, Macy's. Now, with a modest $10 million to his name, he owned the lot (Macy — his name nonetheless immortalized — seems to have been mislaid somewhere along the line). Benjamin Guggenheim, the banker and close associate of J. Pierpont Morgan, was present with his valet in attendance. Without too much trouble, Mr Guggenheim could reach out and grasp $95 million. Morgan himself was not on board.

The man who had bought the White Star Line in 1902 for a cool $10 million had other matters that required his attention. He had, however, witnessed the launching of the *Titanic* on 1 June of the previous year. Whilst lesser beings, such as the press and senior executives, were lunched at Belfast's Grand Central Hotel, he had been entertained by Lord Pirrie in his personal dining room at the shipyard. Afterwards, he and his friends were taken back to Liverpool in the recently completed *Olympic*.

On the voyage, the owners were represented by the line's chairman, J. Bruce Ismay; and the builders by Thomas Andrews, Lord Pirrie's nephew and builder of this palace of delight. Whereas Ismay's duties were undemanding — he had merely to satisfy himself about the excellence of his and Morgan's latest acquisition — Andrews had work to do. His task was to diagnose any shortcomings that might become apparent as the liner proceeded westwards, and to see that they were put right.

The sorrow of it was that the one major fault became clear only after the *Titanic* had hit the berg — and then it was rather too late to do anything about it. It was Andrews who, within a few minutes of the impact, informed Captain Smith that his ship was doomed, and he who died when his creation died. Andrews was rewarded — if that is the right word — with a reputation for heroism. Ismay, who survived, was accused of cowardice. Despite the opinion of Lord Mersey at the British inquiry that 'had he not jumped in [to a collapsible boat] he would merely have added one more life, namely his own, to the number of those lost', the public took a more severe view. Haunted by abuse and shame, Ismay fled to exile in Ireland and never came back. Still, he could afford early retirement and the life of a resident landlord. He is said to have been worth $40 million.

Anyone who can remember Noël Coward's *Cavalcade* may recall a brief scene in which a honeymoon couple are leaning over a liner's rail. Beyond, the night is clear and starlit. They murmur the sweet nothings about happiness and mutual esteem that honeymooners are supposed to murmur. Then they turn and go below decks. The girl has deposited her wrap over a rail. As she removes it, a lifebuoy is revealed. On it is written the one word *TITANIC*. *Tabs*, as they say in the theatre.

Since the theme of *Cavalcade* seems to be the ability of the British upper classes to maintain stiff upper lips no matter how adverse the circumstances may be, it is reasonable to suppose that the young couple met their fate with dignity. Both vanish from the script at this point, and the girl must be accounted unfortunate. One hundred and forty out of the 144 women travelling first class survived — or 97.22 per cent. She, surely, should have been escorted to the safety of a boat by her attentive spouse, who would then have vanished into the crowd.

The stiffness of the affluent upper lip in the instance of the *Titanic* has become a matter of legend. We find Mrs Isador Straus refusing to be parted from her husband: 'We have lived for forty years together, and will not part now in old age.' There was a precedent for such an attitude thirty-nine years earlier, when the *Atlantic* stampeded on to the rocks near Halifax. A Mr and Mrs Fisher were in the saloon. On this occasion, Mrs Fisher told her husband, 'Go — save yourself', and he replied, 'No. We will remain together and meet in a better world.' Then they sat down on a settee and held hands. No doubt the Straus couple did something very similar.

Benjamin Guggenheim sent a message to his wife in New York via a steward in one of the boats. 'If anything happens to me,' he instructed, 'tell my wife I have done my best in doing my duty.' It was all very well for Nelson to utter such pen-ultimate words; but what, one asks, was the duty that Mr Guggenheim had performed? That of leaving a vacant space in one of the lifeboats? But the eminent banker appears to have been in the mood for rather theatrical gestures that night. Having made this request, he retired to his stateroom where he and his valet both put on evening dress. As he is said to have remarked, 'We've dressed in our best, and are prepared to go down like gentlemen.'

Colonel J.J. Astor assisted Mrs Astor into a boat, said 'Goodbye, dearie — I will join you later', and casually lit a cigarette. The distinguished newspaper editor W.T. Stead picked up the magazine he'd been reading and returned to its pages with no more concern than if a train in which he was travelling had just pulled out of a station. A party of card players resumed their game. Even Captain Smith, who knew the awful truth, gave the only clue to his anxiety by chewing rather vigorously on a toothpick.

Astor's lighting of a cigarette is an interesting fragment of social history — especially to students of light fiction. When an heroic figure was facing the prospect of extermination, he was apt to 'light a nonchalant cigarette'. In real life, Commander C.E. Glasfurd of the destroyer HMS *Acasta* did so when, after a fearful battering from the German battle-cruiser *Scharnhorst* in June 1940, his ship was about to founder. 'When I was in the water,' a leading seaman recalled, 'I saw the Captain, leaning over the bridge, take a cigarette from a case and light it.' (Upper-class villains behaved differently. Those who were well-dressed — and most of them were — tended to remove invisible fragments of dust from their immaculate sleeves, dwelling the while upon the horrible fate that lay in store for their victims.)

It would be nice to think that Astor knew his E. Phillips Oppenheim and William le Queux, and was performing in the approved manner. Alternatively, he may have been more alarmed than his composure suggested, and did it to calm his nerves.

The band played on. Bell boys, lads in their early teens, found themselves released from duty and occupied the time by larking about. In the first-class accommodation at any rate, there seems to have been an atmosphere of relaxation. Ismay was the only one to show any display of urgency, and he expressed it by trying to help with the lifeboats. His intentions were no doubt excellent, but experience of board-room politics is of no use on such occasions. He merely got in the way and, in the end, was sharply ordered by a junior officer to desist and take himself off elsewhere.

One has to remind oneself that the only evidence of this apparent unconcern comes from survivors. At 12.05 a.m. Smith ordered the lifeboats to be uncovered. At 12.20 a.m., they were swung outwards, though there were still comparatively few people on deck. At 12.30 a.m., a number of women and children were told to get into the boats; and, at 12.45, they were lowered 65 feet into the water. Despite the fact that there were insufficient to accommodate everyone, they were by no means completely filled. The reasons given for this were that many were loath to leave the ship; that some were afraid of the long drop to the sea; that some women refused to leave their husbands: and, finally, *that there were hopes of imminent rescue.*

Without wishing to belittle the calm of most people in first class — from the millionaires to the bell-hops — in the face of such peril, it may have been that they did not realize how extreme the peril was. Perhaps Astor really did expect to see his wife later (and not in another world). Perhaps Ben Guggenheim expected the story of his dressing for Judgement Day to circulate in New York society, and that he would be there to utter a self-deprecating laugh. Perhaps, for all the din of steam escaping from the ship's boilers, their belief in the myth of the *Titanic*'s unsinkability remained intact. Indeed, even if it had been slightly shaken, there were comforting lights in the distance: those of the slumbering *Californian* and, until she darkened ship and crept away, the wretched *Samson.*

It was not until Fourth Officer Boxhall sent up the first

rocket at 12.45 a.m. that the real seriousness of the situation dawned on many people. Boxhall also flashed signals in Morse to another vessel that, he thought, was about five or six miles away. The fact that look-outs on the *Californian* didn't see them, and that nobody saw the *Californian's* flashed inquiries, suggests that the Leyland liner really was the nineteen miles away that Captain Lord alleged to be the case. Perhaps Boxhall was unknowingly trying to contact the *Samson* and that Captain Naess was misinterpreting his signals as an order to await a boarding party. So much was never properly explained.

Once the boats had been lowered into the ocean and it became clear that the *Titanic* had not very much longer to live, the conduct of their occupants was somewhat less than heroic. The crews were inclined to blame the passengers; and the passengers to blame the crew. Whichever the case, they showed a distressing reluctance to approach the area of the sinking ship and to pick up those in the water. They were, it appears, frightened that, with so many struggling for survival, they would be overwhelmed. Sir Cosmo Duff Gordon was later accused of offering five-pound notes to the sailors if they would concentrate on the matter in hand: that of getting himself and Lady Gordon safely out of the danger zone. However, at the British inquiry, Lord Mersey ruled that there was no truth in these allegations: that, in fact, Sir Cosmo had encouraged them to return to the scene of the disaster.

(In the case of the *Atlantic*, an elderly man offered $100 to anyone who would save his life. There was no takers.)

When it was all over, only thirteen people had been taken from the sea, and some of them died later. The ship that had betrayed so many hopes sank with a bang rather than a whimper, as her boilers were torn from their emplacements. But this was not the only sound to make the night hideous. As recounted in Wyn Craig Wade's *The Titanic*, one survivor recalled 'a heavy moan as of one being from whom final agony forces a single sound'. Another likened it to 'locusts on a midsummer night', and someone spoke of a 'long continuous wailing chant'. The band stopped playing only when the sea stifled their sounds, though what they were playing at the end remains a matter of speculation. It was certainly not 'Nearer My God to Thee': it was quite likely an Episcopal hymn entitled 'Autumn'. If it was, it was a suitable accompaniment to the devotions of one hundred or so Catholics in one of the lounges, who were on their knees and receiving the all too final sacrament from two priests.

When the list of survivors was assembled, it read:

First Class
Adult males: 57 of the 175 on board were saved — or 32.57 per cent
Women: 140 of the 144 were saved — 97.22 per cent
Male children: five — which is to say all of them
Female children: one — again, all.

Second Class
Adult males: 14 out of 168 saved — 8.33 per cent
Women: 80 out of 93 saved — 86.02 per cent
Male children: 11 — all of them
Female children: 13 — all of them

Third Class
Adult males: 75 out of 462 saved — 16.23 per cent
Women: 76 out of 165 saved — 46.06 per cent
Male children: 13 out of 48 saved — 27.08 per cent
Female children: 14 out of 31 saved — 45.16 per cent

One officer, who was superintending the loading of the boats, lost his head when assessing the priorities and tried to ban all males — even if they were very small boys. Colonel Astor almost certainly saved one ten-year-old's life when, seeing a little girl's hat lying on the deck, he picked it up and placed it on the youngster's head. 'Now he's a girl,' he told the officer, 'and he can go.'

Another male passenger, in this case one of the survivors, almost certainly saved the life of a steward named Sidney Daniels — simply by giving him some good advice. Mr Daniels had begun his career at sea just under a year previously, when he joined the *Olympic* for her maiden voyage. Greatly to his pride, he was transferred to the *Titanic* when she was nearing completion at Belfast.

He was asleep when the liner collided with the iceberg. A night-watchman roused him: told him to put on his life-jacket and report for duty at lifeboat number thirteen. At first, he and his companions thought it was a routine drill for the crew. When he arrived on deck, however, he could see that some rather more serious situation had arisen. 'Shortly afterwards', he recalled, 'we had orders to swing out the boats and prepare for lowering. Then came an order for passengers to be put in, and I was sent down below to get all the passengers I saw to go on deck with their lifebelts — which I did.'

When he returned to the boat deck, he found that number thirteen had already departed. He walked over to a group of men, near one of the funnel casings, who were trying to clear a collapsible for launching. 'Somebody called out for a knife to cut the lashings,' he said, 'and I passed up my pocket knife. But there was no room for me to help any more, and so I climbed down to the deck again and went over to the starboard side.' Everything was strangely quiet. The boats had all gone and there was nobody in sight. The water, he noticed, 'was coming up the companionway pretty quickly, but I could feel no motion of the ship — although she had listed well to port and was down at the head. Then I realized that I had to do something for myself.'

One of the problems, he decided, was to get clear away from the ship 'to avoid being sucked down as she sank ... I just jumped out into the darkness and swam away as far as I could. How long I swam I don't know, but I found a lifebuoy with a man clinging to it, and I held on to that for a while. As I turned back to look, I could see the stern of the *Titanic* standing almost straight up in the air. With the thought of the suction still in mind, I said to the man with me, "We had better go farther away." He did not answer: he may not have spoken English — so I turned away and just swam.'

After swimming for goodness knows how long, he came across a number of people clinging to a capsized collapsible: the very one, it turned out, for which his knife had been the instrument of liberation. Somehow they all managed to clamber on to its keel, and there they were: twenty-five souls perched upon the wrong side of a disturbingly unseaworthy craft. During the night, one of them died from exposure.

'I think I should have died, too,' Mr Daniels recalled, 'had it not been for a passenger sitting next to me. I said, "I'm tired: I must go to sleep." But he said, "For God's sake, son, don't go to sleep", and I soon realized that, had I done so, it would have been my last sleep — for the icy wind would have got me. Soon afterwards, someone started swearing and cursing for some unknown reason, but another voice said, "This is not the time for swearing, but for saying our prayers", which we promptly did. We said the Lord's Prayer.'

A glance at the figures shows that casualties among third-class passengers considerably out-numbered those travelling in first and second classes. There were, of course, more of them on board. Nevertheless, the percentages show that (with the exception of adult males in second class) the rate was higher. The British inquiry attributed this to their unwillingness to become separated from their baggage; their reluctance to leave the ship for the unknown perils of the sea outside; and the difficulty of getting to the boat deck from their quarters at the extreme ends of the ship.

To these factors can be added the problem of communication (quite apart from the lack of a public address system, some — indeed, many — of these passengers were unable to understand English). Nor was getting to what might have been safety as simple as it might have been. To keep the lower orders in their places — and to prevent what might have been a stampede for the lifeboats — a door that should have offered a means of escape was barricaded by a member of the crew. Once the mob (or what was considered to be the mob) had broken through and reached the vicinity of the boats, shots were certainly fired to prevent fear-crazed emigrants from running amok. In one case, a party of men were evicted from a boat at gunpoint.

At the time of the *Titanic* disaster, the priorities were quite simple: women and children first and then, if there were any room left in the boats, men. There was no mention of class, though this was a comparatively recent development. Until as recently as 1908, there had been another category and this was the lowest of them all: third-class passengers. It was a relic of the previous century, when boats were provided only for cabin-class passengers. Those who travelled in steerage (later third class) were considered expendable. In a manner of speaking, and to put the matter cruelly, they were. They were not crossing the ocean to attend business appointments in other lands; they were certainly not going to or returning from holidays. They were travelling because, surplus to the requirements of their own countries, they were trying to discover some sort of future in some other place. They were the emigrants.

The Statue of Liberty in New York harbour has the following words inscribed upon it:

Give me your tired, your poor,
Your huddled masses yearning to breathe free,
The wretched refuse of your teeming shore,
Send these, the homeless, tempest-tossed to me:
I lift my lamp beside the golden door.

They are part of a sonnet written by Emma Lazarus and entitled 'The New Colossus'. The tired and the poor were certainly tempest-tossed by the time they reached North America, and the circumstances of their voyages were appropriate for 'wretched refuse'. Many never reached their destinations at all. Between 1847 and 1851, no fewer than forty-four of the ships that departed from the UK for North America were wrecked, and 1,043 people were drowned. When the emigrant ship *Exmouth* was driven aground on Islay off the west coast of Scotland in 1847, 248 lost their lives. When the White Diamond Line's *Ocean Monarch* caught fire in the River Mersey in the following year, 176 perished. But fire, storm and tempest were not the only hazards that had to be faced by these under-privileged travellers of the seas. There were also disease and starvation.

Carrying emigrants was essentially a one-way business. There were innumerable victims of tyranny, neglect, or simply hard times, in Europe, who wished to settle in the United States or in Canada. On the other hand, citizens of the New World were reasonably contented, and had no wish to migrate eastwards. Consequently, a ship that had carried people from, say, Liverpool to New York, had to transport freight on the return trip to make the voyage profitable. The vessels were seldom cleaned out properly afterwards; the space that had served well enough for cargo was badly adapted for the accommodation of human beings. Indeed, there were some who said that slave ships provided better conditions: their captains at

least had a vested interest in delivering the captives alive and
fit enough to work.

Long after steamships had come into service on the North
Atlantic, emigrant ships continued to depend on sails. The one
certain thing was that a trip would take longer than anyone
expected. A crossing made by the *Cumberland Lass* from
Belfast with 139 on board lasted for 66 days, but this was not
the record. In 1841 a brig named the *Lady Hood* set out from
Stornaway in the Hebrides and reached New York 78 days
later. By a coincidence, 78 people were crammed into her
meagre cargo space.

Inevitably, the passengers' own supplies of food ran out.
The captain was usually prepared to sell replenishments — at a
price. In the case of the *Cumberland Lass*, he had only potatoes
to offer and then they, too, were exhausted. When the ship
reached her destination, there was no food at all on board.

With so many people crammed into so little space, the
opportunities for germs to multiply were enormous. Cholera
and typhus flourished: in 1847 (the year of the Irish potato
famine) no fewer than 17,445 emigrants died in transit. When
a quarantine station was opened on Grosse Isle in the St
Lawrence that year, they said that you could anticipate the
arrival of an emigrant ship by 'the smell alone at gunshot
range'. Soon these vessels became dubbed the 'fever ships', and
the description was apt. The station had been in business for
only twenty-four days, when its hospital was crammed with
856 cases of typhoid fever and dysentery — with a further 470
still awaiting disembarkation.

On one ship in which an epidemic of typhus had broken out,
a young Scotsman saw fifty-three corpses, including those of
his mother and sister, thrown without ceremony into the sea.
'One got used to it,' he wrote afterwards.

It was nothing but splash, splash, splash all day long — first
one, then another. There was one Martin on board, I
remember, with a wife and nine children ... Well, first his
wife died, and they threw *her* into the sea, and then *he* died,
and they threw *him* into the sea, and then the children, one
after another, till only two were left. The eldest, a girl of
about thirteen who had nursed them all, one after another,

and seen them die — well, she died, and then there was only the little fellow left.

By contrast, if you had the money, you could catch a regular packet boat from Liverpool to New York on the 1st, 8th, 16th and 24th of every month. Before the advent of steam, the westward passage was accomplished in about 38 days (25 days for eastbound ships). The fare was 35 guineas: the food was very tolerable and wines and spirits were included.

In spite of the passing of a succession of Passenger Acts by the British Parliament, the awfulness continued for most of the nineteenth century. Germany, and the Hamburg-Amerika Line in particular, was the originator of better conditions. A special village for the departure of emigrants was built beside the Elbe and the ships employed in the trade were at least sanitary. But the real breakthrough was initiated by the White Star Line with the building of the *Olympic* and the *Titanic*. Emigrants (or 'steerage', or third-class passengers) were given cabins. They had a dining saloon with its own galley, and they were waited upon at table by stewards. It was not altogether an act of philanthropy. As the line's management shrewdly thought, some of these travellers to the United States might achieve success. If they had been treated decently on the way out, they would probably patronize White Star for any return visits they might make to Europe. And, this time, they would travel first class.

Any discussion of the *Titanic* disaster seems to centre on the lack of adequate lifeboat accommodation. There is no denying this, but it has to be accompanied by the question of why such boats as there were had so many vacant seats — and why, indeed, were two not used at all? The only way in which to survive was by finding sanctuary in a boat. There were 2,201 people on board the ship. There were sufficient lifeboats to evacuate 1,178, which creates the alarming figure of 1,023 for whom there was no escape. But only 712 were picked up by the Cunarder *Carpathia*. A simple sum suggests that, for some reason, a bad situation was rendered even worse: or that 466 died unnecessarily.

With regard to her quota of lifeboats, however, the *Titanic* conformed to the laws administered by the British Board of Trade. In fact, she did more than this: she exceeded their requirements by carrying four Engelhardt collapsibles, each with a capacity of 47. How, then, was it possible that, even if every boat had been used, and if every boat had been filled to its limits, 1,023 (the entire population of a large village) would have been condemned to death, and nobody need have been called to account for it?

The answer lies in the sheer bumbling inefficiency of government and officialdom. The matter of lifeboats had last been seriously considered in 1894. The Passenger Act of 1855 had ruled that lifeboat accommodation for no more than 216 people need be provided (the ships, to be sure, were small). Forty years later, the situation was reviewed and new regulations formulated. It now became necessary for vessels of 15,000 tons or more to carry a minimum of sixteen boats. This may have been sufficient at the time: the crack Cunarders *Campania* and *Lucania* each registered no more than 12,950 tons — though there were already changes taking place in the shipyards. In 1899, the 17,274-ton White Star liner *Oceanic* was launched; followed in 1901 by the 20,904-ton *Celtic*. In 1907 the *Lusitania* (32,500 tons) was completed; and her sister, the *Mauretania,* followed in November 1908. Thus, even before the *Olympic* and the *Titanic* had become thoughts on a drawing-board, the Board of Trade's 15,000 tons had become a nonsense. The White Star giants were three times as large and ought, it might have been imagined, to have carried three times the minimum number of boats. But, despite the accounts published in newspapers, or the visible evidence available to anyone who went to Southampton or Liverpool, the thought seems to have escaped the Board of Trade.

It had not, however, been unremarked elsewhere. In 1910 a Member of the House of Commons asked whether 'the attention of the President of the Board of Trade has been called to the fact that the *Olympic* is provided with only 14 lifeboats?' The reply, which was far from satisfactory, was that she had, indeed, 14 lifeboats plus two 'ordinary boats' — providing a total capacity of 9,752 cubic feet. Possibly because he was unable to translate this statistic into terms of human occupancy, the Member did not press his point.

Next year, on 15 February, another politician asked when the rules governing lifeboats had last been reviewed. He was shamelessly told that the year was 1894; but, a little vaguely, he was assured that 'the matter is under consideration'. By this time, the process of fitting-out the *Olympic* had almost been completed, and the *Titanic* was within three and a half months of being launched.

Sir Alfred Chambers, Nautical Adviser to the Board of Trade from 1896 until 1911, expressed the rather silly view that 'The great object is so to build a ship that, in the event of a disaster, she should be her own lifeboat.' Even after the loss of the *Titanic*, which must surely have shown him the folly of such an idea, he was unrepentant. 'It was,' he said, 'quite evident to me that, if you went on crowding the ships with boats, you would require a crew which were not required otherwise for the safe navigation of the ship, or for the proper upkeep of the ship, but you are providing a crew which would be carried uselessly across the ocean, that would never be required to man the boats.'

If Sir Alfred emerges from the discussion as something of a buffoon, there are others who do not. Alexander Carlisle, the designer of the *Olympic* and the *Titanic*, is said to have proposed that each ship should carry 50 boats — which, with a capacity of 65 people in each, would have been sufficient. Possibly he did not argue his case forcibly enough; possibly the barrier of prejudices was too great. At all events, the White Star directors turned his suggestion down. He had to be content with the addition of those four collapsibles.

Captain E.J. Smith himself seems to have been less than happy about the situation. During an Atlantic crossing the *Olympic*, a passenger is said to have remarked to him on how few lifeboats there were. If this account is to be believed, he replied: 'If this ship should strike a submerged derelict or iceberg that would cut through several of the watertight compartments, we would not have enough boats or rafts aboard to take care of more than one-third of the passengers. The *Titanic*, too, is no better equipped.'

It hardly sounds like the kind of reassuring observation that captains are supposed to make to anxious passengers, but it may be true. Carlisle, the brain behind the ship, did not believe that either the *Olympic* or the *Titanic* were unsinkable.

John Maxtone-Graham in *The North Atlantic Run* (in the United States entitled *The Only Way to Cross*) refers to 'a paralysis of command' during the *Titanic*'s dying hours. Conceivably, Captain Smith was preoccupied by the impossibility of dividing 2,201 into 1,178, and wondering who, apart from himself, should be sacrificed to the lassitude of the Board of Trade and the cupidity of his owners. They had, indeed, spent the ransoms of several kings on luxurious accommodation, but they had refused Carlisle those extra lifeboats he wanted. Luxury is something that can be marketed; safety is somehow taken for granted.

Even nowadays, when the public is possibly better informed, this is so. John Lancaster-Smith, Director of the Passenger Shipping Association, said:

> Safety is not a factor. People don't worry about going in a ship, other than that they might be seasick. They don't worry about the safety factor until we get an accident. In the last two weeks [summer 1984], we've had a ship run on to the rocks in Alaska, and 750 passengers had to be taken off. That sort of thing concentrates the mind a little on the safety angle, and might inhibit passengers. But it's only when something happens that people think about it. Nine times out of ten they get on to a ship and — unlike in an aircraft — they don't worry about the safety angle of it.

Neither, if the advertisements reflect any reality at all, do aeroplane passengers, despite Mr Lancaster-Smith's suggestion. They concentrate on the quality of the in-flight food, the comeliness of the stewardesses, and the space in which tired executives can increase their fatigue by going through papers. One cannot imagine a slogan such as: 'British Airways Gets You There — Alive'.

Of course, regulations concerning safety at sea have improved beyond all recognition since the days of the *Titanic*. But even in those days, if we are to believe Hugo P. Frear, naval contractor to the Union Iron Works, matters were better arranged in America than in Britain. Writing in the San Francisco *Examiner*, Mr Frear asserted that, had the *Titanic* been under the supervision of the United States government, the White Star Line would have been compelled to provide at least 42 lifeboats. Between them, they would have accommodated 2,367 people.

Nevertheless, the United States must take the blame for one circumstance in the *Titanic* that impeded the passage of third-class passengers to the safety of the boats: the locking of the doors that confined them to their parts of the ship. The law that stipulated this was not conceived with the idea of keeping the lower orders where they belonged, or of making sure that they never strayed beyond the accommodation for which they had paid. Doubtless recollecting the state of affairs on board emigrant ships in the nineteenth century, it assumed the less than affluent travellers to be subject to ill-health. If they were isolated, so, too, would their germs be, and the spread of infection would be contained.

In fact, though it was probably not intended, the flow of people to the boat deck in an emergency would be controlled. The first-class passengers would obviously get there first; and, if time were short, would stand a better chance of being taken to safety. Those in the third class would be the last to arrive and have the least chance. The rule of women and children first, then first-class men, and then the rest, may have been modified. But, in effect, it still applied.

Nowadays, passengers are required by international law to carry out boat drill. From Mr Lancaster-Smith:

In the old days, passengers mustered at lifeboat stations. In practice, this was fine until we had a number of accidents in which, for one reason or another, ships took on a list and they couldn't muster there. Or, even if they did manage to muster by the boats, the ship might have been damaged in some way that made some of the boats unserviceable. Now, under IMO [the International Maritime Organization] regulations, passengers converge on a muster station that is usually in a lounge or somewhere. They are briefed by an officer, or by the captain over the Tannoy. Sometimes they are taken out to the boat stations so they know where to go. But nine times out of ten they are not. They are shown how to put on life-jackets and told about the safety procedures. It varies from ship to ship. Sometimes it's good; sometimes it's bad.

In the case of the *Titanic*, it was non-existent. The crew had received only the most perfunctory training in boat drill; the passengers did not have any at all. On this voyage, of all voyages, Captain Smith had overlooked it. Was he so anxious that his customers should hold faith in his liner's unsinkability that he considered such a precaution to be a retrograde step?

This must surely have been the main reason why, despite the calmness of the sea, despite *Titanic*'s consideration in taking so long to die, the boats were not filled to capacity and two were not used at all. Perhaps it was 'paralysis of command'. It was certainly chaos.

After the disaster, shipowners were compelled to look to their complements of boats and to ensure that they were sufficient. This was among the recommendations of the British inquiry. The lifeboat and raft accommodation, its members suggested, should be based on the number of persons carried — and not on the tonnage. There was, however, an escape clause. When, in the opinion of the Board of Trade, this requirement is impracticable, they said, it 'may be modified as the Board may think right'.

Writing nearly two years after the event, Adam W. Kirkaldy — author of *British Shipping* — was inclined to excuse the Board of Trade for its laxity in bringing its ideas up to date.

An event like the loss of the *Titanic*, [Mr Kirkaldy wrote] comes as a great shock to the public conscience, and necessitates a very considerable jettisoning of old ideas. It is discovered that the question of boats for all has not been in the official mind; probably the conviction that the unsinkable ship had been constructed had lessened the belief in the utility of boats. In fact it is only very occasionally that boats, even though needed, can be used to advantage ... It is of very rare occurrence that a vessel founders on a fine still night, giving the opportunity to lower every available boat.

No doubt he was correct. The *Titanic* disaster was undoubtedly a turning point in the attitude to safety at sea. But this did not stop the occurrences of tragedies — even in vessels where there were 'boats for all'.

The *Titanic* was only the beginning. Within a period of just over three years, three transatlantic liners — the *Titanic* herself, the *Empress of Ireland*, and the *Lusitania* — sank and accounted for a total of 3,712 lives. For whatever it may be worth, this can be compared to the crashing of eight Boeing 747s in the latest version, or fourteen DC10s, or about thirty Concordes — each filled to capacity and in every instance with no survivors. The toll of the *Titanic* is inexcusable. The night was clear and calm, two other ships were reasonably nearby: if there had been sufficient boats, and if matters had been handled better — which means to say if all the passengers had known where to go, and the crew had been properly practised in what to do — the casualties need only have been few. There was, after all, plenty of time.

When the *Lusitania* sank within sight of land on that early summer afternoon in 1915, this precious commodity was denied to Captain Turner. Within twenty minutes of being struck by the torpedo, the great Cunarder had sunk. Charles Frohman, the famous New York theatrical producer, is said to have quoted that line from James Barrie's *Peter Pan*: 'Why fear death? It is the most beautiful adventure in life.' If he did, it must have come very readily to mind, and Mr Frohman must have been uncommonly philosophical. Few people confront the ends of their particular worlds with such equanimity. Nor, indeed, do circumstances such as these cause the majority to indulge in reflection. They are far too busy trying to save their skins.

Of the 159 Americans on board, Frohman, the millionaire Alfred Vanderbilt, and nine others had been sent telegrams warning them not to sail. They turned out to have emanated from the office of the *Providence Journal*, a newspaper published on Rhode Island which became famous for its war-time scoops (no doubt helped by payments said to have been paid to its editor by British Naval Intelligence). Once their source had been established, the messages were dismissed as journalistic stunts and not delivered. In any case, the intended recipients and nearly everybody else aboard the *Lusitania* had already been warned. On the morning of sailing day (1 May) there had been a strange juxtaposition of advertisements in the New York press. One of them, by Cunard, announced that the *Lusitania,* the 'fastest and largest steamer now in Atlantic service', would be sailing for Liverpool. The other had been paid for by the Imperial German Embassy. Headlined simply 'Notice!', it read:

> Travellers intending to embark on the Atlantic voyage are reminded that a state of war exists between Germany and her allies and Great Britain and her allies; that the zone of war includes the waters adjacent to the British Isles; that, in accordance with formal notice given by the Imperial German Government, vessels flying the flag of Great Britain, or of any of her allies, are liable to destruction in those waters and that travellers sailing into the war zone on ships of Great Britain or her allies do so at their own risk.

In spite of this declaration, 1,251 passengers embarked for the voyage: among them Vanderbilt (who was on his way to a horse show in Britain), Frohman, Elbert Hubbert (an abrasive writer who was travelling to Europe in the hope of interviewing the Kaiser), and Charles Lauriat (a wealthy bookseller with branches in Boston and London).

The second sitting of luncheon was just over when the U20's torpedo struck the ship. It exploded at a point just behind the bridge and put the engines out of action. Unassisted, it would not have been sufficient to sink the ship; but, a few seconds later, there was another explosion, which ripped the bottom out of the forepart of the liner. The British Admiralty always maintained that the U20's commander, Walther Schweiger, fired two torpedoes. Schweiger's records, on the other hand, mention only one, and he had no reason to lie. His stock was nearly exhausted, and he wanted to keep the last one in hand in case a promising target presented itself on the trip back to Germany.

On the other hand, as Colin Simpson shows in *Lusitania,* the liner was carrying a good deal of contraband war material — including a considerable quantity of high explosives. It was beyond any shadow of reasonable doubt that these delivered the *coup de grâce.* If cargo can be regarded as an intrinsic part of a ship, the *Lusitania*'s mortal wound was self-inflicted.

There was pandemonium. The din of escaping steam drowned many of Captain Turner's orders. He was, for instance, accused afterwards by one passenger of saying, 'Don't lower the boats.' In fact, he had instructed, 'Don't lower the boats into the water;' for the perfectly sensible reason that the ship still had way on her. Many of the passengers didn't know how to put on their life-jackets (some of them were drowned because they had put them on upside down); at least two of the lifeboats dropped from their falls when they were 20 feet above the sea; the portholes on D deck had been left open (the sea rushed in eagerly, helping the effects of the explosion); and the ship listed so far over to starboard that it was impossible to use the davits on the port side.

Vanderbilt and Frohman tried to save the lives of a number of babies by tying life-jackets to Moses baskets found in the ship's nursery (the effort failed: the jackets were ripped off by the turbulence created by the rapidly settling ship). At one point, the comforting shape of the elderly cruiser HMS *Juno* appeared in the distance as if on a rescue mission. But then, unaccountably, she turned round and returned to her base at Queenstown (now Cobh). It later transpired that she had been recalled by the Admiralty: her system of construction was so obsolete that she was considered to be perfect U-boat fodder. It was not until two hours after the explosion that help arrived — and most of this was from Irish fishermen.

Only 754 survived the sinking — only six of the liner's 48 boats reached Queenstown. Vanderbilt was drowned, Frohman was drowned, and 122 other American citizens died. It can have been little comfort to their relatives to know that, when it was all over and corpses were being washed up on the Irish shore, there were rewards to be had from finding them. The going rate was £1 each for a non-American, £2 for an American, with a macabre jackpot of £1,000 for anyone who discovered the earthly remains of Alfred Vanderbilt.

The ocean is a theatre of war. Man, on the whole, is better at sinking ships than nature is: though nature, with her armoury of tempest, icebergs and rocks, has not done too badly. As recently as 1980, despite so many rules to be obeyed and such

ingenious instruments to assist the mariner, 387 vessels of over
100 tons were lost; and, in the following year, no fewer than
1,094 died in shipping disasters. But none of these were transatlantic liners and none of the casualties could be attributed to
the sinking of such great ships. This is of no particular credit to
the owners and crews of these giants: as a regular means of
communication between Europe and North America, they had
virtually become extinct.

More significantly, the years between the First and Second
World Wars were quiet years. Since the *Lusitania* disaster was
the work of a hostile submarine, it may have seemed that the
loss of the *Empress of Ireland* marked the end of an age when
the weather (using the weapon of fog) and man (by making a
misjudgement) created such a substantial casualty list. After
the war, when the big ships resumed their traffic, most
passengers may have concluded that the hazards of ocean
travel were the province of historians and of no concern to the
contemporary traveller.

The Second World War — like most of the major conflicts in
relatively modern times — had created quite a lot of technical
progress. Radar was one example. It could detect objects
obscured by fog; it could warn the captain of dangers in the
vicinity — whether they were icebergs, the rocks of an all too
nearby coast, or another vessel. When a master mariner
pushed on with undiminished speed through what many would
have thought to be dangerous conditions, he was no longer
guilty of recklessness. Nor need he depend too much on prayer
or on whatever sixth sense these seafarers may have seemed to
possess.

That was what people thought. Unhappily they were wrong.
In 1956, radar had been installed in merchant ships for a mere
two years, and its performance was still limited. Admittedly, it
could show that some sort of obstacle was in the vicinity, but
this was not sufficient. The information that it imparted
required interpretation. This was something that the captains
of the 29,083-ton Italian liner *Andrea Doria* and the Swedish
ship *Stockholm* (registering 12,644 tons, she was the smallest
passenger ship in transatlantic service) seem to have overlooked as they converged upon each other in thick fog. On 7
July 1956 the *Andrea Doria* had sailed from Genoa on passage

to New York. With no less than three outdoor swimming pools, three cinemas, and interior decorations of unparalleled splendour, she was the pride of the Italian merchant navy. As might have been expected, the long haul of the voyage was without incident. But then, on the night of the 25th, everything went sadly wrong, and the lives of the 1,134 passengers and the 572 members of the crew were put in jeopardy. The great liner was nearing the end of her crossing: Nantucket Island lay some short distance away to port and, closer to hand, the Nantucket lightship marked the perilous shoals. Thick fog enclosed the scene.

The *Stockholm*, which had left New York for Sweden that morning, showed up as a blip on the *Andrea Doria*'s radar screen, but the latter's master, Captain Piero Calamai, at first mistook it for a fishing boat. This was not his only mistake. The liner was not on the course he supposed her to be taking, and she was travelling much faster than he thought (her speed was 22 knots). By the time he realized his errors, it was too late. The *Stockholm* lunged into the *Andrea Doria*'s flank. It was the old story: if you must hit something, strike it head-on and pray that the collision bulkhead will hold fast.

Nothing, indeed, had changed — at least in this respect. The *Stockholm* escaped with a crumpled bow, which could be replaced. The *Andrea Doria* had come to the end of her five-year-old life.

Having delivered what amounted to a death blow, the Swedish ship withdrew and slipped quietly into the murk. On board the doomed liner, Captain Calamai seemed to be unaware of how severe the damage was; at all events, he announced that he proposed to run his ship on to the nearest beach. It was now 11.30 p.m. For fear of creating panic, he refused to sound the alarms. But the deception could not be maintained for long. The liner was shipping water through a 30-foot gash in her side and, before very long, she was markedly listing to starboard.

Richardson Dilworth, the Mayor of Philadelphia, and his wife were both thrown from their beds by the impact. Mrs Dilworth suggested that the ship had struck an iceberg 'like the *Titanic*'. Mr Dilworth pointed out that this was improbable: you didn't get icebergs so far south as off the coast of Massachusetts. The ship's senior surgeon, Dr Bruno Donati, concluded that one of the boilers had burst. Morris Novik, president of New York's Italian-language radio station, WOV, decided with admirable calm that, 'It's really nothing.' Ruth Roman, the movie star, had been dancing in the first-class lounge. Now she ran to her cabin, gathered up her three-year-old son, and told him: 'We're going on a picnic.' The little boy didn't seem to think it strange that they should go picnicking in a now sadly lopsided ship in the middle of the night. Betsy Drake, the current wife of Cary Grant, walked to a lifeboat on the starboard side, and found that, owing to the already pronounced cant of the ship, it could not be launched.

In the lounge, the orchestra played 'Arrivederci Roma' and then played it again — and again. It appeared as good a way as any to keep up morale — though Roma seemed very far away.

Nothing, apparently, could maintain morale in the tourist-class cinema, where an audience had been watching *Foxfire* starring Jane Russell and Jeff Chandler. Some ran. Some wept. Some went down upon their knees and said their prayers. But the panic subsided, and one feature of the disaster was the well-disciplined way in which most people did as they were told.

Some had lucky escapes. The wife of an oil executive had been reluctant to go to bed. She fancied another cup of coffee, a quiet smoke, a chat about this and that. Her husband fretted: he was tired. But he did what most husbands do under such circumstances and surrendered. It was as well. Their cabin was very close to the point of impact. Had they been in it, they would certainly have been killed.

In a few instances, a matter of feet made all the difference between life and death. A lawyer and banker named Walter G. Carlin went into the bathroom to clean his teeth. When he staggered back into what had once been his stateroom, he discovered that his wife was missing. The place was a shambles of destruction and there was a large hole in the side of the ship. A chiropractor named Thure Petersen actually had a glimpse of the *Stockholm*'s prow before he passed out. He survived the experience.

All told, there were 52 fatal casualties; nearly all of them caused by the impact and its damage to the *Andrea Doria*'s starboard side. The miracle is that there were not many more; for, since the liner was now listing heavily to starboard, it was impossible to launch more than a fraction of the ship's complement of lifeboats. Nor was the *Stockholm* eager to contribute any of hers. As her master, Captain Nordenson, not unreasonably pointed out, he might well need them for his own people.

Reluctant though Captain Calamai may have been to inform his passengers of the emergency, he had no misgivings about broadcasting his ship's plight to the world beyond. The 6,600-ton United Fruit Company's ship *Cape Ann* picked up the SOS and hurried to offer assistance; and so did the troopship *Private William H. Thomas* (homeward bound with servicemen from Europe), and so did several other vessels. But the most effective help of all came from the French liner *Ile de France*, commanded by the aristocratic Captain Baron Raoul de Beaudéan.

There were 940 passengers attended by a crew of 826 aboard the *Ile de France*. At 10.34 that night, the ship had passed six miles to the south of the Nantucket lightship and then set course along her normal route for the Le Havre trip. Now de Beaudéan had to decide whether to turn his ship round and track back, or whether to continue on his journey to Europe. One result of the *Titanic* disaster was the formation of the International Convention for the Safety of Life at Sea (commonly known as SOLAS). Its meetings are attended by government representatives of all maritime nations, and it is greatly concerned with regulations for preventing collisions.

In 1929, SOLAS had decreed that any ship picking up an SOS should proceed immediately to the injured vessel, unless, for some reason, the victim's captain turned down the offer of help. However, in 1948, this regulation was modified. Providing there were other ships hastening to the disaster, it was left to the master's discretion.

Beaudéan knew that other vessels had gone to the scene of the *Andrea Doria*'s final anguish. He knew that to turn back would cost him time and his employers a good deal of money. He therefore radioed his position at 11.40 p.m. and asked, 'Do you need assistance?' The reply was quick and uncompromising: 'Need immediate assistance.' For some unexplained reason, this never reached the *Ile de France*, but Beaudéan did not feel released from his possible obligation. He called up the *Stockholm*, asking for guidance. Nordenson explained his own problem and pointed out the need for lifeboats. The radio officer in the *Cape Ann* was even more specific. 'Doria wants to disembark 1,500 passengers and crew,' he transmitted. 'Suggest strongly you have all your lifeboats ready to assist.' Beaudéan needed no further bidding. He turned his ship round and, at 2 a.m., the massive French liner reached the sinking Italian ship.

There was more time than anyone could have hoped for: the *Andrea Doria* did not sink until 10.09 that morning. There were good communications. There was no panic. Beaudéan retained 17 boats for his own passengers in case they might be needed, and dispatched 11 to the stricken giant. Somehow passengers and crew negotiated the obstacles of the slanting liner; somehow they slithered down her side. Some needed encouragement to go, but they received it and they went. The most reluctant of all was Captain Calamai. But, eventually, the ship's second officer persuaded him. The ship, he agreed, was lost, but there was no reason why the two of them should die with her. Calamai sadly agreed.

One thousand six hundred and fifty-four lives were saved. By 5 a.m., the work was done, and the *Ile de France* proceeded at full speed to New York. In theory, something very similar could have been accomplished by the *Californian* in the case of the *Titanic*.

But ...

The Greek cruise liner *Lakonia* was an old ship when she sailed from Southampton on 19 December 1963 for a winter's journey that should have taken her 657 passengers (most of them English) to Madeira, Tenerife and Las Palmas. Launched in 1929, this 20,238-ton property of Greek Lines SA had originally been named the *Johan van Oldenbarnvelt* and was owned by a Dutch company. Since then, she had been bought by at least one other shipping line in the Netherlands, which, in 1959, had refitted her and converted her into a one-class ship.

It seems unlikely that she was commercially successful. In 1962 Greek Lines SA were able to purchase her for a knock-down price that only marginally exceeded her value as scrap.

She was adapted for cruising at Genoa and every expense was spared; every short cut that could be taken was taken. For example, no diagrams of the electrical circuits were submitted to the Bureau Véritas for the simple reason that the French classification society did not ask to see them. Nor did representatives of the Bureau Véritas inspect the new accommodation — in this instance, because the owners considered it none of the society's concern.

One day in March 1963 two officials of the Greek Shipping Directorate went on board, had a quick look round, and duly issued the ship with a safety certificate. It acknowledged that the safety equipment had been properly renewed; that the fire detection system and the fire-fighting equipment were in good order. And that the lifeboats exceeded the number insisted upon by SOLAS by the ratio of 1 to 4.

There were, indeed, plenty of lifeboats, though several of the davits were in less than perfect shape. When it had a mind to, the fire-detection system could detect fire. There was not, however, any sprinkler system to extinguish the flames. By and large, one has to take the view that the *Lakonia* (as she was now called in deference to her Greek ownership: Cunard must have hated it — they had owned at least two very successful ships named *Laconia*) was rather like a student who has passed an examination by one mark — and that with the help of a sympathetic invigilator.

But it's amazing what you can get away with if you apply a few coats of paint. Those passengers who embarked at Southampton in the hope of spending Christmas in the sunshine knew nothing of these imperfections. Nor did they know that a fairly high proportion of the sailors were novices. Had anyone been connected with the sea, however, he might have cast a critical eye at the accommodation ladders. Instead of having been taken in, they remained lashed to the outside of the hull. Such neglect did not argue well for the quality of seamanship.

The first few days passed pleasantly enough. Those who wished to buy last-minute Christmas presents could avail themselves of a gift shop. Next to it, there was a lady's hairdresser and a barber's shop for the gentlemen. The supply of perfumes, the eau de Cologne, the lacquer, the brilliantine, and all the other unguents, potions, and similar aids to a sweet-smelling, well-groomed humanity, was impressive. So, indeed, was its inflammatory content. Ignite the lot and you could generate enough fire to set a small island ablaze from end to end. This might have been acceptable — most such establishments stock a similar range without ill effects — had it been possible to seal off these salons; had the fire detectors been in the correct places and in working order; had there been a sprinkler device; and, in the event of a fire, had anyone known what was the right thing to do.

At 10.15 on the first morning at sea, what passed for boat-drill took place. Several passengers didn't bother to attend. A number were given the wrong directions about how to put on their life-jackets; there was little said about how to behave in an emergency and nothing about what to do in the unpleasant event of having to throw oneself into the sea from a great height.

There was, however, a notice in each cabin informing the occupant of his or her allocated lifeboat, and there were signs showing how to get there. The *Lakonia*'s master, Captain Matthew Zarbis may have satisfied himself that a sufficient quorum of passengers had been present: enough to justify his entering the occasion in the log without impugning his integrity.

On the evening of 22 December the elderly ship was steaming at 16 knots about 180 miles to the north of Madeira. The wind was blowing at force 4 from the north-east: a slight swell was running. Life on board had settled down to what promised to be a pleasant conclusion to the day. The two hairdressing establishments had closed at six o'clock, just as they always did. The gift shop next door normally shut at 6.30; but, on this occasion, it had remained open until 9.30. The staff were busy putting up Christmas decorations.

Up in the Lakonia Room on the promenade deck, Captain Zarbis was attending a masked ball that the cruise manager, George Herbert, had organized. He was obviously enjoying himself until, at 11.00 p.m., somebody noticed smoke drifting up the central staircase. Zarbis quickly excused himself and went up to the bridge. It was now five minutes since the fire had been discovered, but the staff captain did not seem to be worried.

At 10.55 p.m., the night-patrol fire watchman had noticed smoke seeping through the sides of the door to the hairdressing salon. Thinking that a personal visit would be quicker than using a telephone, he ran up to the wheelhouse and informed the officer of the watch. Whatever the cause might be, he said, it must have occurred within the previous hour. When he had passed that way at 9.55, everything had seemed to be in good order.

There followed a series of mistakes and frustrations which, if the results had not been so tragic, would have been the stuff of slapstick comedy. The door of the salon was locked. In too much of a hurry to get the key from the hairdresser's cabin, the purser — assisted by a German steward — battered it down. This, of course, unleashed the blaze and enabled the flames to travel wherever they would. It also revealed immense quantities of thick, choking, black smoke that obscured the centre of the inferno. Consequently it was impossible to judge correctly where best to concentrate the puny counter-attack by the ship's far from sufficient fire-fighting equipment.

Had the fire detectors in the hairdresser's shop been properly installed, the blaze would have been detected at birth. But no — hardly anything on board the *Lakonia* seemed to be in good order that night.

Nevertheless, the staff captain believed that the flames could be contained by using extinguishers and, if the need arose, by water. But, he cautioned, don't make too much noise. It would be a mistake to alarm the passengers.

The passengers were already alarmed — especially those whose cabins were near the small shopping centre, and those who, a few minutes earlier, had been dancing in the Lakonia Room. Zarbis was aware of this. He rang down 'stop engines' and picked up the microphone of the public address system. He judged the situation to be sufficiently serious to order everyone on deck. But the public address system had broken down. It was left to Mr Herbert — who had overheard somebody say 'fire' or 'smoke', he wasn't sure which — to warn the revellers at the ball. He urged them to remain calm: to go out on to the deck and inhale the fresh air.

Confusion followed. According to one source, it was Mr Herbert who gave the next instruction; according to another, it was the stewards. At all events, the passengers were now told to muster in the dining room three decks below. About one hundred obeyed. They remained there for about ten minutes; then they were advised to retrace their steps and make for the promenade deck.

Meanwhile, on the bridge, Zarbis had told the staff captain to keep him informed of the situation while he worked out the ship's position and radioed for help. Four vessels in the vicinity responded. The Argentinian *Salta* was the first to arrive; then the British freighter *Montcalm*, followed by the American *Rio Grande* and the Pakistan cargo ship *Mehdi*. The intentions of their captains may have been admirable, though they kept their distance. The nearest hove to about four miles away which, under the circumstances, was four miles too far.

The fire now had complete control of the *Lakonia*. At 11.25 p.m., Zarbis capitulated. The fire-fighting attempts were clearly having no success: it would surely not be long before he had to abandon ship. At this point, Mr Herbert came up to the bridge. He was told that the public address system was out of action, and asked to do the best he could. At the same time, a party of stewards was sent below to search the cabins in case anyone was still unaware of the emergency.

George Herbert paced the promenade deck, calling at the top of his voice, 'On captain's order, as the loudspeakers do not function, you are requested to go to your positions near your boats.' At 11.38, as if to complete the chaos, the ship's telephone system broke down.

At midnight, and then again at ten minutes past midnight, Zarbis instructed Herbert to 'tell the passengers to enter boats — first on the starboard side'. The rolling of the ship made things more difficult, and those accommodation ladders that had never been taken inboard created an obstacle to embarkation. Somebody commented on the danger of 'the passengers smashing their limbs between the ship's rail and the boats'. Two boats, near the stern, were lowered by winches. The operation seemed to be going well enough until, in each case, a member of the crew forgot to unhitch one of the tackles. The result was that each boat hung suspended from one davit, and that everyone on board was tipped into the sea.

In another boat, two of the sailors were too seasick to row;

and, for want of any better method, one of the passengers had to make pathetic attempts to attract attention by using his cigarette lighter. When they saw another lifeboat overturn some distance astern, there was not enough manpower to go back and rescue the occupants.

According to the evidence of the Greek inquiry, when the last boat had departed, about 150 passengers and 80 members of the crew (including the captain, the chief engineer and the staff captain) were still on board and the fire was manifestly out of control. But this may have been an exaggeration. The total death toll was 128 — 95 passengers and 33 crew members. The blame, predictably, was levelled at Zarbis and his senior officers, which may seem to be unfair. The owners had skimped money in the conversion of the *Lakonia* into a cruise liner. She was by no means a safe ship and, with the breakdown of the address system, it may seem surprising that a majority did survive.

But this is one of the problems of safety at sea. Because the *Lakonia* had been built before the 1949 SOLAS conference, she was exempt from its regulations. Similarly, at a convention held in 1983, new requirements were formulated. They concerned the provision of lifeboats, inflatable and rigid life-rafts, improved personal life-saving appliances, and they reflected an awareness that, nowadays, the greatest danger in an accident at sea is not drowning but death from hypothermia. But many of them will apply only to ships that have been laid down on or after 1 July 1986. Those responsible for safety in the *Titanic* made no attempt to advance this aspect of ocean travel in pace with the development of larger, faster, ships. Now, at least, they are trying. In today's cruise ship — which, apart from two liners that run a seasonal service between Europe and North America and one that travels to Cape Town, is the only reminder of the great ocean-going passenger ships — the passenger's lot is invariably comfortable. More important, though, it is as safe as anything to do with such a determined opponent as the sea can ever be.

—5—

The Navigator's Story

Captain Edward J. Smith had begun his career in square-rigged sailing ships, moved on into steamers and, as a culmination of all those years at sea, had attained command of the largest, possibly the most luxurious, and undoubtedly the most talked-about liner of the day. Smith's journey up the ladder might not unreasonably be related to the progress of passenger vessels. His responsibilities had enlarged as they had become bigger; as the ships became more complex, so did his job.

The elegantly appointed *Titanic* was as luxurious as any hotel on land; but, as Smith must sometimes have told himself, she was still a ship. Her purpose was to carry people across the ocean with the promptness and regularity of a railway express. This was expected of all the crack liners and, by and large, they fulfilled the expectation. On one occasion, the White Star's *Oceanic* made the round transatlantic trip with less than a minute's difference between the time taken for the west-bound passage and that for the east-bound.

It is reasonable to run trains according to an exact timetable, even if they do not always maintain it. But trains do not have to contend with gales and fog and icebergs. Nevertheless, the masters of these ocean expresses managed to keep to the schedule — although sometimes at the cost of prudence. They frequently cut corners: as certain captains frankly told the

British inquiry, they were prepared to blunder through fog and ice in the mistaken assumption that the faster you travel through danger, the more quickly you escape from it.

The *Titanic* was powered by a pair of steam reciprocating engines and a turbine. Whilst she was not so fast as her Cunard competitors, she was by no means slow. This, perhaps, was progress. Her accommodation — even that of her third-class passengers — was as magnificent as that of any ship on the North Atlantic run, and better than most. This too, perhaps, was progress. She was in touch with the world beyond by means of wireless (which was more than you could say of many vessels in the year 1912), but there remained a department in which everything was much as it had been for the previous half-century or more: navigation.

If a captain from Smith's days in square-riggers had wandered on to *Titanic*'s bridge; if he had explored the wheel-house and the chart room, he might have been mildly surprised. The atmosphere would have been different. Every-thing would have been on a much grander scale (they didn't *have* wheelhouses in those old sailing ships), but the essentials had not changed. A magnetic compass was still used (though a gyroscopic compass — which, among other advantages, points to true north rather than to the magnetic pole — was being developed). Each officer still had a sextant, and on the chart room table, you could still see those tools of the navigator's trade, parallel rules, dividers, a protractor, and so on.

The methods had not altered, either. When you could see the sun and the stars, you could pinpoint your position with very reasonable accuracy. When you could not — which is commonplace on the North Atlantic — you had to rely on dead reckoning. You knew how far you had travelled in a certain time and on what course. You made allowances for the push of the wind and the set of the currents, and from this data you attempted to establish your position. Usually the result was rather less than accurate.

Indeed, any master mariner who was honest with himself would have admitted that there had to be luck. Another White Star captain, Thomas Jones, had once brought the liner *Bovic* from the Tusker Rock (opposite Wexford in the south of the Irish Sea) to the Nantucket Shoals lightship (at the approaches to New York) in eight days. Throughout the trip the sky was obscured by cloud: he never so much as glimpsed the sun or the stars. Just the same, he made a commendably precise landfall.

Was he, then, a more than usually talented navigator? The answer must be no. On 17 March 1907, when he was in command of the *Suevic* — the finest of the White Star ships employed on its service to Australia — he was struggling up the English Channel in fog and opposed by heavy seas. At about 10.30 that night one of the look-outs reported the beam of a lighthouse on the southernmost tip of the Lizard. Jones went out on to a wing of the bridge to study it. It came from a point higher than he had expected it to be. He must, he judged, be too close inshore. Turning to the wheelhouse, he ordered the quartermaster to go hard-a-port. But it was too late. A strong current was running: before the liner was able to respond to her helm, she had been thrown forward on to rocks.

One and a half minutes had elapsed since the first sighting of the light.

Afterwards, a passenger recalled:

I was in my bunk, when I heard a grating noise. We were told that the vessel was ashore. I rushed out and could see the glimmer of the lighthouse lights ahead. The crew responded to the orders of the captain nobly. They gave us life-jackets, and we were told to go into the library. Hot coffee and other warm food was brought to us, and the liner's boats were then launched. We were let down the side, one by one. It was terrible in the darkness and we had to wait for the lifeboat to be hurled near the ship before we could get on board. The lifeboat crews worked bravely, but the weather was awful.

Happily there were no casualties. Nevertheless, the court of inquiry ruled that 'the vessel was not navigated with proper and seamanlike care after 10 p.m. on March 17th last'. Jones's master's certificate was suspended for three months. But, although the court's verdict ended Captain Jones's career as a master mariner, the disaster was by no means the end of the *Suevic*. The liner's afterpart was later salvaged and taken to her builders, Harland & Wolff at Belfast, where a new forepart was constructed. She soldiered on at sea in various roles until

1942, when she was scuttled to avoid capture by a German warship.

As the White Star liner was driven on to the Lizard on that fog-wrapped, gale-tormented night in 1907, another calamity was taking place farther up the Channel. The Elder Dempster ship *Jebba* was homeward bound from the west coast of Africa with 79 passengers. She was due to call at Plymouth, then to retrace her course to Land's End, steam up the Irish Sea and dock at Liverpool. Her master, Captain J.J.C. Mills, sat huddled in a corner of the wheelhouse with his eyes on the starboard horizon. If only the fog would clear — just for a second or two (it wasn't asking for very much) — he could probably catch a glimpse of the Eddystone light. This would enable him to fix his position with some (though far from total) accuracy. But the fog did not clear and the light flashed its warning beam unseen.

Though he did not realize it, Captain Mills was lost. He thought he knew where he was. He was sufficiently certain to maintain a speed of 11 knots — which, under the circumstances, might have been regarded as foolhardy. Mills, as any other experienced mariner, must have been aware of the folly of trusting dead reckoning, but there you are. The *Jebba* steamed on through the night with a sailor taking soundings as the only concession to the far from friendly circumstances.

Mills first became aware that all was not quite as it should have been when the leadsman reported a depth of 11 fathoms. This did not tally with his calculations: it should have been more. He ordered a reduction of speed to $5\frac{1}{2}$ knots and checked the course. Had he known it, he had already overshot the approaches to Plymouth Sound by nearly 13 miles. Eddystone was making its unheeded signals 18 miles away to the south-west, and the ship was much too close inshore. She was, indeed, steaming towards disaster in the shape of a promontory named Bolt Tail.

To say that a wave took hold of the *Jebba* and threw her on to the rocks at the foot of Bolt Tail may be an overstatement. Yet this is what seemed to happen. Some of the passengers had already packed and were waiting to disembark at Plymouth. Others were preparing to turn in. And then, very suddenly, there was chaos. Within three minutes of going aground, water was flooding into the cabins; soon afterwards, the floors of the public rooms were awash.

Two of the ladies on board fainted, but a missionary travelling home on leave was made of stronger stuff. Sitting at a piano with water up to his knees, he deftly rendered a selection of popular pantomime tunes. If death had to be on the way, at least it would be heralded by the sound of cheerful music.

In spite of the fog, the *Jebba*'s distress signals were seen. The lifeboat from neighbouring Hope Cove put to sea within minutes of the calamity, but there was nothing that its crew could do. The waves were too tall, the wind too strong, for it to come close. The *Jebba*'s own boats were swung out, but they were never used. It was probably just as well. After about half an hour, somebody saw lights moving about on top of the headland. Presently a green one and then a red one appeared. A sailor shouted, 'They're going to send a rocket.' Dragging a trail of flame in its wake, this perfectly aimed harbinger of deliverance landed amidships. The second mate grabbed the line attached to it, and secured it to the mainmast. Patiently, praying that the fabric of the ship would be strong enough to survive the hammering of the sea, the 79 passengers and then the crew were lifted to safety by breeches buoy.

As in the case of the *Suevic*, there were no casualties. Nor, again, did the ship have to be written off. When the wind's energy had become spent, and when the fog had dispersed, a team of tugs dislodged the stranded liner and towed her to Southampton for repairs. The only victim was Captain Mills. The court of inquiry decided that he had 'not navigated with proper and seamanlike care'. As with Jones, his master's ticket was suspended for three months. It was his penalty for relying on dead reckoning (though what other kind of reckoning could there have been?), and for the *Jebba* having been nudged seven miles north-north-east of her intended course 'by an unusual current'. There was no speculation about where she might have made a landfall had it not been for this mischievous current.

Until the *Olympic* made her début on the North Atlantic, the White Star Line's flagship on the run to New York had been the 17,274-ton *Oceanic*, which was launched in 1899. Apart from a spell of troop-carrying during the Boer War, she plied uncomplaining across the Atlantic, causing nobody any trouble and accommodating her passengers in very tolerable comfort. By no means the least of her admirers was J.P. Morgan himself, who often used her on his travels to Europe.

The British government, unlike its relationship with Cunard, did nothing to fund the building of the White Star ships. It did, however, contribute to their upkeep upon the understanding that, in the event of war, they should be made available as armed merchant cruisers. Consequently, when the *Oceanic* steamed into Southampton at the end of an eastbound passage in August 1914, she was taken over by the Admiralty. Within a month, she had been equipped with 4.7-inch guns and assigned to patrol the sea between the northernmost coast of Scotland and the Faroe Islands — paying particular attention to the waters around Shetland. Her captain had discretionary powers to stop any merchantman and search it for German subjects or for freight intended for Germany.

All this was clear enough. There was, however, one question that was far from certain: who precisely *was* the captain? Henry Smith had been the ship's master for the previous two years. Like most of those commanding the big ships on the North Atlantic route, he held a commission in the Royal Naval Reserve. The converted liner's duties did not appear to be very demanding from a military point of view. To most people, there seemed to be no reason why Captain Smith should not change into naval uniform and carry on with his job, even if the circumstances might be rather different.

The Admiralty did not agree. Since the former liner was now HMS *Oceanic*, there had to be a Royal Navy officer on board. Indeed, there were several, but the matter of contention was the appointment of Captain William Slayter RN. Who, then, was master? Whitehall was vague. Slayter was to have the ultimate responsibility, but Smith was to be some kind of consultant. Quite what he was supposed to do in this advisory role was never made clear.

Such confusion was not the happiest of beginnings. Smith, quite rightly, regarded the *Oceanic* as *his* ship, whilst Slayter knew that she was his. Eventually, they seem to have reached a kind of compromise by which the one had charge by day and the other by night. This might have worked had they been in agreement about how best to run the ship. They were not.

In early September 1914 the *Oceanic* made her appearance at Lerwick on the Shetland mainland. She impressed the islanders and decorated the port with her appearance, and then, on the 6th, she set off on patrol. Her course lay to the westward of the Shetlands and thence to Fair Isle. On her journey, she would pass by Foula — 20 miles from the mainland and the westernmost inhabited island of the Shetland group. Two miles east of this small slab of land there was a reef called the Shaalds of Foula. Any mariner in his right mind gave it a wide berth.

To say that the *Oceanic* was being navigated by dead reckoning may not be strictly true. The sky was clear; the sea was calm; and there was land to be seen. Even an amateur yachtsman of only moderate experience should have been able to find his way without difficulty and certainly without endangering his boat. On the evening of 7 September the officer of the watch took bearings on the north and south ends of the small island. At their intersection, there you would (or should) have found the *Oceanic*. Slayter, who was, so to speak, doing the night shift, had no misgivings. Early next morning, he said something about 'steer for Foula' and went to bed.

But where, precisely, were they? Both captains had checked the position the previous evening, and this was one of those rare occasions when Slayter agreed with Smith and Smith with Slayter. Next morning, when Slayter was enjoying his slumber and Smith had taken over the bridge, fog came down. Sensibly, he stopped the ship while he thought things over. He had a great deal of knowledge about how to cope with the capricious anger of the North Atlantic, but he was less at home in these cramped and rock-strewn waters. Thinking that his ship (or was it Slayter's ship?) was to the south of Foula, he presently ordered the helmsman to steer due west: making, that is to say, for the much more spacious — and, under the circumstances, safer — waters of the ocean. It might have worked, even though there had been a lot of miscalculating, and the *Oceanic* was now 14 miles to the north of what was assumed to be her position. Furthermore, as quite a number of people must have been asking themselves, where was Foula? Islands do not move by night any more than they do by day. But ships do, and a cry from the look-out in the crow's nest soon alerted Captain Smith to the fact that matters had gone singularly awry. The man had sighted the silhouette of land in quite the wrong place. It was neither to the north (which, according to the Smith/Slayter reckoning, was where it should have been), nor to the east (where it would have given no cause for concern) but to the west. The *Oceanic* was making towards what was to be her final resting place: the Shaalds of Foula.

Smith, to give him credit, ordered the liner to go full astern on a reciprocal course, but then Slayter came into the wheel-house. Acting presumably on the assumption that any instruction his colleague gave must be wrong, he immediately countermanded it. He told the officer of the watch, Davy Blair, to take a fix on the land and to have the wheel put hard-a-starboard. This was the worst possible thing to do, and its consequences became very clear a minute or two later when, helped by the tide, HMS *Oceanic* quietly dumped herself on the reef.

The crew were taken off in the boats and carried to a trawler that was standing by. At 4.30 that afternoon, a cruiser, HMS *Forward*, attempted to pull the stranded liner off her perch, but the tide was running strong and the *Oceanic* had made a good job of wedging herself securely in position. She refused to budge.

Not long afterwards, the weather, which had been so calm for so long, changed its mood. By the 29th, all traces of the one-time darling of the Atlantic had disappeared. The only people to benefit from the disaster were the inhabitants of Foula, who had helped themselves lavishly from this unexpected gift that had landed so unexpectedly on what was almost literally their doorstep.

Surprisingly, Captains Slayter and Smith were acquitted at the court martial that followed — though the unfortunate Blair was reprimanded for not taking soundings.

Nowadays, the only liner to run anything like a regular transatlantic service is the *Stefan Batory* of the Polish Ocean Lines. So long as the St Lawrence and its approaches are free from ice, she runs a scheduled service between Gdynia, Rotterdam and Tilbury and Montreal. She is equipped with the

most modern aids to navigation and her master, Captain
Telesfor Bielicz, is a very experienced North Atlantic hand.
Nevertheless, Captain Bielicz will tell you:

> At sea we can't do anything against nature. We can't fight
> nature. But if we understand nature, then we can take all
> precautions to reduce its dangerous influence on the ship.
> But, first of all, we must understand it. Then, later, it's more
> easy. Some captains make mistakes because they have tried
> to go against nature.

One captain who seems to have treated nature with rather
less than respect was E.J. Smith of the *Titanic.*

When people discuss matters to do with navigation, you may
hear such names as Mercator (he of the projection), Kelvin
(compasses and sounding apparatus) and Galileo (the tele-
scope) bandied about. You are unlikely, however, to hear
Matthew Fontaine Maury of the United States Navy mentioned. This, perhaps, is to do his memory less than justice. His
books on the subject and his work on hydrography and meteorology contributed much to the knowledge of the art. Furthermore, he sailed round the world in USS *Vincennes* when
circumnavigation implied rather more than the ability to buy
an expensive ticket in the *QE2.*

In the present context, however, the importance of being
Maury manifested itself not long before his death in 1873. He
had noticed the increasing traffic across the North Atlantic and
he envisaged the possibility of, say, an eastbound ship colliding
with a westbound. In many ways it was a problem that has
since become familiar to the air transport industry. It may even
be that air traffic control owes more than it might readily
acknowledge to Maury's solution, for it was he who devised the
principle of lane separation. In other words, there should be
one route for vessels travelling to North America, and another
for those travelling away from it. They would not, he stressed,
necessarily be the best in terms of shortness, but they would be
in terms of maximum safety.

But collision with another ship is by no means the only
danger. At certain seasons of the year, icebergs are another

hazard. With such topics on the agenda, a meeting of the principal steamship companies took place on 15 January 1898. Ironically, it was chaired by Bruce Ismay. From its deliberations, two westbound routes to the United States, and two eastbound were devised. In each case, there was one for the period 15 January to 14 August, when the iceberg peril was judged to be most acute, and one from 15 August until 14 January, when it was minimal. For Canada, the tracks were more complex; but then so, too, is the situation concerning ice. The lanes were modified in 1913 following the *Titanic* disaster, but Captain E.J. Smith's course was by the Great Circle from the Fastnet lightship to 42°N 47°W — a point known as 'The Corner', which master mariners in a hurry were reprehensibly apt to cut. Thereafter, it was by rhumb-line to Sandy Hook lightship. (The Great Circle route is the one that looks longer on a chart. In fact, it is the shortest since it follows the curvature of the earth. It requires constant changes of course — while in the case of rhumb-line navigation, a vessel can proceed in a straight line. This may seem to be less distance; but, the globe being a globe, it is actually greater.)

After her departure from Queenstown, the *Titanic* sighted the Fastnet and Captain Smith ordered the quartermaster to steer S68°W. Thereafter, nothing remarkable happened until the afternoon before the catastrophe. Then, at 5.50 p.m., Smith ordered a change of course from S60°W to S86°W. Normally, he would have done this half an hour earlier. The effect was to take him well clear of the ice reported by the *Baltic* and sufficiently far south of that mentioned by the *Caronia.*

This would certainly have seemed a prudent thing to do. It was, however, a point on which Captain Smith's reputation was later to depend. Was it, as Lord Mersey avowed, a matter of small importance? Or was it, as Lord Justice Vaughan Williams asserted on 9 February 1914, when White Star took the case to the Court of Appeal, evidence of Smith's awareness of the perils in his path? 'The diversion from the "lane" by Captain Smith,' said Vaughan Williams, 'was itself clear evidence that he himself recognized the seriousness of the danger ahead of which he had notice, and a recognition of the fact that even on a clear night you cannot always maintain course and speed in a region made dangerous by ice.'

Considering the tolerant attitude of Lord Mersey, it may seem strange that White Star bothered to appeal. Lord Justice Vaughan Williams was a far tougher nut, and the shipping company left the court-room with its reputation more scarred than it had been when it came in. Nor was poor Smith allowed to rest easy in his North Atlantic grave. His conduct had amounted to negligence and there was nothing left to gainsay the accusation.

Up to this point, his conduct of the ship had been beyond reproach. The fact that he had deliberately delayed altering course is beyond dispute. Fourth Officer Boxhall noticed the instruction, written in the night order book, when he came on duty at 4 p.m. He commented on it to the officer of the watch, Chief Officer Henry Wilde, and remarked that they would overshoot the normal turning point at 'The Corner'. The only possible reason for this was to steer clear of the ice zone.

Did Smith imagine that, by taking this precaution, he was avoiding the danger area? If he did, his attitude was strangely unrealistic. As he must have been aware, the wireless officer had received reports only of ice *known* to exist. They certainly did not establish any limit to it. He must have realized that there were more bergs that year, and that their penetration of the shipping lanes was unusually far south. There was still the need for caution and, as Vaughan Williams implied, Smith's place throughout that evening and into the night, was on the bridge. Living it up with the transatlantic gentry was hardly in order when the ocean might yet be cluttered with bergs that other ships had *not* yet seen or had not yet reported. Indeed, there *were* other warnings still to come.

Captain Bielicz of the *Stefan Batory* (to take only one example) has no staff captain to assist in the running of his ship, and you will certainly find him mingling sociably with the customers when such mingling is in order. As he said:

I am captain. I am responsible for everything: for navigating the ship as well as for administration. But I have on board the 'second captain' — the chief officer, who has a master's certificate. I can't stay on duty round-the-clock every day. I need some rest. In that case, the chief officer can run the ship. *But if my presence on the bridge is required, there can be no socializing. Safety comes first.*

Smith's presence was clearly needed on the bridge that evening, but he was elsewhere. Had he been given the message received from the *Mesaba* at 7.30 p.m., he might have changed his mind. It reported bergs between 42°N and 41°25'W and between 49°W and 50°30'W. In other words, it would have made nonsense of any idea he might have entertained about being beyond the danger zone. But, owing to the backlog of telegrams handed in by passengers, the chief wireless operator, Jack Phillips, never sent it to the bridge.

But where, exactly was the *Titanic* when she struck the berg? At 7.30 p.m. her position was established by astral navigation; at 8 p.m. by dead reckoning. In the first distress signal from the wireless office, the latter was updated to take into account the liner's course and speed. It established her at 41°44'N, 50°24'W. Soon afterwards, the more accurate star position was brought up to date by the same method, and this put her at 41°46'N, 50°14'W. But it was now more than four hours since the star sight had been taken. Since then, the ship had been steaming at $22\frac{1}{2}$ knots — her fastest speed during the entire trip — and had covered more than 104 miles.

If this chapter has not suggested how misleading dead reckoning can be, it has so far achieved very little. When the *Carpathia* came steaming to the rescue, her look-outs sighted the boats and some debris 16 miles to the south-east of the reported position. Under the circumstances, such an error would not have been impossible. It was, indeed, more than commonly fortunate that the Cunarder had to travel over this particular point in the ocean to reach what was believed to be the *Titanic*'s location.

So where, if you will allow the question to be repeated, *was* she? There have been several attempts to locate the wreck and now, at last, one of them has succeeded. In the late summer of 1985, an expedition mounted by America and France discovered the liner's remains at a depth of 13,120 feet (2.25 miles). Using a robot submarine named the *Argo*, they were actually able to take photographs. But the team's leader, Dr Robert Ballard of the Woods Hole Oceanographic Institute,

Massachusetts, refused to reveal the precise position. Quite
rightly, he insisted that the spot should be treated with the
reverence due to a resting place of the dead. To provide such
details would be to invite a flock of scavengers, each of them
eager to profit by his findings. As Dr Ballard pointed out, the
object had been to test out new underwater equipment and
little else. Inevitably, denied facts, the media resorted to
guesswork. Some papers put the scene at 375 miles south of
Newfoundland; others (the majority) suggested 500 miles.
When warned of a spotter aircraft's approach, Dr Ballard
headed his ship — the United States Navy's survey vessel USS
Knorr — for home. In any case, the season of gales was
approaching and this was no less than prudent. However, he
insisted that he and his colleagues would return in 1986 for a
more detailed examination.

First reports suggested that the liner was in surprisingly
good shape — despite the fact that she must have hit the seabed at a speed of 50 mph. It soon became clear, however, that
her boilers had broken loose and were now lying beside the
hull. It also transpired that the stern had yet to be discovered.
Nevertheless, this did not deter the salvage enthusiasts — some
of whom announced schemes that can only be regarded as
bizarre. If Dr Ballard maintains his silence, he will not only
protect the restful dead: he will save a number of hare-brained
entrepreneurs considerable money.

It may seem strange to anyone of a fanciful disposition that
a ship, so flamboyant during her brief life, should (for seventy-
three years, at any rate) have slid so totally into obscurity —
though the word is used in its literal sense. The world — or that
of the media in whatever form — has made certain that the
dead liner should be granted immortality. There have been
books and films galore about her. Indeed, on the very day of
writing this, one newspaper informed its readers that a
chamberpot bearing the *Titanic*'s name had been discovered in
an attic, and offered to the maritime museum at Southampton.

But, for those that die at sea, there are no tombstones — and
this includes the vessels in which they perish. Against poor
Captain Smith it might be said that he relied too much on
others. The second officer (in this case Lightoller) was the
navigating officer. But, from Captain Bielicz: 'I check all the

positions given by my navigation aids to make sure they are not failing. If they are, I should know. The second officer is not in charge of navigation, but he is responsible for all the equipment, the charts, the books, for everything we need.'

The first responsibility of a master, then, is the safety of his ship. He is the navigator. No matter how much his affluent and sometimes influential passengers may jostle for seats at his table in the dining saloon; no matter how much they may seek his company as the uncelebrated seek that of the celebrated, they must forgo his attentions when his more professional duties require this small sacrifice. Their safekeeping, even their lives, depends upon it. That evening, as the *Titanic* approached the tail of the Grand Banks, Smith seems to have turned his back on nature. Captain Bielicz would never approve of that.

But, in Smith's defence (and his reputation has already been sufficiently tarnished without any help from these pages) we must return to the beginning of this chapter. He was entrusted with the navigation of the most sophisticated floating environment the world had yet seen (if one excludes the construction of its hull). And yet the techniques and equipment at his disposal — the essential tools for guiding his liner across the large and uninformative ocean — these were no different from those used by the skippers of the windjammers in which Captain Smith had graduated. The body of the ship was huge. Its mind (if this is not too implausible a word for it) had not grown in proportion.

Just as time has been neatly parcelled into two packages, BC and AD, so might that of the North Atlantic be classified as BT and PT. BT would be 'Before *Titanic*' and PT 'Post *Titanic*.' After that night of 14/15 April 1912, nothing was quite the same as it had been. The changes did not all happen at once: indeed, a large span of years lay between the primitive navigational aids that Smith used and the electronic wizardry that avails Captain Bielicz. But changes there certainly were, and it is a rather sad reflection that it needed the loss of a great liner and a lot of lives to improve an attitude — and a couple of world wars to produce the hardware.

The problem, initially, was to ensure that vessels in the neighbourhood of the Grand Banks — or anywhere north of them — no longer blundered into bergs. The United States government acted with remarkable promptness by dispatching the scout cruisers USS *Chester* and USS *Birmingham* to patrol the Grand Banks for the remaining months of 1912. But these were warships and the Navy Department couldn't accept this responsibility for too long. Consequently, on the instructions of the President, it was taken over by the Revenue Cutter Service (later called the United States Coast Guard) in 1913. The cruisers were replaced by a pair of cutters named the *Seneca* and *Miami*. In the meantime, in London, representatives of thirteen nations with interests in transatlantic navigation debated the *Titanic* affair. They were determined to ensure that there would be no repeat performance with some other ship as its tragic star. As a result of their deliberations, the first SOLAS Convention (The International Convention for the Safety of Life at Sea) took place in early 1914. Among the subjects that engaged its members' attentions were sufficient standards of navigation, the provision of watertight and fire-resistant bulkheads, life-saving appliances, the importance of radiotelegraphy (without it, the *Titanic*'s casualty list would have been even larger), and the establishment of a North Atlantic ice patrol.

Since the Revenue Cutter Service had already accumulated some experience of such work, it was invited to take charge of it. Specifically, it was to concern itself with patrolling the ice region during the dangerous period of the year, making ice observations, and keeping the shipping lanes free from derelicts and other hazards. The cost was to be defrayed by the thirteen nations concerned.

The United States Coast Guard (we may as well call it by its present name) originated in 1789, when the United States Lighthouse Service was taken over by the Treasury. During the following year, the Revenue Cutter Service — created to combat smuggling — was added to its responsibilities. Since the law-breakers occasionally fought back, it assumed a para-military role. In both world wars, its members served with the armed forces — partly to augment the strength of the US Navy with men and ships, and partly to undertake special missions for which its peacetime operations provided unique skills. As an example of the former, six cutters were stationed at Gibraltar immediately after the United States had joined the

Allies in the 1914-18 war. They carried out escort duties between Gibraltar and Britain, and in the Mediterranean. One of them, the *Tampa,* was sunk — presumably by a German submarine. All the 115 officers and enlisted men on board were killed. One hundred and eleven of them were Coast Guard personnel. With the exception of the USS *Cyclops* — which vanished on 4 March 1918, in the so-called Bermuda Triangle when on passage from Barbados to Newport, Virginia, with the death of 309 naval personnel — this was the largest loss of life incurred by any US naval unit during the First World War.

As the British Admiralty wrote to Rear-Admiral William Sims, USN: 'Her [the *Tampa*'s] record since she has been employed in European waters has been remarkable. She has acted in the capacity of ocean escort to no less than 18 convoys from Gibraltar comprising 350 vessels, with a loss of only two ships through enemy action ...'

In the Second World War, the Coast Guard was active in both the Pacific and European theatres of operations. Understandably, it was concerned with amphibious operations — though its members also smashed enemy radio-weather stations in Greenland and rescued more than 1,500 survivors from ships torpedoed near the United States seaboard.

Nowadays, the Coast Guard's responsibility for the protection of life at sea is enormous. As one of its publications puts it, 'The Coast Guard maintains 47,600 aids to navigation of all classes along 47,000 miles of coast, lakes, and rivers — a length equal to nearly twice the circumference of the earth. If placed along the equator, there would be an aid every half mile.'

Well, now ... There have, of course, been changes. For instance, in the early part of this century, there used to be 100 manned lightship stations. Now there is only one: the Nantucket Shoals at the approach to New York. On 16 May 1934, the *Titanic*'s sister, the *Olympic,* was on passage to New York steering on a radio beam transmitted by the light vessel. The idea was that it would guide the liner towards it. Once the lightship had been sighted, the liner would change course and steer for the next floating beacon — the Ambrose lightship. But then, with the suddenness that is so characteristic of these waters, fog came down. Although the big ship's speed was reduced to two (possibly, three) knots, she charged into the side of the lightship, which sank instantly. The seven men on board were all drowned. In its fifty-six years of service, the Ambrose light was hit four times, though never before with such severe consequences.

One Coast Guard project, which lasted for thirty years, was the establishment of 'Ocean Stations'. In 1944, there were thirteen of them in the North Atlantic and, by the end of the war, another twenty-four in the Pacific. They were manned by cutters (vessels comparable to frigates), which were responsible for issuing weather reports and providing a rescue service for crashed aircraft. Once the hostilities were over, only three were retained.

Their purpose now was entirely that of feeding meteorological information to the forecasters — a task in which they were joined by vessels belonging to other nations. The adapted warships were replaced by purpose-built vessels, but the coming of satellites added to the score of redundancies. At the time of writing, there are only three weather ships (not just American) on station in the North Atlantic, and the day is clearly in sight when there will be none at all. Nevertheless, to revert to 1947, in October of that year, Ocean Station 'Charlie' — where the US Coast Guard cutter *Bibb* was currently on duty — had its moment of glory, and revived memories of more violent days when rescue was by no means the least of the roles.

On 14 October, a Boeing flying-boat named *Bermuda Sky Queen* had taken off from Foynes in Ireland *en route* for Gander. On board were a crew of seven and 62 passengers. Soon after departure, the aircraft flew into vile weather with punishing headwinds. When he had completed just over half his journey, the pilot calculated that he would run out of fuel five minutes short of his destination. As a result, he made the daring, and perhaps foolhardy, decision to ditch at a spot precisely half-way across the ocean, where the *Bibb* was positioned.

He picked up the station's radio call sign of BBBB and homed on it. The manoeuvre was observed by the captain of a Constellation airliner bound for Prestwick. 'It made a dandy landing in spite of the very heavy sea,' he recalled. 'We came down to about 3,500 feet to circle the cutter and watch the flying-boat drawing closer to it. We saw the ship's crew putting out floats and heard the flying-boat's radio calmly telling the ship, "Everything is OK." When we left after circling for an hour, the flying-boat was within 200 feet of the ship.'

Later, the following message was received by USCG headquarters in New York from Captain Paul Cronk, master of the *Bibb*:

Darkness approaching. Plane leaking. Passengers mostly prostrated by seasickness. Winds of gale force. Three passengers removed unharmed with small life-raft. Second successful boat and raft operation brings total saved this far to five men, two women, two little boys and one baby. Baby appeared to have stood ordeal better than the rest.

The rescue operation was interrupted by darkness. At dawn on 15 October, it began again and, by six a.m., all the passengers and crew were safely on board the *Bibb*. On several occasions, the operation came close to disaster. The landing itself was something of a miracle. The Coast Guard cutter swung round in an attempt to break the waves and provide some shelter. The flying-boat, the Constellation pilot remembered, 'made a dummy run and then came in to land, making straight for the ship. The keel struck a wave. Then there was a tremendous splash. The whole aircraft seemed to disappear under the water and then, like a whale, reappeared through the spray.'

A motor lifeboat towing a raft became submerged and 20 people, all of them weak from seasickness, were flung into the sea. But, with consummate seamanship, Captain Cronk caused the *Bibb* to drift alongside them, and they were all fished out. At another time, a rubber raft burst and sank.

Soon after the rescue had been completed, the cutter *Duane* relieved the *Bibb*, which steamed to Boston and landed her cargo of 69 bedraggled survivors. The *Bermuda Sky Queen*, still afloat, was sunk by gunfire to prevent its becoming a hazard to shipping.

It seemed to be a singular example of how much better and safer flying-boats were compared to land-based aircraft for transatlantic air traffic. The British government, which had been losing interest in them, promptly took up the cause again and approved development work on another generation.

But the real marvel was the *Bermuda Sky Queen*'s pilot's ability to pick up the call sign, follow it, and to make such a splendid landing. At the subsequent inquiry by the US Civil Aeronautics Board, it transpired that he had logged only 60 hours' experience of flying the North Atlantic, and all of them as a co-pilot. As for the first officer, who was also required to act as deputy pilot and chief navigator, his experience of air navigation over sea was limited to one transatlantic trip. However, as he protested to the Board, he had spent ten years crewing in ocean racing yachts. Neither he nor his captain were aware of broadcasts from New York that reported on the weather and winds likely to be encountered by aircraft in flight. Nor, it must seem, had they very much knowledge of the logistics of fuel and its consumption — and the proposition that, on a flight such as this, there must not be just sufficient to reach a destination, but considerably more than enough.

For many travellers, the affair of the *Bermuda Sky Queen* must have been convincing evidence that, time-saving though air travel might be, a liner was still the best way in which to cross.

However: to the matter of the International Ice Patrol. I have given credit (or should it be blame?) to the Disko glacier on the west coast of Greenland for producing the berg that slew the *Titanic*. This may be self-indulgent, for there are twenty glaciers on this side of the island producing these potentially lethal islands of frozen water. Some of them — and the amount varies from year to year — reach the meeting point of the Labrador current and the Gulf Stream. Since the temperature of the former is about 20°C colder than that of the latter, it follows with grim inevitability that there shall be fog, and fog there most certainly is — for something between 40 and 50 per cent of the year. As a representative of the ice patrol told me, 'The fog, the accumulation of bergs, severe storm conditions and a great deal of shipping make this one of the most dangerous marine areas in the world.'

It is impossible to be precise about anything to do with icebergs. Nature, so rightly respected by Captain Bielicz, makes her own rules and, although man tries to be privy to them, he does not always succeed. The longest iceberg season on record was that of 1972, which lasted from 29 February until 4 September — 189 days. Nobody has recorded the shortest, though it was undoubtedly long enough. On average, something like 1,000 bergs get as far south as Belle Isle off the north coast of Newfoundland, but this is not a figure to be taken too seriously. In 1929, the Ice Patrol counted 1,350 in the vicinity of the Grand Banks, which was some kind of record. It was, however, beaten in 1972, when 1,587 were seen to exist in the patrol area, which extends from 40°N–52°N, 39°W–57°W. This was roughly five times the number that normally venture south of latitude 48°N (a few miles north of St John's, Newfoundland) every year. On the other hand, there have been years such as 1966 when no bergs at all were detected south of the line.

As for the icebergs themselves, they refuse to conform to any pattern. The largest ever seen by an Ice Patrol observer was 550 feet above water level — it was recorded by the US Coast Guard Icebreaker *Eastwind* in 1957. It may sound impressive, but it was one of the more benign intruders into the shipping lanes. With such ample dimensions, it showed up clearly on a radar screen and at some considerable distance. A growler, however, is unlikely to be more than three feet high, but anyone who scorns it does so at his peril. Its underwater depth will probably be 12 feet and its total mass will weigh more than 100 tons. This will not be so quick to catch the eye of radar, but its capacity for destruction is just as great.

In return for $2.5 million subscribed by the twenty signatories of the 1960 SOLAS Convention, the International Ice Patrol has to locate these hazards, keep track of them, and warn shipping of their positions. To do this, it has a staff of sixteen military and civilian personnel working in an ice operations centre adjoining the US Coast Guard Research and Development Centre at Groton, Connecticut. During the season, which usually lasts from 1 March until 31 August, the Coast Guard Air Station at Elizabeth City, North Carolina, contributes an HC-130 Hercules aircraft equipped with side-looking radar (SLAR). It is manned by a crew of anything from nine to twelve plus three ice observers.

The HC-130 makes three or four flights every week. On each, it searches an expanse of 33,000 square miles — which, as the Coast Guard informs us, is 'roughly the size of the state of Pennsylvania'. But, all the time, information is being contributed by ships travelling through the area, by oil rigs hoping to discover petroleum in the depths of the Grand Banks, civilian air crews, the Canadian Atmospheric Environment Service, and the Canadian Coast Guard. The last of these — which, in contrast to the US Coast Guard, is staffed by civilians — carries out ice operations all the year round.

All this data is fed into a carefully programmed computer at the operations centre. So, too, is information concerning the ocean current and the wind. Thus the drift of the bergs is predicted; and, every twelve hours, the limit of all known ice is estimated. This limit, with the locations of a few of the more critical bergs, is broadcast twice daily as an 'Ice Bulletin' from stations in the United States, Canada, and in Europe. In addition to this, ships that carry the equipment receive a radio facsimile chart of the ice area showing the positions of ice. This service is transmitted once a day.

Captain Bielicz, whose destination is Montreal, has a choice of two routes as he nears the end of his journey. He can either take the northern passage along the Strait of Belle Isle and so into the Gulf of St Lawrence, or he can keep to the south of Newfoundland, go past Cape Race and up the Cabot Strait.

> It depends [he said] on the time of year and the weather conditions. The northern route is open at the end of June or the beginning of July. Then there is no pack ice, and the ship can pass through. But the southern route, via Cape Race, is clear at the beginning of May. This year [1984] though, there was very thick pack ice. We can always pick up bergs on the radar; but, when there's wind and rain, then it's difficult to find some of the growlers. I have the two radar sets manned all the time when we are approaching the danger zone.

He receives all the information transmitted by the International Ice Patrol, but he confesses to finding it 'very limited' (possibly because, when he takes the Belle Isle route, he is passing through the northern edge of its responsibility). However, he asks 'St John's for information on ice conditions; and, as I approach Newfoundland, I am sending information to St

John's about ice every four hours.'

Nowadays, he said,

there are not fixed routes across the North Atlantic. It depends on which route is chosen by the captain. Nobody can tell me to go this road or that road or any other road. I get weather reports every few hours [on a facsimile chart]. I get a picture of the barometer situation. The lows always bring strong winds and big waves. If I know the tracks of the lows, then I can take a chance to go more to the north, or more to the south. Of course, we take the Great Circle route if the weather permits, but it is not always that we can do this. Sometimes we have to make more miles and get better weather.

Captain Bielicz contentedly recalled an occasion when the *QE2*, westbound for New York, was delayed for 24 hours by high winds, but the *Stefan Batory* arrived at Montreal punctually. ('It was not a gale, but it was strong. I am never held up by the weather. This is a good ship — that is important; but I think there's always some luck, though.')

A slow smile wrinkled his face, and he leaned forward. 'The weather,' he said, 'is like a woman, you know. It's changeable.' One felt that he had made this remark several times before, but it has lost none of its punch.

On 30 April 1865 Rear-Admiral Robert Fitzroy retired to the bathroom, took out his razor, and cut his throat. It was a tragic end to a life that had been more than commonly useful; a career that deserved greater recognition than it received. Fitzroy had been commander of the 240-ton brig *Beagle*, which took Darwin to the Magellan Straits; and, on a second voyage, around the world. But he was a highly strung man, plagued by his rather too active conscience, and nearly always overworked.

In 1850, wretched with ill health and tormented by 'private affairs' upon which he refused to elaborate, he asked for retirement from the navy. Four years later, when it was decided to set up a meteorological department at the British Board of Trade, he accepted the appointment of superintendent. It is

significant that it coincided with a period of considerable
development in the use of electric telegraph (in 1850 a cable
was laid across the Dover Strait, linking England with France).
After all, even the most brilliant weather forecast is useless, if it
cannot be communicated.

Fitzroy must, as it happens, receive credit for *creating* the
expression 'weather forecast'. He preferred it to such terms as
'foretelling' or 'predicting' — which, he felt, gave a wrong
impression and smacked of soothsaying. He was also notable
for drawing up the first synoptic charts displaying weather
patterns (he called them his 'wind stars' because the shape of
the diagrams roughly suggested a star), and for the introduction of storm warnings to Britain. In the United States, the
telegraph had already been used to transmit news of impending
gales to the various port authorities. In the UK, Fitzroy devised
the system of cones which, according to whether they point
upwards or downwards, give an idea of the wind's direction.

Not the least of his problems was that, while there was no
difficulty in warning mariners before they set out, there was no
means of communicating with them at sea. In the early
autumn of 1859, the emigrant ship *Royal Charter* was homeward bound after a passage to Melbourne. She called briefly at
Holyhead on Anglesey, and then set course for Liverpool. High
winds were now approaching gale force and the master,
Captain Taylor, decided to drop anchor and ride out the storm.

But the weather had not yet finished its performance. A
cyclone developed. Gusts of over 100 miles per hour struck the
Royal Charter. Her masts were torn down; her anchor cables
snapped; and she was driven on to a shoal, where she broke in
half. Four hundred and thirty-eight passengers and crew were
killed — only 18 survived.

The *Royal Charter* disaster haunted Fitzroy. He was
convinced that such tragedies could be avoided: it just needed a
more urgent and bolder approach. Upon one thing he was
certain: the captain of every vessel should have a barometer. It
was not enough to have faith in such jingles as 'When rain
comes before wind, Halyards, sheets, and braces mind.' He was
also disturbed by the fact that, since all the information he
received came from ships that had recently docked, it was out
of date. The storms about which their masters should have

been warned were those through which they had already passed.

In an attempt to improve the situation, he set up twenty-four weather stations: eighteen of them in the UK and six in Europe at points ranging from Copenhagen to Lisbon. Reports from these places, telegraphed to London, provided essential data for his charts.

On 1 August 1861 *The Times* published its first daily forecast (it promised fine weather for the whole of the UK). The Prince Consort had already taken an interest in his work, and Fitzroy seemed to be achieving his goal. But presently things took a decided turn for the worse — ironically from the two bodies that had done most to champion his cause. The Royal Society had recommended him for the appointment; now its members turned against him and actually advocated the suspension of gale warnings. *The Times* weighed in with a couple of anti-Fitzroy articles and disclaimed all responsibility for the forecasts it printed. Even that other pioneer, Captain Matthew Maury, who was now living in Britain as a refugee from the American Civil War, seemed to be hostile.

Poor Fitzroy: his only crime was one that is still perpetrated by those who attempt to forecast the weather. Sometimes he got it wrong. Suicide may seem to be a severe penalty to inflict upon oneself for making errors it is impossible to avoid.

The father of modern forecasting might, quite possibly, be a scientist named Dr L.R. Richardson who, in 1916, worked out a system using equations based on physical laws. It was good, sound stuff. The trouble was that Dr Richardson did not have the means to carry it out. According to one estimate, and in the light of calculating machines available at the time, it would have needed 64,000 mathematicians, working continuously round the clock, to produce results. Since then, there has not been an immense increase in the number of mathematicians who can work forever without sleep. On the other hand, the computer has been invented. Not only can it solve sums in the twinkling of an eye: it can also point out mistakes.

In Britain, the Meteorological Office now comes under the Ministry of Defence. It is situated in a large building at Bracknell, Berkshire; and, predictably, you will find computers at its heart. Coded data (the code eliminates language problems) is fed into them from just about every part of the world: from weather stations, ships, aircraft, balloons, satellites, and from other meteorological authorities. It is, indeed, comforting to discover that, whilst humanity seems to be divided into two intransigent blocs — that of the West and that of the East — weather forecasting is a civilized example of international co-operation. There is an occasional interruption — as, for example, during the Falklands hostilities, when Britain was denied information from a large part of South America. 'Somebody must have pulled the plug out somewhere,' a Met. Office official told me. 'But, under normal circumstances, there's a free interchange in a very civilized manner.'

This is essential, for everything that happens in the atmosphere is interrelated. You cannot shrug off a storm in the Pacific as a matter of no importance. It will cause other things to occur that may eventually affect the Atlantic, or Africa, or the USSR, or anywhere else. It is rather like that tired old cliché about the stone on the beach of John o' Groats that, when shifted, will eventually cause another stone to move at Land's End. The difference is that, in the case of the weather, it is true.

Among the Meteorological Office's prodigious output is that of issuing weather charts for the North Atlantic every six hours. So far as icebergs are concerned, it would not dream of usurping the role of the International Ice Patrol. But it does take credit for being the first such establishment to issue ice charts, in 1961.

The captains of most ships — certainly those registered in North American and in the northern European countries — can reasonably claim to be meteorologists. They have, after all, taken an examination in the subject to qualify for their masters' certificates. Thus, port meteorological officers in Britain are liable to approach them with the question: would their owners object to their taking certain instruments on board. As the official said:

The officers of the watch are trained as observers — they have to know about the weather, anyway. If we can get good observations from merchant ships all the way across the Atlantic — not just from one point — then we are augmenting the information we receive. This, of course, applies just as much to the South Atlantic and the Far East. By various means, it all finds its way into our telecommunications circuit, and then it is exchanged internationally.

And then there are the satellites: two of them. Meteosat is part of the European Space Agency, which has its headquarters at Darmstadt in Germany. NOAA 7 and 8 are American. Meteosat is on station 36,000 kilometres up: its orbit coincides with the speed of the earth's rotation — with the result that it is positioned permanently at a point over the equator.

NOAA 7 and NOAA 8 pass over the north and south poles at heights varying from 700 kilometres to 1,500 kilometres (they come closest to earth as they travel over the poles). Both broadcast pictures that show the world's weather at the time of transmission. If they are placed side-by-side, a pattern is revealed.

There are three agencies that offer services to mariners: two international companies — Ocean Routes and Noble Denton — and the British Meteorological Office. Appropriately, the men employed on running the last of these are all certificated master mariners who, in their time, have commanded ships of their own. As one of them said:

If you sail the North Atlantic, you've got to be prepared for almost anything. The majority of British shipping companies leave the decision of whether to use our service to the ship's captain. Foreign ships use us, too — but mainly because somebody has chartered them and he insists on it. We charge a fee for each crossing, but if all a company's ships are to be routed for the next twelve months, we come to some sort of other arrangement. We always *advise*; we never *tell* the shipmaster what to do — he'd throw it straight back at us, if we did.'

In the beginning (say for a vessel on passage from Bremen to New York), there is a North Atlantic weather chart. Further facsimile charts are issued over the radio at intervals of every six hours. 'We have the limits of all known ice daily,' the member of the Ship Routeing Service continued:

If a lot of icebergs are coming down into the area, we'll have to advise him to come further south to clear the area. Or if, for example [pointing to a chart], this low moves over to there, we'll tell him about it and suggest he moves a bit farther south — out of the stronger winds. It's partly a matter of economy, for headwinds will slow the vessel down.

These container ships are very, very time conscious. They have a booking at the container terminal for a certain time. If they fall behind, they've lost their slot and they'll have to lie off for perhaps a day before they can get alongside. Times are vital. These chappies are now carrying containers stacked five high on deck: that's a lot of wind resistance, and if the sea hits them, they could lose them. That's a lot of money. There was an occasion a little while ago where one container alone was valued at £½ million, so losing them gets the insurance underwriters a bit upset.

I wouldn't say that the majority take risks to save time. They don't go blindly into the North Atlantic. After all, a master has been at sea for fifteen years or so before he gets a command. He's rather more aware of the weather than a land person would be, because it's been with him all his working life. With our knowledge of shipmasters backed up by the knowledge of our senior forecasters, we believe we can provide a better service than any other routeing agency.

Cruise vessels do not invest in it, though ships of a British fruit-carrying company have used it. These, nowadays, are charming anomalies — leftovers, so to say, from the days of passenger cargo liners. They might be described as 'banana boats', for that is their trade.

But the main consideration [I was told] is the comfort of their passengers — and making sure none of them is injured. If you carry twelve passengers — nearly all of them elderly — they don't like being thrown about too much. We've routed them from the West Indies — sometimes to the east of the Azores. It takes longer, but it produces a much more pleasant voyage. Time, fuel consumption, avoidance of any damage to vessels, and insurance claims from passengers: these are four reasons for ship routing.

And, from my original informant:

I think of the weather almost as something that's alive —
not in terms of people: you can't talk to it. But — yes: it is a
constantly changing pattern of creation. One becomes aware
of the vast forces that are involved and the amount of power
that is generated — it is very, very large indeed, and it is
constantly changing. Although I talk about a weather
pattern being maintained, there are small-scale processes
changing all the time — right down to little gusts of wind
here at Bracknell. At the same time, in the atmosphere,
there are umpteen thunderstorms going on at this very
minute. There are large-scale depressions developing somewhere, and there are high-pressure static areas. It all inter-
relates into a great big picture over the entire globe; and, in
some way, each bit interacts back on to another bit. It's very
much a living, changing, thing.

Captain E.J. Smith had to contend with the weather — just as
other shipmasters had done over the centuries. But he had no
routeing service to guide him; no facsimile weather charts
transmitted to his wireless office; and no ice charts.

Neither did he have radar or any of the navigational aids
that have since become available. The equipment at his
disposal added up to charts, sailing directions, tide tables, lists
of lights, a sextant, a chronometer, a log, sounding apparatus,
and, of course, a compass. With a few exceptions, the situation
remained the same until the Second World War. Nevertheless,
the scientists were working on improvements and the first
evidence of this was to be seen as early as 1912, when the
Mauretania was fitted with an experimental radio direction
finder.

The trouble with the early sets was that the ship had to
transmit the signals: shore stations took bearings on them,
worked out a sum, and then informed her captain of his
position. From a military point of view, this was less than satisfactory, for it meant breaking radio silence. From a practical
point of view, it also consumed rather a lot of time.

After the First World War, British and German scientists got
to work on it independently, and each team produced a version

in which, instead of receiving the signals, the shore stations transmitted them. It was tried out in the *Olympic* in 1924, and her master was pleased with it. He found it particularly useful when the English Channel was fog wrapped, and he was even able to take bearings on other ships. Later, more than 160 other merchant ships were equipped with it.

'Radio direction finder' was, indeed, the name that was first given to radar by the British. It suggested considerable opportunities for confusion and this was certainly so. In 1943, it was changed to 'radar' — a word, dreamed up by a commander in the US Navy named S.M. Tucker, that was already being used in the United States. Once you saw it, it was simple. It stood for 'radio direction and range' or, if you prefer it, 'Radio Direction And Range'.

Conceivably, Guglielmo Marconi might deserve the distinction for first seeing the possibility of inventing radar. In 1933, he happened to notice that, if a car passed through a microwave, a humming noise was heard in the receiver. This led him to the conclusion that an object encountered by any such beam reflected sufficient energy to be detected by a receiver placed near the transmitter. The thought suggested military applications and, in 1934 and 1935, he worked with the Italian navy and the Italian Marconi Company to investigate the possibilities. The project was put on the secret list. Rumours circulated that experiments on death rays were being carried out, and nobody knows where it might all have ended. But Marconi was in poor health. He had many other things on his mind, and he lost interest in the matter.

With Marconi out of the running, there was no true originator of the system. In 1934, the United States and Germany were both applying themselves to research. Germany was marginally the leader for, in 1933, Dr Rudolph Kühnold, head of the German navy's Signals Research Department, began construction on a primitive set. By 20 March of the following year, it was ready for tests in Kiel harbour. An elderly battleship named the *Hessen* was used as a target: and signals were successfully bounced off her at a range of 600 yards. That October, at Pelzerhaken near Lübeck, Kühnold did even better, when he produced echoes from a ship seven miles away. The German top brass was impressed. Seventy thousand Reichmarks (or £11,500 or $57,500 at the current rate

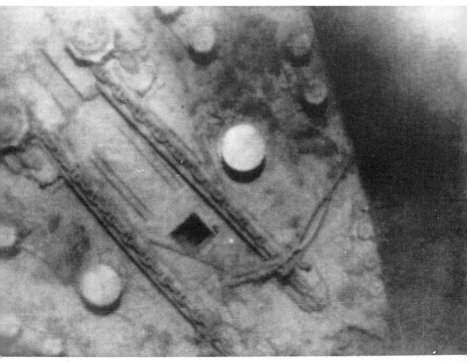

Top: The dream: a model of the *Titanic* is raised from the shallow waters of Marsaxlokk harbour, Malta. Previously it had starred in Lord Grade's monumental loss-maker, *Raise the Titanic!*

The reality: the remains of the *Titanic*, 12,000 feet deep, as photographed in 1985 by the mini-submarine *Argo*.

Top: An early casualty of the North Atlantic steamship trade, the Collins liner *Arctic.*
Contrary to the suggestion inherent in her name, she was the victim of a collision: a
sacrifice, as the *Liverpool Albion* put it, 'offered to the great Moloch of the day – speed'.
Two years later, in 1856, her sister ship, the *Pacific,* foundered after smashing into an
iceberg.

If you must strike an iceberg, the answer must be to strike it head-on. The Guion liner
Arizona did it this way in 1879. With her bow crushed to pieces, she was yet able to travel,
stern-first, to safety, and lived to sail again.

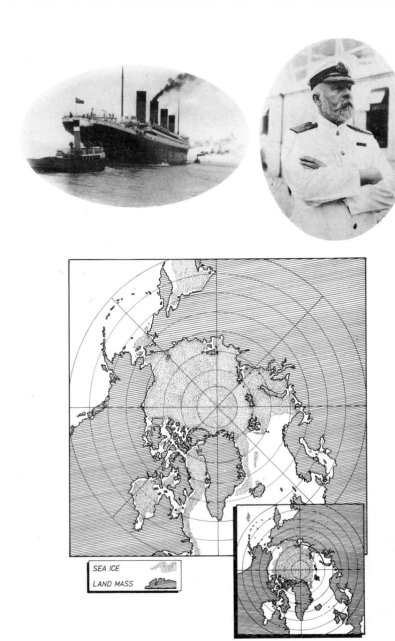

Top: The victims: the *Titanic (left)* sailing from Southampton on her first and last voyage on Wednesday 10 April 1912. *(Right)* Her captain, Edward J. Smith: was he a hero or a dupe? Although he once told a newsman that he was 'not very good material for a story', the debate continues.

The spread of Arctic polar ice: a satellite's-eye view. As the ice creeps southwards—notably down the coasts of Greenland—the ends of the glaciers at the edges snap off into the sea as icebergs—the process known as calving.

The main map shows the distribution of sea ice after winter (April 1979); the inset shows the same region in September, after warmer months of almost continual daylight.

The Davis Strait *(top)* is the highway of newly calved icebergs, which travel up the coast of Greenland, go round the top and then make their way southwards along the Canadian seaboard. Here a convoy is being escorted through the strait by the Canadian Coast Guard.

In April 1924 the International Ice Patrol conducted a memorial service at the spot where the *Titanic* sank. The iceberg seen here bears an uncanny resemblance to the one (photographed at the same spot not many hours after the sinking) that may have sunk the White Star giant. A coincidence?

Top: The lifts in the *Titanic*'s first-class accommodation area. It was here that the bell-boys frolicked, still not really believing that the end was nigh.

The ghost ship. The lights of the Norwegian sealer *Samson* caused a lot of misunderstanding, and her furtive departure did nothing to help matters. 'If we had known, what might we not have done?' her captain later lamented.

The Leyland liner *Californian* (*top*): she might have saved so many lives, but her captain slept, unaware of the drama that was taking place not many miles away. By the time she arrived on the scene it was too late to pick up any survivors.

The *Carpathia*, on the other hand, was the undisputed hero of the incident, steaming at full power through massive icefields on her rescue mission: only later did her master, Captain Arthur Rostron, admit how anxious he had been for the safety of his ship and her passengers. Here, the *Titanic*'s lifeboats arrive alongside the *Carpathia*.

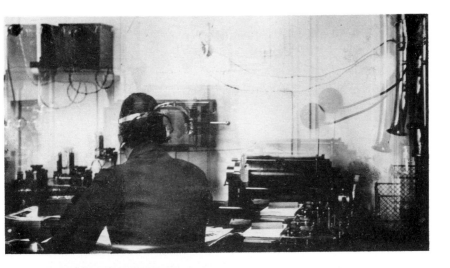

Had it not been for wireless, it seems unlikely that anyone would have survived the *Titanic* tragedy. The wireless operator whose call for help was picked up by the *Carpathia* died, but his assistant, Harold Bride—seen here *(top)* in the *Titanic's* Marconi office—was rescued, and assisted with the wireless transmissions from the *Carpathia*.

Marconi was one of the few people to emerge from the *Titanic* disaster with an enhanced reputation. Newspaper cartoonists were quick to give him the credit he deserved: this drawing appeared four days after the sinking.

One of the first transatlantic liners to be equipped by Marconi was the American Line's *Philadelphia* (formerly the *City of Paris*). On one occasion this ship played a game with the *Etruria* in mid-ocean. It was all done by wireless: the game, which was inconclusive, lasted for five hours.

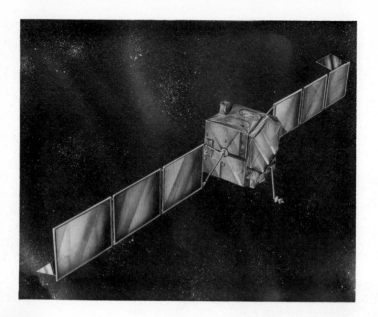

Nowadays the radio facilities are rather more sophisticated. Many shipping lines take advantage of INMARSAT—the International Maritime Satellite Organization—which enables signals to be transmitted via satellite *(top)*, swiftly and with little interference, to radio stations on land.

An early and important step taken after the incident of the *Titanic* was the formation of the International Ice Patrol. Run by the United States Coast Guard, its facilities now include aircraft as well as ships: this picture, taken from a US Coast Guard helicopter, shows one of their cutters keeping a not necessarily friendly eye on an iceberg.

Ice is by no means the only enemy of shipping. On a foggy night in 1907 the White Star liner *Suevic* (*top*), struggling against heavy seas, ran on to rocks off the Lizard.

Some captains still get it wrong—as in the case of the cruise liner *Sundancer* which, in June 1984, on her way from Alaska to Vancouver, ran aground on Vancouver Island. There were no casualties, but the cost of the repairs caused the ship to be written off.

Top: The problem with ship's boats in the early part of the century was that, if the vessel developed a list, it was impossible to launch them. Even now, the difficulty has not been completely overcome. This drawing shows the situation on board the *Empress of Ireland* after she had collided with a freighter in the St Lawrence in 1914. Fewer than a third of those on board survived after she sank minutes later.

Like the *Empress of Ireland*, the *Lusitania* was adequately equipped with lifeboats. She too, however, had similar problems when she was sunk by a U-boat in 1915, and more than a thousand died.

Pioneered in 1850, early weather forecasting was less than reliable, particularly as warnings could not be communicated to mariners at sea. In more modern times, weather forecasters still sometimes make mistakes, even with aids such as this METEOSAT satellite *(top)*, controlled by the European Space Agency.

The British inquiry into the loss of the *Titanic* has been harshly criticized as a whitewash job. So, too, has the American. Nevertheless, these proceedings marked a turning point in the history of safety at sea.

The White Star Line took some steps to improve safety at sea after the *Titanic* sank, and—although it was probably little more than a cosmetic job—spent six months strengthening her sister, the *Olympic*, as advertised here.

The first portent (though not recognized as such) that the age of Atlantic sea crossings might one day come to an end came in 1919. (*Top*) The first non-stop transatlantic flight was made by John Alcock (*right*) and Arthur Whitten Brown in the Vickers Vimy shown in the inset.

After the historic transatlantic flight, Brown expressed his certainty of an aircraft service across the Atlantic: aeroplanes, however, would be 'impracticable', he said—the answer was airships. But airships became unacceptable after the *Hindenburg* burst into flames on arrival at Lakehurst, New Jersey, on 6 May 1937.

Top: Fire is also a hazard on board ship, especially if the vessel is as disgracefully run as was the *Morro Castle,* much of which was consumed by flames in September 1934.

Nowadays, providing it is within range, a helicopter plucks survivors from the deep. Such was the case when the Dutch cruise ship *Prinsendam (above)* caught fire in the Gulf of Alaska in 1980. *Below:* a US Coast Guard helicopter approaches one of the *Prinsendam*'s lifeboats. There were no casualties.

Top: In the British search-and-rescue region of the North Atlantic, RAF Nimrods are used for locating casualties and for rescue co-ordination. They also carry out anti-submarine patrols in wartime.

The US Coast Guard uses HC-130-B Hercules aircraft, based at St John's Newfoundland, to locate icebergs and for search-and-rescue operations. This one has touched down at a Greenland airfield to refuel.

Top: The last recorded major victim of an iceberg was the Danish ferry *Hans Hedtoft*, which foundered 37 miles off Cape Farewell on 30 January 1959. None of her 130 passengers and crew survived.

When a bomb alert took place on the *QE2* on 18 May 1972, British Army explosives experts were dropped by parachute in mid-Atlantic. The scare was later revealed to be a hoax.

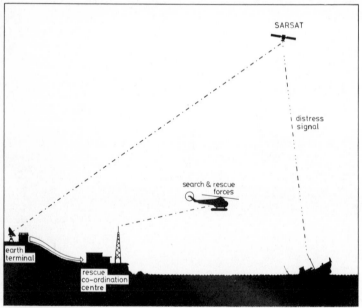

Top: The last of the transatlantic liners, the Polish ship *Stefan Batory*, which plies between Europe and Canada for as long as the ice allows. The *Stefan Batory*'s days are numbered; but, when her end comes, she will be replaced.

SARSAT—'Search and Rescue Satellite-Aided Tracking'—a system used to detect and pinpoint ships or aircraft in trouble, and thus speed up the rescue operation. The distress signal is received by the satellite, transmitted to a terminal on earth, which relays it (here by land-line) to the local Maritime Rescue Co-ordination Centre from where rescue craft are swiftly sent out to the wrecked vessel.

of exchange — whichever you prefer) were allocated for development purposes. Not surprisingly, the first ship to receive it as standard equipment was a unit in the German navy: the 'pocket-battleship' *Graf Spee* — though it was used only for gun-ranging.

One day in January 1935 Sir Robert Watson-Watt, Superintendent of the Radio Research Laboratory at Ditton Park, in England, received a strange letter. The committee for the Scientific Survey of Air Defence invited him to examine the possibility of inventing a death ray. (Had its members been listening to Italian gossip?) Sir Robert dismissed the idea for the nonsense it then was and, instead, submitted a paper entitled 'Detection and Location of Aircraft by Radio Methods'. He demonstrated his thesis on 26 February when a Heyford bomber, flying at 6,000 feet, was identified eight miles away on a cathode-ray tube resting in the back of a Morris van.

The first British vessels to be fitted with radar were the battleship HMS *Rodney* and the cruiser HMS *Sheffield*.

Just as the Second World War hastened the development of radar and put it to good use, so did it produce the genesis of hyperbolic navigational systems. The word is derived from 'hyperbola', which means to say that the radio waves supplying the data travel in curves. The father of them all was a device popularly known as Gee. With considerable exactitude, it guided British bombers to their targets on the Continent. By 1942, the Americans had manufactured something not unlike it. They called it 'Loran'. As its name (LOng RAnge Navigation) may suggest, it was (still is) used over long distances. Both were modified for use in ships; and, by D-Day in 1944, a newcomer had arrived — the Decca Navigator (or QM as it was referred to at the time). To make sure that the troops arrived in the right places, an exceptionally accurate aid to inshore navigation was required. This was precisely what Decca supplied.

Although each is different from the others, the principle behind them all is similar. All radio waves travel at the same speed: 300,000 kilometres a second. Thus, if you know the location of, say, two transmitting stations, you can compare the time taken to receive a signal from one with that from the other. This, perhaps, is to oversimplify the matter, but to go

deeper into it would be to stray into a technical jungle. The
point is that the systems work. With computers making the
necessary calculations, and providing that they are functioning
properly, there is no reason why any navigator should
complain of being lost.

On board the *Stefan Batory*, Captain Bielicz has a Decca
Navigator for European waters and (a more recent arrival)
Omega for the long haul across the Atlantic. Also available on
the market is a system known as TRANSIT in which five satellites are used. They provide a fix accurate to 0.2 nautical miles
at intervals of between thirty minutes and two hours. But
Bielicz prefers his Omega. Whilst Decca requires the use of
charts — with arcs printed in green, red and purple upon them
— Omega clocks up the ship's position in much the manner of
a tripmeter on a car. 'With it,' he said, 'I can get a position
every minute' — though he admits that 'satellite is also very
good, and some captains prefer it.'

Were he going to the United States, he would have to use
Loran C, for such are the current Coast Guard regulations.
Nevertheless, there may be changes. Omega, which was introduced in 1966, was developed by the US Navy Electronics
Laboratory; and, indeed, the United States Navy has already
adopted it — to the extent of placing a considerable order with
its manufacturers. Not the least of the reasons is that it is less
expensive. By its ability to give worldwide coverage from eight
stations, it eliminates the costly need to extend the Loran C
network, which, at present, covers only parts of the North
Atlantic and North Pacific and nowhere south of the equator.

This, of course, is all very nice for Omega, but we must
return to Captain Bielicz. 'You are checking your position,' he
said, 're-checking it and re-checking it. We still use sextants,
because they are a very dependable way to make a position —
also dead reckoning. I get a position from Omega, say. I check
to make sure the Omega is not failing. I check, check, check.'

Captain E.J. Smith did not check sufficiently. Nor do some
masters today. Radar, for example, may seem to be the
ultimate weapon against collisions at sea, but it can only serve
this purpose if people know how to use it properly. Unhappily,
there are still many that do not. The radar-assisted collision
has become a cliché, and when a study was carried out by the

Maritime Research Institute of the Netherlands and the US Coast Guard, it transpired that 75 per cent of all accidents at sea result from human error.

Whether the *Titanic* would have reached New York if she had been equipped with the aids that serve the *Stefan Batory* is a point that can be endlessly debated. As things were, the most sophisticated equipment at Smith's disposal was the means to call for help.

—6—

The Wireless Operator's Story

'It is a capital mistake,' Holmes once said to Watson, 'to theorize before one has data.' It is also a mistake — more than that, an offence — to find a man guilty before one has considered all the evidence. The inquiries on both sides of the Atlantic into the loss of the *Titanic* suggested that Captain E.J. Smith's conduct had been less prudent than might have been expected of a master mariner in dangerous circumstances. The verdict of the appeal court was more emphatic. It left the unhappy Smith's reputation in tatters.

Since he was not able to plead, it is only fair to search for mitigating circumstances. In an article entitled 'The Psychology of Plane Crashes' (*New Society*, 8 March 1984), Maryon Tysoe points out that 'Psychologists say that once a sequence of actions has become very well learnt, it runs off quite automatically, like a computer program (in fact, they call it a 'motor program'), with the occasional bit of monitoring from the cortex (which handles conscious control). But mistakes can occur.'

The sequence of actions required to cross the North Atlantic had become very well learnt by Captain Smith. Even so, a mistake did occur, and it was caused by an uncommonly large number of bergs drifting unusually far south that April. Had Smith's cortex been performing its duties properly, it should have monitored his routine to the extent of increasing the number of look-outs, reducing speed, and being on the bridge of his ship. If it is possible to compare the actions of a steamship's master with those of an aircraft pilot, this may offer an explanation, if not an excuse, for his apparent negligence. The fact that no theory upon such lines was advanced at any of the investigations is not surprising. The human mind is territory that has still to be properly explored.

On the other hand, there may have been circumstances that mitigated his conduct and which depended less on theory. Smith's cortex was monitoring his actions sufficiently to cause him to delay the liner's change of course at 'The Corner'. This, he may have decided, should have taken him beyond the limits of the ice and into clear water. Having done this, he was swept into the social hub of the ship; and, from that moment onwards, no more ice warnings reached him.

In fact, there were two more and neither was given to the officer of the watch — let alone to the politely revelling master. One was received from the *Mesaba*, and one should have been received (but was not) from the *Californian*. If Smith had been aware of either, he would surely have extracted himself from the throng of expensive passengers. Without the need of assistance from his mental monitoring system, the genial representative of the White Star Line would have resumed his more important role of navigator.

But there must, it seems, be a culprit, and the finger of accusation now points in the direction of the chief Marconi operator, Jack Phillips. Mr Phillips, had he survived, might certainly have suggested mitigating circumstance, though his fault was not unlike Captain Smith's. He put the fads and fancies of the customers before the welfare of the ship. A few of the messages that he dutifully tapped out to the station at Cape Race, Newfoundland (from which they were telegraphed to their destinations by land-line), may have been urgent. But nothing can usurp the safekeeping of a ship on which 2,201 lives depend.

Nowadays, people marvel at the speed with which computer technology has developed, but this seems slow when compared

to wireless. A mere fifteen years separated Guglielmo
Marconi's early experiments from the launching of the *Titanic*.
During this period, Marconi had achieved international fame.
He had established stations on both sides of the Atlantic and
elsewhere in the world; and he had founded companies that
offered shipping lines packaged deals providing personnel as
well as equipment.

At sea, the wireless operator was in a curious and not very
comfortable situation. He did not rank with the ship's officers;
nor was he a member of the crew. He lived a detached, rather
lonely, life, appearing on the bridge only when he had something to tell the officer of the watch. One or two people (such
as Charles Groves, third officer of the *Californian*) used sometimes to visit the wireless office — simply because they were
interested in the new science. But, on the whole, most of the
Marconi employees' companionship came from other operators
in other ships, with whom they chatted in Morse code. It is,
perhaps, significant that, in the shorthand of the ether, the
letters OM appeared frequently. They stood for 'old man': an
address that is now seldom used, but which used to imply a
degree of friendship.

In a passenger liner, the sheer novelty of wireless appealed
to the customers. No attempts were made to discourage their
interest, for it was their messages — a few of them important,
but mostly manifestations of the craze generated by any
innovation — that produced the profits. To have received a
telegram dispatched from a liner such as the *Titanic* on her
maiden voyage was, indeed, something to tell the neighbours.
To have actually sent one was to put oneself well ahead in the
social scramble.

The *Titanic* had two operators on board: Jack Phillips and
his assistant, Harold ('Judy') Bride. They shared sleeping
accommodation that was separated from their two-roomed
working quarters by a green curtain. Bride was twenty-two
years old and had graduated from the British School of
Telegraphy in the previous July. Phillips, aged twenty-five, was
considered to be a veteran. Both men had begun their careers
as Post Office telegraphists.

Passengers who wished to send messages handed them in at
the purser's office, from which they were sent to the wireless

room by means of a pneumatic tube. Not the least of the problems facing Phillips and Bride was the fact that the range over which signals could be transmitted varied according to whether it was day or night. Everything destined for the United States mainland had to be routed via Cape Race and, for most of the voyage, the shore station could only be reached after it was dark.

Normally, the influx of messages could have been coped with, considerable though it was. But on the evening of 13/14 April, a transformer in the equipment broke down, and Phillips was up for most of the night carrying out repairs while the paper mountain grew higher than ever. Next evening, he had not only to clear this very considerable backlog; he had also to bring his accounts up to date. He was tired when he came on duty and he had no attention to spare for anything that might interrupt his conversations with Cape Race. To him, the message from the *Mesaba* was just such an interruption. He scribbled the ice warning down, made a mental note to deliver it to the bridge later, and (as is the way with so many mental notes) forgot about it. The *Californian*'s attempt to acquaint Captain Smith with the danger that was now so imminent received even shorter shrift. The well-meaning Evans was told to 'Shut up, shut up, I am busy; I am working Cape Race; you are jamming me.' Unfortunately, Evans did as he was told, though the departure from the courtesies normally observed when one operator spoke to another must have surprised him. Phillips, obviously, was in a state of considerable stress.

'Judy' Bride had been in his bunk when the *Titanic* hit the berg. He was due to come on duty at 2 a.m. However, he realized the strain under which Phillips had been working, and he very considerately decided to relieve him two hours or so earlier. He was not aware that anything untoward had occurred as he slipped a dressing gown over his pyjamas and wandered into the office. Phillips remarked that the engines had stopped: that something must have broken down and that they would probably have to return to Belfast. He, too, had not been conscious of any impact. He was relieved that, at last, he had cleared the Cape Race traffic and mildly surprised by the silence, the total lack of vibration, which informed him that the liner was now at a standstill.

The weary senior wireless operator rose from his chair and was about to go to bed, when Captain Smith appeared at the door. Such a visitor was unusual enough to cause comment; the reason for his presence was even more remarkable — and, indeed, alarming. 'We've struck an iceberg,' he said. 'Be ready to call for assistance, but do nothing until I tell you.' They did not have to wait for long: at 11.50 p.m. — ten minutes after the collision — the first plea for help was transmitted. It was heard by the Norddeutscher Lloyd's *Frankfurt,* by the Canadian Pacific's *Mount Temple,* by the Allan liner *Virginian,* by the Russian cargo vessel *Birma,* and (very faintly) by an enthusiast on the roof of Wanamaker's department store in New York, who excitedly passed on the information to receivers closer to hand.

It was not heard by the *Carpathia,* whose operator, Harold Cottam, was on the bridge at the time. It was, indeed, only by good fortune that the *Carpathia* ever knew of the desperate drama that was taking place 58 miles away. Cottam was ready to turn in for the night. On impulse, however, he walked back to his office. A miners' strike was taking place in England, and he decided to call up Cape Cod in case there was any news of a settlement. Then he remembered having heard that there was a mass of messages awaiting the *Titanic* from Cape Race, and he wondered whether Phillips knew about them. It might be as well to inform him — and, while he was about it, to work out his accounts. Then he heard: 'Come at once. We have struck a berg. It's a CQD, old man. Position 41°46N 50°14′W.'

Cottam replied by asking whether he should tell the captain. The answer was short and the more urgent by its very brevity. 'Yes: quick,' Phillips tapped out. Five minutes later, Cottam was equally succinct. 'Coming hard,' he Morsed.

Of all the ships that replied to the *Titanic*'s signals, the *Carpathia* was the only one that seemed to have any conception of how desperate the situation was. The *Frankfurt* in her first acknowledgement did not even give her position, which left Smith in considerable doubt about whether she was to be taken seriously as a potential rescuer. Later, her operator asked what was wrong (reply: 'Tell your captain to come to our help. We are on ice'); and, later still, he requested more details (reply: 'Stand by and keep off').

At the time of the disaster, four companies were competing for supremacy in the field of wireless: Marconi, Lee de Forest and United Wireless in North America, and the Telefunken company in Germany. The last of them had the personal backing of the Kaiser who, while building a fleet in an attempt to rule the waves of the sea, was also intent upon ruling those of the air. The rivalry between them all was bitter — even to the extent of jamming one another's transmissions whenever possible. Since the *Frankfurt* was equipped by Telefunken, there were insinuations afterwards that her operator had been deliberately obtuse. But these, surely, must be discounted. Commercial competition, tough though it may be, stops short at putting lives in danger. One has to assume that the *Frankfurt*'s man really did not understand how serious things were. Possibly he, too, had been convinced by the myth of unsinkability.

Nor, in any case, was the *Frankfurt* the only ship that failed to grasp how grave the situation was at 41°46′N 50°14′W. The *Titanic*'s sister, the *Olympic* was 500 miles away. She, too, eventually picked up Phillips's signals, and she, too, displayed a remarkable lack of comprehension. At 1.25 a.m., her operator transmitted: 'Are you steering to meet us?' There was no time to go into details, and Phillips stated, simply, that 'We are putting the women off in boats.' It was more than sufficiently concise, and the *Olympic*'s master can have been in no doubt that he was much too far away to render any assistance. Twenty minutes later, Phillips was telling Cottam: 'Come as quickly as possible, old man; engine-room filling up to boilers.'

All the messages ended with the letters MGY, which was the *Titanic*'s call sign. Many of them were prefixed by CQD — the commonly used code for an extreme emergency. Later that night, however, the initials SOS were used. Bride is reputed to have suggested to Phillips that he use it. 'It's new,' he recalled saying, 'and it may be your last chance to send it.' This has given rise to the belief that the *Titanic* was the first ship to transmit SOS, which is by no means the case. The second part of Bride's remark turned out to be sadly true: it *was* Phillips's last chance (or very nearly the last) to transmit any signal at all, but SOS was by no means new. It had been introduced nearly three years earlier, and it is surprising that Bride does not seem to have been aware of that.

CQD was devised by Marconi, who intended it to mean 'All Stations — Urgent'. In fact, many people were misled by the initials and interpreted it as 'Come Quick — Danger'. Consequently, an international convention replaced it by SOS in 1910. In that year, the master of the 10,606-ton Cunarder *Slavonia,* Captain Alfred George Dunning, got things very wrong on a trip that was intended to take the liner from New York to Naples. His owners' instructions were that the Azores should be given a wide berth, even though it increased the time and the cost of the passage.

Dunning does not seem to have agreed with this. After seven days plodding across the Atlantic, he felt that his passengers would enjoy a glimpse of land and, a fact that the Cunard company must surely have applauded, it would save money. After all, German liners went via the Azores to save time, and none of them had come to grief.

It was the sad old story: currents that had no business to be where they were, and that most capricious of hazards, patchy fog. On 11 July the voyage of the *Slavonia* — and, indeed, the liner herself — came to a sudden end, as she ran on to a reef two miles south of Flores, the westernmost island of the Azores group. Dunning had been mistaken about his position: he was driving his ship too hard, he had disobeyed his owners' instructions — there were few errors that he had not committed. It is not surprising that the episode cost him his ticket, even though there were no casualties. The German liners *Prinzess Irene* and *Batavia* were prompt in answering the signal 'Slavonia ashore, please assist': a call that was prefixed by SOS. It seems strange that neither Phillips nor Bride appears to have been aware of it.

During the last two hours of the *Titanic*'s life, Phillips continued to tap out signals at fifteen words a minute, though it seems improbable that anyone heard them. Evans in the *Californian* was sound asleep. At 12.10 a.m., Cottam wrote in his log, '*Titanic* calling CQD. His power appears to be greatly reduced;' and, later, '*Titanic* calls CQD; his signals blurred and end abruptly;' until: 'Continued to call at frequent intervals, keeping close watch for him, but nothing further heard.'

Throughout this period, Smith made many visits to the

wireless office, and Bride acted as a courier between Phillips and the bridge. At one point, Phillips noticed that his assistant was still clad only in his pyjamas and suggested that it might be a good idea if he got dressed. Bride, back in uniform, brought a coat and a life-jacket from their sleeping quarters and draped them around his colleague's shoulders. At another time, Phillips asked him to go on deck to see whether all the boats had gone. They had, but he noticed a group of men trying to launch a collapsible from the roof of the officers' quarters. Later, he went again to their cabin and collected his and Phillips's money. On his return, Bride observed a stoker creep up behind his superior in an attempt to remove his life-jacket. He grabbed the man while Phillips, suddenly aware of the situation, sprang to his feet and knocked him out. (It is some measure of how ill-equipped the liner was to cope with disaster. The man, surely, should have had a life-jacket of his own, and, at this stage, he should have been wearing it. But, in theory, there would have been no room for him in the boats. The alternatives seem to have been death by drowning or death by remaining afloat in the water and succumbing to hypothermia. Of the two, the former may, perhaps, be regarded as the less unpleasant. But, whatever the case, stokers, one has to assume, were expendable.)

At 2.05 a.m., Captain Smith came again to the office. They had, he said, done enough and they could go. Phillips sent one last message. Amazingly, the ship's generators were still producing electricity — there appeared no need to resort to the accumulators that were available for an emergency. (Though, if this were so, why wasn't the *Carpathia* receiving her signals?) The water was now slopping through the door into the office. Phillips rose wearily from his chair and turned to Bride. 'Come on,' he said. 'Let's clear out.'

Out on deck, the two men parted. Phillips walked to the afterpart of the ship: it was the last that Bride ever saw of him. The younger Marconi operator remembered the group that, under the direction of Second Officer Lightoller, was trying to launch the Englehardt collapsible from its position above the officers' quarters. Rather to his surprise, the men were still engaged in what must now have appeared an impossible task. He went over to lend a hand.

The next few minutes were a confusion of impressions: a montage of experiences such as, thankfully, one can normally discover only in a singularly bad dream. It is, indeed, to 'Judy' Bride that we owe the ghastly minutiae of the *Titanic*'s final agony. It was he who saw Captain Smith dive into the sea from a wing of the bridge. It was he who recalled the band, still bravely playing, cease its repertoire of ragtime numbers and embark upon its sombre finale — the hymn, 'Autumn'.

> Saviour, look on Thy beloved,
> Triumph over all my foes;
> Turn to heavenly joy my mourning,
> Turn to gladness all my woes;
> Live or die, or work or suffer,
> Let my weary soul abide,
> In all changes whatsoever,
> Sure and steadfast by Thy side.

... and so on. Conrad called it 'music to get drowned by'; Maxtone-Graham, that literary guru of North Atlantic passenger traffic, described the entire performance as 'a numbing charade of normality'.

But Bride was not in a reflective mood: the problem of survival gave him more than enough to think about. The collapsible, which had remained obdurate for so long, suddenly gave way. It tumbled into the sea; but, as if to show that its capacity for being difficult was not yet expended, it landed upside down. For some minutes — less, perhaps, for time is relative and, in such circumstances, moments seem to become hours — Bride was trapped beneath it, encased in a bubble of air. Somehow, he managed to scramble free and join the small group standing on its top (which is to say its bottom). By the time the *Carpathia* reached them, he was suffering from frost-bite in both feet. When, at last, he was hauled aboard the Cunarder, he fainted.

Harold Cottam found it hard to remember when he had last slept. He was now dreadfully tired and when, brought back to consciousness and refreshed, Bride offered to relieve him, he thankfully accepted. When the *Carpathia* docked at New York, he was still transmitting the names of survivors. He stopped only when a quiet voice from behind him said, 'Hardly worth sending now, boy'. It was Guglielmo Marconi. In words heavy with grief, Bride replied, 'You know, Mr Marconi, Phillips is dead.'

Ironically, Marconi himself might have been among those for whom the bells were tolling. The White Star Line had invited him and his wife, Bea, to travel in the *Titanic* as its guests. They would probably have accepted, but he had urgent business to attend to in New York, and he departed a few days earlier in the *Lusitania*. Bea and their daughter, Degna, had watched the doomed liner depart from the top of a folly at Eaglehurst, a house near Fawley on Southampton Water, which the Marconis used when they were in England and in which his personal assistant, a former sailor named George Kemp, had rigged up a laboratory.

Had it not been for the inventiveness and business thrust of Guglielmo Marconi, the toll of *Titanic*'s casualties would have undoubtedly been greater. In all probability there would have been no survivors at all. This remarkable Italian was born at Bologna on 25 April 1874, the son of a country gentleman who had eloped with Annie Jameson, the daughter of a resident of County Wexford in Ireland. As a child, Guglielmo showed a singular interest in anything mechanical. Thinking, perhaps, that his attention might be better employed, his father disapproved. Marconi Senior continued to disapprove for many years to come, and it was not until his (to his way of thinking) wayward son had achieved a precociously early success, that he relented to the extent of investing a few hundred pounds in his enterprise. Whether this could be regarded as an act of reconciliation, or whether he was sufficiently shrewd to recognize a sound business proposition, may be doubtful. The certain thing is that the younger Marconi owed all his early encouragement, and some of his commercial success, to his imaginative, determined, and entirely delightful mother.

It was she who overcame the objections of her husband when Guglielmo proposed to turn the attic of their home at Bologna, the Villa Grifone, into a workshop for his experiments. It was she who countered her husband's impatience, when he described young Guglielmo as feckless and lacking in ambition. And it was she who, when the boy failed to get into the Naval Academy and, after a course at Leghorn Technical Institute, muffed the entrance exam for the University of Bologna, smoothed things over. Indeed, in the latter case, she did rather more than this. She persuaded one of the professors to tutor him and to advise him.

The starting point of Marconi's experiments was the discovery, in 1887, by the German physicist Heinrich Hertz, that electrical energy could be radiated through space from one point to another. As the young Italian was to discover, 'Hertzian waves' (as they were called) were electromagnetic and they could be transmitted by an electric spark. In order to receive them, a so-called coherer was required. This was the forerunner of the magnetic detector which, since its clockwork mechanism had not been wound up, prevented the *Californian* from picking up the *Titanic*'s distress signals. (Ironically, had Third Officer Groves known it, it could be cranked by hand.) In the beginning, however, it was a glass tube filled with metal dust.

By the end of 1894 Guglielmo was ready to demonstrate his progress. With the adoring Annie as the only member of the audience, he pressed a key in the attic and caused a buzzer, situated 30 feet away, to function. After this, events moved quickly. Almost by accident, he placed a metal slab into the earth and set up another a few feet from the ground. As he wrote, 'With this arrangement the signals became so strong that they permitted me to increase the sending distance to a kilometre.' What, in fact, he had discovered was that, to cover any appreciable distance, an aerial and an earth were required. Shortly afterwards, he replaced the second metal slab with a pole to which several copper wires were attached. They were anchored to the ground by empty petrol cans filled with stones.

His next achievement was carried out with the help of his brother who was on the receiving end about a mile away on the far side of a hill. Again, it worked. 'The waves,' he wrote, 'were going through or over the hill. It is my belief that they went through, but I do not wish to state it as a fact.' It was just as well: time was to show that they went *over* it.

By the end of September 1895 he had developed a crude but nonetheless effective system of wireless telegraphy. He had also reached a point beyond which his work at home, and his own handiwork, could go no further. He needed a backer and the obvious one was the Italian Ministry of Post and Telegraphs. The Ministry was not impressed. There was, he was told, a perfectly adequate network of cables and nobody saw any reason why it should be superceded by some newfangled device. The fact that, in the event of a war, the submarine cables could quite easily have been cut by a hostile power does not seem to have occurred to the authorities. Nor did anyone suggest that the Italian navy might be more receptive to his ideas.

Marconi was never one to give up easily and nor was his faithful mama. She remembered that one of her relatives, Henry Jameson-Davis, was an engineer in London. Perhaps he could help. Burdened with a mass of apparatus and their own baggage, the two of them set off for England in February 1896. They exchanged the comforts of the Villa Grifone for rooms in the English capital's Bayswater Road.

Henry Jameson-Davis proved to be an excellent ally. He was on friendly terms with a research scientist who was acquainted with the chief engineer of the Post Office, William (later Sir William) Preece. Clearly, a demonstration was needed to engage Preece's interest, but this was no problem. The young Italian had become adept at putting on such shows, and they availed him well throughout most of his life. Whilst other people might argue a point, Marconi gave visible evidence to which there could be little contradiction.

For Preece he erected his apparatus on the roof of the General Post Office building near St Paul's Cathedral, and put up another set on top of a post office in Queen Victoria Street — just under a mile away. It worked faultlessly. Afterwards, Preece said, 'Young man, you have done something truly exceptional. I congratulate you on it.' This was nice, but, more to the point, he promised him the co-operation that the Italian Ministry of Post and Telegraphs had so thick-headedly refused.

The first experiments took place on Salisbury Plain, with the range becoming longer and then longer. He discovered that the higher the aerial, the better the results and that, by using a kite, an aerial could be very high indeed. Within two years of his tyro efforts in the attic of the Villa Grifone, he was sending and receiving over a distance of 8.7 miles, but this was just another beginning. In 1897, he exchanged signals from Alum Bay on the Isle of Wight with a tug in the Solent. The weather was horrible, and this serves to show one of the reasons why people liked working for Marconi. He never took the soft option which, in this case, would have been to remain snugly ashore. He insisted on being present on the wave-racked tug.

Next year, he provided the *Dublin Daily Express* with a major scoop by enabling the Kingstown (now Dun Laoghaire) regatta to be reported by on-the-spot observers. Not the least of the advantages was that the progress of the events could be relayed to land when the boats were out-of-sight. Later, during Cowes Week, the Prince of Wales was on board the Royal Yacht off the Isle of Wight while Queen Victoria was staying at Osborne. HRH had injured his knee, and the Queen insisted on daily reports of his progress. To receive them, a pole, 100 feet high, was erected in the grounds of Osborne and a smaller aerial was attached to one of the *Victoria and Albert*'s masts. A sample exchange of messages is:

> The Queen wishes to know how the Prince slept; how he is this morning; and if he had any news about the Queen [of Denmark: the Prince's mother-in-law, who was seriously ill].

To which the reply was:

> HRH the Prince of Wales received last night from the Princess of Wales an account of the Queen of Denmark which on the whole is fairly favourable. The Prince slept very well indeed last night and is feeling very well today.

One story has it that, while on his way to inspect the aerial at Osborne, Marconi was stopped by a gardener. He was told that Her Majesty was enjoying a stroll and that she would be angry if her privacy were invaded. Marconi paid no attention and continued on his way. When the matter was reported to the Queen, she snapped 'Get another electrician.'

By 1899 both the Italian and British navies were beginning to take an interest in the possibility of wireless telegraphy. In the latter, three cruisers — HMS *Juno*, HMS *Alexandra*, and HMS *Europa* — were equipped with sets. And, on the North Atlantic, the American Line's *St Paul* now had Marconi equipment on board. As she passed about 70 miles from the station at Alum Bay, her operator was able to exchange signals. As a result of this conversation, the first issue of *The Transatlantic Times* was printed and issued to passengers. Most of the news had to do with the Boer War. The two main items were:

Ladysmith, Kimberly, and Mafeking holding out well. No big battle. 15,000 men recently landed.

And:

At Ladysmith no more killed. Bombardment at Kimberley effective the destruction of ONE TIN POT. It was auctioned for £200. It is felt that period of anxiety and strain is over, and that our turn has come.

It may sound rather along the lines of that journalistic classic of non-news: 'Small earthquake in Peru. Few people injured.' But at least it was a beginning.

The climax of Marconi's work at this time was to be the sending of a signal across the Atlantic. There were many who said that it was impossible: according to this school of thought, the curvature of the earth would block the transmissions. Marconi was unimpressed by the theory and, in October 1900, he began work on a station for this purpose at Poldhu Bay on the western side of the Lizard in Cornwall. He erected a ring of masts, 200 feet in diameter, and set up his apparatus in a large hotel nearby. Then he departed across the ocean to Cape Cod to find a location for a base on the American side.

Alas, the weather was far from helpful. On 15 September of the following year, a gale sent the Poldhu masts crashing down. This was far from being a major disaster: within a week, the debris had been cleared away and rather more simple replacements erected. This, however, was by no means the end of the matter. About two months later, the wind was blowing hard at Cape Cod and the aerial there collapsed. The site was abandoned, and Marconi moved to St John's, Newfoundland. He took over a cluster of what had once been military buildings on Signal Hill overlooking the town.

St John's in December is bitterly cold and swept by high winds. On Tuesday, 10 December, however, Marconi decided that it was as moderate as it was ever likely to be at this time of year, and sent a cablegram to Poldhu, telling the men there to begin transmitting next day. The idea was that they should send the letter S (... in Morse) for three hours every afternoon. Normally the Marconi call sign was D (_...), but S was preferred. It was simpler and, by substituting a dot for the dash in D, less consuming of energy.

A balloon 14 feet in diameter was used to hold the aerial aloft and it was experiencing no end of difficulty. The more gentle weather of the previous day had gone; in its place, the worst excesses of meteorological villainy were raging over Signal Hill. Marconi sat in one of the old military buildings, making continual adjustments and listening hard as he tried to coax a signal out of the ether. At last he got it: there, against the cacophony of atmospherics, was S. And again. And once more. It was weak, admittedly, but it was undoubtedly audible. Then, as if its mission was accomplished and it might now dismiss, the balloon sheared away from its moorings and was thrust into space.

Next day, they used a kite, which performed a magnificent selection of aerobatics, but nevertheless delivered the three dots at 12.30 p.m., 1.10 p.m. and 2.20 p.m. The weather worsened, which was something that seemed impossible, but it managed. To send a kite into the sky under these conditions would merely be a good way in which to lose it. The valiant Kemp managed to take an aerial from the top of Signal Hill and attach it to an iceberg stranded on the shore below. As an example of human endeavour, it may have been impressive; as a means of trapping an S or two that had made the journey from Cornwall, it was useless.

Marconi decided that enough was enough. He had done it — though he would have liked better evidence of his feat. There were, indeed, those who doubted it — people who said that the transmission must have come from a station in the United States, or from a steamer chartered by Marconi and positioned not too far from the shore. But, on the whole, public opinion seemed to be satisfied. The Canadian government was certainly impressed; and so, we must assume, was the Anglo–American Telegraph Company.

Newfoundland, it may be remembered, was independent of Canada until 1949, when a referendum was held and its citizens elected to join the rather larger Commonwealth country. The Anglo–American Telegraph Company asserted that it had the monopoly of all communications within the small dominion and, unless Signor Marconi took himself and his apparatus elsewhere, it promised to sue. Marconi surely had suffered worries enough, and he could have done without this unkind cut. However, a trip to Ottawa improved his spirits. The Canadian authorities offered him a site at Glace Bay on Cape Breton Island, Nova Scotia. It should be perfectly suitable for his work. Moreover, on the train journey, he may have reflected with pleasure that, within the small span of five years, he had extended the range of wireless telegraphy from just over two miles to a good deal more than 2,000.

Whatever the merits of wireless telegraphy on land, there was a far greater need for it at sea. The first vessel to be equipped with it on a permanent (as opposed to experimental) basis was the East Goodwin lightship ten miles offshore from Deal in Kent. The set was installed on Christmas Eve 1898. It was put to good use on 28 April of the following year. A thick fog had come down over the Goodwin Sands and a slattern of the seas, a charmless freighter named the *R.F. Matthews*, which lumbered from port to port in search of cargo, was groping her way from London to goodness knows where. The *R.F. Matthews* more or less stumbled across the East Goodwin lightship and smashed into her bows. Captain Clayson, the light vessel's master, applied himself to the Marconi equipment and carefully tapped out a message to Marconi's assistant, Mr Bullock, who was running an experimental station in the South Foreland lighthouse. The message ran: 'We have just been run into by the steamer *R.F. Matthews*. Steamship is standing by. Our bows very badly damaged.'

There were no casualties; the damage turned out to be less than Captain Clayson had imagined; and the lightship was able to remain on station. But, as an illustration of wireless as a potential life-saver, it was impressive. Captain Clayson was particularly enthusiastic. 'I had not the slightest trouble,' he said. 'I called the South Foreland up about two minutes after the steamer got clear of us, while she was still standing by, and I got a reply immediately from Mr Bullock, to whom I telegraphed briefly the particulars of the collision.'

There is more to ocean rescue, however, than sending a message to a lighthouse about ten miles away. Having demonstrated to the satisfaction of himself and a good many other people that his wireless could send signals across the Atlantic, Marconi applied himself to its use in ships crossing the ocean. Again he sought help from the American Line and again that company agreed to co-operate. In 1902, the liner *Philadelphia* was fitted with a set for a passage between Southampton and New York. The object was to maintain contact with the station at Poldhu. An aerial reaching more than 60 metres above sea level was attached to the mainmast, and the incoming signals were recorded on tape. It turned out to be possible to receive readable messages at distances of up to 1,551 miles, and test letters up to 2,009 miles. To ensure that there was no suggestion of cheating, the liner's master, Captain Mills, and his chief officer verified the results and signed them. Mills also marked on a chart the positions of the ship when the signals arrived from Poldhu.

In 1909, ten years after the incident involving the *R.F. Matthews* and the East Goodwin lightship, wireless and, in particular, one of Marconi's operators, made their first dramatic appearances as saviours of life at sea. On 22 January, a thick fog settled over New York and the sea and coastline in the vicinity. The White Star liner *Republic* (15,377 tons) was outward bound for the Mediterranean. On board were 461 passengers and a crew of 300. The value of her cargo, which included supplies for the United States' Mediterranean fleet, was estimated at half a million pounds. Much of it was needed for the victims of an earthquake that had devastated Sicily and Calabria.

The *Republic*'s master, Captain Sealby, had delayed his departure in the hope that the fog might clear. Shortly after midnight, he decided that he could wait no longer. The *Republic* cast off from the pier and headed eastwards along Long Island sound. Feeling her way through the murk and accompanied by deep blasts from her whistle, the liner passed the light vessel at the approach to the Ambrose Channel and set course for the Atlantic. Coming towards her was the Italian liner *Florida*. She was carrying 800 emigrants — most of them refugees from the earthquake who, having lost their homes and most of their belongings, were hoping to make a fresh start in America.

At 5.30 on the morning of 23 January the two ships collided. At the subsequent inquiry, the *Florida*'s master asserted that his own vessel had been travelling at reduced speed, whilst the *Republic* was making no concessions to the weather. Sealby denied this.

Captain Sealby's first reaction to the emergency was the traditional appeal of mariners in distress: he sent up rockets. It was, of course, futile. In such thick fog, nobody would be able to see them. Then he became aware that he had on board a priceless collection of equipment designed for just such a situation — wireless. The impact of the crash had put the dynamos out of action and shattered the wall of Marconi operator Jack Binns's office. However, both the reserve accumulators were undamaged and Mr Binns was able to transmit. He prefaced the message CQD and then tapped out: 'Am in distress and need assistance.' It was quickly answered by the French liner *Lorraine*, which replied with the encouraging words, 'I am coming.' Her master advised Sealby to 'make all the noise you can', and pointed out that he was 120 miles away. According to his calculations, the Cunarder *Lucania* was nearer; he would, he promised, pass on the message to her.

On board the badly damaged White Star liner, everything was taking place with commendable calm. All the passengers had been asleep at the time: some had been flung from their berths by the shock of collision. Four people had been killed, and four more had died in the *Florida*. It seemed probable that everyone in the *Republic* would be transferred to the Italian liner which, apart from having had the shape of her bows drastically modified, did not seem to be too badly damaged.

The early morning air was now alive with the chatter of Morse. Two stations on shore picked up the signals and relayed them. Jack Binns was working in complete darkness. As well as the office wall, the transmitting key had been damaged; but, for so long as the aerial remained in position and there was life in the accumulators, he proposed to remain on duty. One message was sent to the station at Vineyard Haven (at the entrance to Nantucket Sound) for onward transmission to the

White Star office in New York. It read: 'When 20 miles south of Nantucket lightship this morning, we were run into by an unknown vessel. The engine-room is full of water. Can remain afloat. No danger. No lives lost.' He had clearly not heard of the four casualties and the statement 'Can remain afloat' was wildly optimistic. The *Republic* had not much longer to live.

However, several ships were rushing to the liner's assistance. The *New York* came out to escort the *Florida* into New York. The White Star's *Baltic* was inward-bound from Europe. At 6 a.m. just as she was passing the Nantucket light, her master, Captain Ransome, received news of his colleague's plight from the wireless station on shore. He promptly turned his ship around and headed for the *Republic*. The *Lucania* was still searching for the stricken liner, her look-outs confused by what might have been the appeals of the *Republic*'s whistle and what could have been the groan of the lightship's fog horn. Two United States Coast Guard cutters, the *Gresham* and the *Seneca* were also making haste to the disaster.

The *Baltic* got there first, and the passengers were transferred to her in a well-disciplined operation that was remarkable only for its lack of incident. At one o'clock that afternoon, they were landed in New York. They seemed to be in surprisingly good order. As one bystander observed, 'It was hard to tell the difference between those who had been rescued and those who had not.' And, from another: 'Barring general mourning for the loss of baggage, everybody is in good spirits. It was wonderful to have the wireless at hand, otherwise it would have been a terrible calamity.'

Out at sea, the drama was approaching its conclusion. Captain Sealby, Marconi operator Binns, and a volunteer crew of officers and ratings were still aboard the *Republic*. The two Coast Guard cutters tried to take the liner in tow and, for a short period, it looked as though they might be successful. At eight o'clock that evening, however, it seemed horribly certain that the ship was about to sink. The cutters launched boats to take off those who had remained behind. Sealby and his chief officer were picked up clinging to a grating, as their ship slid to her grave in 45 fathoms of water off Martha's Vineyard.

Captain Sealby and Jack Binns arrived in New York to heroes' welcomes. A party of White Star stewards and seamen carried them on their shoulders to the company's offices. The two seemed to be embarrassed by so much attention, though they may have been pleased by the editorial in one newspaper, which paid tribute to 'The men of steady nerves and courageous hearts who, patiently and skilfully, directed the splendid rescue — and who are willingly sharing the thankfulness and gratitude of the country with Mr Marconi, whose wireless telegraphy made it possible.'

Eighteen months later, Marconi's invention demonstrated its importance in a very different situation. Dr Crippen, having disposed of Mrs Crippen beneath the ground floor of his house in North London, left for the Continent with his mistress, Ethel Le Neve. The couple travelled to Holland and thence to Antwerp, where they boarded the Canadian Pacific liner *Montrose*, which was about to depart for Quebec. Miss Le Neve was rather thinly disguised as a young man, and they described themselves as 'Mr Robinson and son'. The *Montrose*'s master, Captain Kendall, had read about the case in the newspapers. He could not help remarking upon the resemblance of Mr Robinson to the much wanted Crippen. Furthermore, the man and the lad demonstrated a curious affection for each other. It was not, Captain Kendall told himself, the attitude that fathers and sons usually adopt.

When the liner was some way out into the Atlantic, he decided to voice his suspicions in a series of wireless messages to Scotland Yard. All told, there were thirteen of them. One read: 'Have suspicion that Crippen, London cellar murderer, and accomplice are among saloon passengers. Moustache taken off, grown a beard. Accomplice dressed as a boy. Voice, manner and build undoubtedly a girl...' And: 'I feel even more convinced it is him ... they have no luggage except small cheap grip ... Is still letting beard grow and shaved upper lip. Managed to examine his grey felt hat while at lunch ... noticed accomplice using safety pin on pants.'

The CID advised Captain Kendall to do nothing that might alarm the 'Robinsons'. The *Laurentic*, a faster liner than the *Montrose*, was due to sail from Liverpool for the St Lawrence and passages were booked for Inspector Dew and two detective constables. They arrived ahead of the CPR liner, disguised themselves as pilots and, as the *Montrose* steamed up river, went aboard her. Dew identified his man. He made a discreet signal to his colleagues and, without any fuss, Crippen and Miss Le Neve were arrested. Dew's wireless telegram to Scotland Yard was in austere contrast to Captain Kendall's profusion of messages. It stated briefly, 'Crippen and Le Neve arrested wire later — Dew.'

According to an almost certainly apocryphal story that circulated afterwards, Crippen flew into a rage when Dew confronted him. He cursed Kendall; he cursed the ship; and he cursed the spot in the Saint Lawrence where the liner had paused to take on the detectives. According to the *Daily Telegraph*, his actual words were 'I am rather glad the anxiety is over.' Miss Le Neve was less sanguine, but she was hysterical rather than melodramatic. It is, perhaps, a pity that the unhappy 'doctor' did not put the evil eye upon the trio, for, had he done so, it would have been a nice example of black magic's power: Kendall was master of the *Empress of Ireland* when she sank following a collision with a Norwegian collier. The sinking took place at this very location. As for the *Montrose*, her future was not to be entirely happy.

When the First World War broke out, the *Montrose* and the *Montreal* were berthed at Antwerp. The latter was undergoing engine repairs, but Kendall (now Canadian Pacific's marine superintendent at the Belgian port) decided that the sooner the two were out of the way, the better it would be. Thus the *Montrose*, her decks crowded with refugees, struggled across the North Sea with her maimed sister in tow. She handed her over to tugs at the mouth of the Thames and steamed up river to Gravesend. There she suffered the unhappy experience of having her holds filled with concrete and a chaos of gantries erected on her decks. The idea was that she should proceed to Dover, where she would be sunk at the harbour approaches to discourage marauding U-boats. Things did not go quite according on plan. On the night of 28 December 1914, when she was on station but not yet scuttled, a gale blew up. She was wrenched from her moorings, sent scudding through a mine-field, and eventually pulled up short on the Goodwin Sands. Her remains rested there until 22 June 1963. Trinity House, it seems, found her mast a useful marker when carrying out surveys.

Returning to Kendall and his adept sleuthing in the Crippen case, this not altogether fortunate mariner was next to use wireless in far more disastrous circumstances — when the *Empress of Ireland* was sinking after her collision with the collier *Storstad*. The signal was picked up by the Marconi station on shore, and promptly relayed to two Canadian Coast Guard ships, the *Eureka* and the *Lady Evelyn*. One of the liner's survivors was the senior Marconi operator, Ronald Ferguson, whose first message was the rather vague statement that 'We have hit something'. Later, he was to send a very much more elaborate report to London from one of the rescue vessels. It was the first news of the disaster to reach the city. Mr Ferguson's assistant, Edward Bamford, also escaped with his life. He was particularly fortunate: as the liner lurched over, he was thrown into a boat and thus escaped an uncomfortable drenching in the ice-cold water of the St Lawrence.

Marconi was fortunate in the timing of at least two of his business trips to America. An earlier engagement in New York had prevented his accepting the White Star's invitation to sail in the *Titanic* — and thus saved him from almost certain death. This, of course, is speculation: would he have felt that the development of radio depended upon his survival, and, consequently, have made sure he found a place in one of the boats? Or would he have conformed to the *Titanic* ethic and died — possibly with earphones on his head? The second occasion was mere chance: he just happened to be returning to the UK from New York at the right time. In late April 1915, he made the westerly passage in the *Lusitania*. Somewhere in the area of the Fastnet lightship, the periscope of a U-boat was observed. The Cunarder increased her speed and hurried out of range before the German captain could fire a torpedo. For his journey back to Europe, Marconi travelled in the *St Paul*. The American liner slipped away from her berth in Manhattan precisely three weeks after the *Lusitania* had departed on her fatal return voyage.

It was at lunchtime on 7 May that, 12 miles off the Old Head of Kinsale on the south coast of Ireland, Kapitän-Leutnant Walter Schweiger looked through his periscope and noticed the *Lusitania* steaming towards him. He was mildly surprised that providence should provide him with such a huge and helpless victim, and fired one torpedo. He was astonished that the grand lady of the Atlantic sank so easily. In thrall though he was to the Fatherland, he had few illusions about the quality of German torpedoes: one ought certainly to have been insufficient; two might have accomplished it, though even this was debatable. He was not, of course, to know that the liner's real enemy was within her own hull: a cargo of high-explosive shells for which the U20's puny missile served as little more than a detonator.

Schweiger's good fortune, if such it was, lay in the relative positions of the two ships. By one of those coincidences that are the very stuff of tragedy, the torpedo happened to strike the liner in (from the U20's viewpoint) exactly the right place.

Until quite recently, truth has not been a feature of the *Lusitania* disaster. The matter of her cargo of war materials was carefully hushed up; documents that should, by now, be in the possession of the Public Record Office have vanished. There have been lies, damned lies, and more damned lies. By no means the least interesting question in this fog of deception is why the great liner was such an easy prey for her killer.

On the face of it, the *Lusitania*'s master, William Turner, did what any captain of a westbound liner might have done under more normal circumstances. During the morning of the 7th, he ran into fog. Coming out of it, he sighted the Old Head of Kinsale and checked his position. Had he been more fortunate he would have changed course shortly afterwards, proceeded up St George's Channel and so through the Irish Sea to Liverpool. The one flaw in his plan was the presence of the U20: a flaw that, whilst the precise position of the submarine was not known, the British Admiralty could well have foreseen.

Why, then, was not Captain Turner properly informed about the hazard? Thanks to the work of a very talented team of officers and civilians working in Room 40 at the Admiralty, nearly all the radio signals of the German High Seas Fleet were overheard and decoded. The movements of every member of the U-boat pack were known — and, in the case of the U20, there had been two very recent sinkings (the merchant ships *Candidate* and *Centurion*) to show that she was there. Yet, despite the fact that there was a division of destroyers at Milford Haven on the south-west corner of Wales, no escort was provided. Nor was anything done to divert the Cunarder from her course.

The *Lusitania* could have avoided the area and made the run to Liverpool by way of the North Passage around the top of Northern Ireland. It had recently been reopened to merchant shipping. It may even have been (hardly anything in this story is for certain) that Captain Turner asked for permission to do this — and was refused. Why? Can it be true that this crack Cunarder was deliberately allowed to proceed on a course to destruction as a ploy to engage America in the war?

The suggestion has been made. Churchill, then First Lord of the Admiralty, is discredited with the authorship, with the First Sea Lord, Admiral John Arbuthnot Fisher, as his accomplice. It was not necessary that the wound should have been fatal: the mere fact that a German warship should have attacked a merchant ship carrying United States citizens might have been sufficient. In fact, grievous as the sinking of the *Lusitania* was, it required another two years and several more sinkings before President Wilson uttered the last of many warnings, and aligned the United States against the Central Powers.

But, whether the loss of the *Lusitania* was caused by ineptitude or by design, a scapegoat had to be found. The victim was the unfortunate Turner. It was alleged that he had been specifically warned of the presence of U-boats. That he had been told to avoid prominent landmarks (headlands, for example) and to keep to mid-channel. That he had been told to zigzag, and that he had been instructed to delay his arrival at the entrance to the Mersey until after nightfall. With the exception of this final requirement, his accusers said, he had taken no notice of these orders.

In fact, his course took him twelve miles from the Old Head of Kinsale when five miles would have sufficed. There is also evidence to suggest that he may have been preparing to put into Queenstown to await a destroyer escort; and that he never received the other instructions. Largely to satisfy Alfred Booth, chairman of Cunard, who was profoundly disturbed by the attacks on the *Candidate* and the *Centurion,* a submarine warning was issued to *all* merchant ships (not specifically to the *Lusitania*) on the 7th. The text of it was: 'U-boats active in southern part of Irish channel.' Since the sea off the south coast of Ireland cannot, by any stretch of the imagination, be called a 'channel', what did this mean? St George's Channel? If it did, it was irrelevant — as anyone who was privy to the reports compiled in Room 40 at the Admiralty must have known.

Turner was hounded relentlessly by Churchill and Fisher, and the harassment of this luckless mariner did not cease with the end of the war. It was, indeed, Churchill's account of the *Lusitania* in *The World Crisis* (1921) that eventually forced him into retirement. Turner was described at the inquiry as 'an old-fashioned sailor man', and he agreed with this description. But, while it may have implied the talents of a wise and experienced seafarer, it did not make him the best of witnesses. Nor can his demeanour in court and his muddled statements, have been helped by his wife's brutal lack of support — or by the presentation, just before the hearing began, of a white feather by some excessively militant woman.

As in the case of the *Titanic*, the inquiry was headed by the Commissioner for Wrecks, Lord Mersey. Mersey was obviously unhappy, and he must have been aware that the evidence that could have cleared Turner's name was missing. There was no record of the wireless signals exchanged between the *Lusitania* and the Admiralty during the liner's voyage across the Atlantic.

There were two Marconi operators in the ship: Robert Leith and David McCormick. Both survived, but unfortunately their radio log did not. What is more, all the copies of the messages received by shore stations and lodged with the Post Office had been removed. Significantly no doubt, McCormick, the junior of the two, who had been on duty at the time of the disaster, was not called as a witness. Leith, who had been resting in his bunk throughout the morning, and who was having lunch when the torpedo struck, was bidden to attend. But his testimony revealed very little. As reported by Colin Simpson in *Lusitania*, it amounted to this:

> Carson   (Sir Edward Carson, the Attorney-General): On Friday morning the 7th did you receive two Government messages?

Leith: Yes.
Carson: Which were from a wireless coast station?
Leith: Yes.
Carson: The first was at about 11.30?
Leith: Approximately.
Carson: And the other one shortly after 1 o'clock?
Leith: Yes.

... and that was that. Nobody can have been very much the wiser.

But if there was a conspiracy: if the *Lusitania* had received the messages that were said to have been transmitted, why did not these two men eventually speak up? And why, indeed, were they not questioned about them at the inquiry? Alternatively, if no such signals had been received, why did they not say so — if only to refurbish Turner's reputation? One reason is that they would have been in a code to which they did not have the key. Another is that, even if they had been able to interpret them, it seems improbable that they would have dared to pit themselves against such powerful opposition. To have done so would probably have meant immediate dismissal from the Marconi Company and a long prospect of unemployment. As for Captain Turner, he was just an 'old-fashioned sailor man'.

Captain Smith's fault was that he received a great many warnings and did not properly heed them. Captain Turner's misfortune seems to have been that, with the exception to that vague reference to U-boats and 'the Irish Channel', he received none at all.

In 1906 the first international radio-telegraph conference took place. It was held in Berlin and, among other obligations, it required all contracting parties to give absolute priority to distress messages and to avoid interference as much as possible. Three months after the loss of the *Titanic*, the delegates met again, on this occasion in London. The inertia of the *Californian* during that terrible night was obviously a matter of considerable preoccupation. Whilst they did not insist that wireless equipment should be installed in all vessels, they agreed that certain ships must maintain a permanent radio watch. (It was this conference, incidentally, that finally put an end to the dilemma of whether to send CQD, or SOS, or both. SOS was, so to speak, made official — not because its letters had any special significance, but, because ...—... is easy to remember and to transmit in Morse code.)

The convention that took place in 1914 carried that of 1912 a stage further by ruling that all vessels carrying more than 50 passengers must be fitted with wireless installations, and that each set must have a range of at least 100 miles. Owing to the outbreak of war, its recommendations were pigeon-holed for the next few years; but, said a spokesman for the International Maritime Organization, 'it established a precedent that was followed by subsequent conferences'.

When a ship sinks, everyone on board is (in an ideal situation) taken off in the lifeboats. But this may be no more than a reprieve. They have simply been transferred from an environment that no longer floats to one that does. To ensure their survival, the boats themselves have to be located. To take only one example, in 1923 the freighter *Trevessa* sank in the Indian Ocean. Before leaving the ship, her wireless operator had sent a distress message, which was acknowledged. But, by the time help arrived, the *Trevessa* was on her downward path to the ocean bed, and there were no signs of the two boats that carried her crew. After voyages of 22 and 27 days respectively, they eventually arrived at Mauritius. Their occupants were half dead from thirst and starvation and it can only be ascribed to good fortune that they made a landfall when they did. They might well have missed the island.

Nine years earlier, in 1914, some of the Cunard liner *Aquitania*'s lifeboats were fitted with wireless, though there was no international requirement for it. The SOLAS Convention of 1929 set matters partially to rights (and some might have said 'about time, too') by insisting that the larger passenger liners must have at least some boats fitted with radio equipment. It was not, perhaps, a very demanding measure — especially since there is nearly always a lapse of several years between the recommendations of these gatherings and their adoption. Indeed, it was not until the convention of 1948, that *all* passenger ships, and cargo vessels of 1,600 gross tons or more, were compelled to carry radio-telegraph equipment.

In 1962 the first communications satellite, Telstar, was put into orbit. The principle was (and is) that messages were transmitted to it and then redirected to stations on earth. Marconi believed that radio waves followed the curvature of the globe. He was later proved to be wrong. They travel to a height of about 200 miles — in other words to the ionosphere, a band of minute, electrically charged, air particles that reflect them back to earth. This is the basis upon which high-frequency radio functions. Given ideal conditions, which are rare, it is satisfactory. But the signals are subjected to a great deal of interference from static electricity, particularly at night. The result for the unhappy operator is that communications are very hard to hear. At times they are virtually drowned by the interference.

A satellite, on the other hand, is immune from such troubles: it enables high-quality speech (and TV pictures, come to that) to be sent instantly from one place to another.

The maritime significance of Telstar was first explored by an American company known as MARISAT Joint Venture. In February 1982 the system was taken over by the International Maritime Satellite Organization, or INMARSAT. By this time, the problems created by the ionosphere and static had been joined by others. The use of radio had become so widespread, and conventional radio facilities so congested, that it was impossible to increase the number of available wavelengths.

At present three geostationary satellites are on station 23,000 miles up over the equator. One is positioned over the Atlantic Ocean, another over the Indian Ocean, and the third over the Pacific. Between them, they cover the globe as far north as 75° and as far south as 75°. Only the polar regions, where shipping is sparse, are not served by the system. The coastal stations on earth, which link the satellites with the conventional telecommunications networks, had increased to about twenty by the end of 1984. The latest available figures show that 1,650 ships, registered in forty-seven countries, were making use of it in 1983.

'Fifty per cent of our ships are equipped with INMARSAT, which provides an instant link,' said an executive of a large fleet of oil tankers. 'Things will get better as it becomes cheaper — it's slowly becoming the norm, but you must still have a radio officer as a watchkeeper. Eventually, he may become an electronics engineer responsible for all the systems.'

Had the wireless office of the *Californian* been equipped with an auto-alarm, the outcome of the *Titanic* disaster might have been very much happier. Unfortunately it was not: not least because this priceless piece of equipment had yet to be invented. However, it had been by 1929, and the SOLAS convention held in that year allowed some exceptions to the rule of radio watchkeeping for ships that were fitted with it. Nowadays, it keys off all the other alarm systems in the vessel, but its use is strictly limited to distress situations.

A present-day ship's wireless office has features that were unknown in the day (one can hardly call it 'days') of the *Titanic*. Most of the messages, for example, are received on a teleprinter that looks very like the ones to be seen in offices ashore and, indeed, uses the same type and the same paper. Nevertheless, a more conventional radio set is used as a back-up, and radio officers can still be observed tapping out messages in Morse code. In this respect, Jack Phillips and his more fortunate colleague 'Judy' Bride would find themselves quite at home in a modern merchant ship. While many shipping lines now employ their own wireless operators, Marconi Marine still offers a package deal that includes one of the company's own men — in such situations, too, they would find the scene familiar. But the most important difference must surely be the auto-alarm. That would have awakened Evans of the *Californian* from his slumber. It might also have caused Captain Lord to have bestirred himself and done something.

—7—

The Rescuers' Story

A character in a play (or was it a book? I forget) said that 'if only' are the two most useless words in the English language. Nevertheless, it is difficult to attempt any study of the *Titanic* disaster without using them. Suppose, for example, Captain Smith had not delayed his change of course for half an hour after passing 'The Corner'? Might this have taken his ship into clearer waters south of the icefield? Suppose Smith had been on the bridge that evening, might he have decided to proceed with greater caution? It is hard to say, for the danger was hidden by darkness. The comparatively still conditions meant that no waves crashed at the bases of the bergs, and there were no revealing splashes of white foam. The only warning, and one that would have required uncommonly sharp eyesight to detect, would have been the glimmer of starshine on their peaks. Moonshine would have been better, but there was no moon. In any case, it seems improbable that Smith would have noticed something that his look-outs and the officer of the watch so disastrously missed. The unreasonable sense of security, which had enabled him to join in the revels, might have accompanied him to the bridge.

Nor would he have been likely to have improved upon First Officer Murdoch's instructions to the quartermaster. In theory, Murdoch did the right thing — realizing that to have struck the berg head on, whatever its advantages in hindsight, would have killed off everyone forward of the collision bulkhead. Yes: Murdoch's action would have been correct had there been enough time, which means to say sufficient space, to steam around the placidly drifting obstacle. His captain might have made the same decision.

Had Smith — or even Murdoch — had sight of the *Mesaba*'s signal received at 7.30 p.m., the outcome might have been less tragic. It reported ice contained in a rectangle extending from 42°N–41°25′N and from 49°W–50°30′W — an area of 3,150 square nautical miles. Considering the facilities at his disposal, it is impossible not to marvel at the extent of the *Mesaba*'s captain's observations. A sceptic might even have questioned them; but the *Titanic* died in the south-westerly corner of this rectangle. It may seem surprising that the tragedy did not occur earlier. When the *Carpathia* entered the area on her rescue mission, Captain Rostron recorded: 'From now on we were passing bergs on either side, and had to alter course several times to keep well clear of them. You may depend on it, we were keyed up pretty tight and keeping a bright look-out.' And, later, 'We soon found our passage blocked by a tremendous icefield. Of course, we had seen this field before, but did not know how compact it was nor the extent of it.' A junior officer, ordered on to the top of the wheelhouse to count the bergs, sighted twenty-five large ones ranging from 150 feet to 200 feet high. As for the smaller ones, there were too many even to form a rough estimate. 'There were,' he said, 'dozens and dozens all over the place.'

But these sightings took place in daylight, whilst the *Titanic* had been hurrying through darkness. Without a doubt, Captain Smith's only sensible course of action was to do what Rostron did. Look-outs should have been stationed on either side of the bow; those in the crow's nest should have been doubled, and there would have been one on each wing of the bridge. He should certainly have reduced speed; and, even more sensibly (as Rostron did on his journey back to New York), changed course to steer around the area. This, if we take the *Carpathia* as an example, would have added 56 miles to the trip (four hours proceeding cautiously, for there were several bergs clear of the pack and potentially hazardous);

indeed, it was what Rostron had expected Smith to do. It would, he agreed, have been 'hard luck on her maiden voyage' — nevertheless, even an ocean greyhound should put survival before anything else.

It would be interesting to feed all the data concerning the *Titanic* affair into a computer and see how many different things *might* have happened. Regarded as a game of chess, the North Atlantic's pawn (in the shape of an iceberg) took the White Star's queen (the liner) and brought the contest to a conclusion. But the game can be played over and over again in the imagination, and the findings of the inquiries on either side of the Atlantic cannot be regarded as definitive accounts of what actually took place. One matter in question is the location of the Leyland ship *Californian* and the conduct (or lack of it) of her captain, Stanley Lord.

Lord Mersey inflicted no penalties on Captain Lord for what, to those who followed the proceedings of the British inquiry, was manifestly a case of negligence. He had no need to: the public could be relied upon to savage the captain's reputation. In fact, it was his spirit and not his career that suffered. He was, admittedly, forced to leave the services of the Leyland Line; but, a year later, he found fresh employment with the Nitrate Producers' Steam Ship Company Ltd, and he worked for them as master of one ship or another until his retirement in 1927.

But Lord felt that he had been ill-used. Time and again, he tried to persuade the British Board of Trade to re-examine his case; and, time and again, the Board of Trade refused. This seems to have been unfair: in the light of evidence that has since emerged, he did have a case that any competent counsel could have stated with a reasonable chance of success.

Stanley Lord was a tough captain and his officers and crew were suitably in awe of him. When he decided to go to bed, it would have required a brave man — or else very firm evidence — to disturb him. In this respect, he was no different from most master mariners, now as much as then. They do not take kindly to having their repose interrupted. Had Evans been at his wireless and picked up the *Titanic*'s CDQ, there would have been a sufficient reason. But Evans, too, was asleep.

The rub of the matter was: where, precisely, was the

Californian in relation to the *Titanic*? Lord noted his position
as 42°5′N 50°7′W: in other words, 19 miles roughly north of
the White Star liner with the icefield that the *Mesaba* reported
in between. Lord Mersey (presumably thinking, if not actually
saying, that he was lying) put the distance at five miles. But
then Lord Mersey was not aware of the intruder *Samson* and
so, for want of any other vessel, the lights seen from the
stricken liner *had* to be those of the *Californian*. And nor, come
to that, was anyone on board the Leyland liner aware of the
skulking seal hunter, which no doubt added to the confusion.

The British inquiry might, however, have taken into
account two factors — possibly three — that would have shown
Captain Lord and his officers in a more favourable light. The
first is that a master of Lord's experience and integrity would
not have fudged his figures; and, after confirming dead reckoning with a star sight, he would not have been 14 miles out in his
position. In any case, on such a clear night, there would have
been no need for radio signals to inform the officer on duty of a
tragedy taking place no more than five miles away. Any man
with a pair of binoculars should have seen the dying agony of
the great liner — and seen it in some detail.

There was also the matter of the rockets. They were
observed, but nobody on board the *Californian* said that he had
heard their explosions. I asked an audiologist how far sound
can travel. He told me that it depends on conditions, especially
on the amount of humidity. But on a night such as this, when
the temperature was below freezing, a range of up to 21 miles
would have been possible. At five miles, they would have been
perfectly audible.

Lord Mersey implied a degree of cowardice: that Lord was
unwilling to steer his ship through comparatively thin ice. But
Rostron's descriptions show that it was far from thin, and he
further supports this by remarking on the Russian steamer
Birma, which was eastbound. 'We saw him attempt to cut
through the ice-pack,' he wrote, 'but he had to turn out again.
And I don't blame him either.' Even Rostron admits that, had
he known how bad conditions were, he might have had second
thoughts about risking his ship and his passengers. It was as
bad as that; but when, early in the morning, Evans awakened,
turned on his wireless set, and found out what had happened,

Lord did not hesitate to make for the scene of the disaster. Evans's fault was that, after a night of silence, he seems to have indulged in an excess of verbosity. His signals were so strong and so frequent, that other ships complained that he was jamming their transmissions.

There is a distressing tendency of *Titanic* students — of which, goodness knows, there have been sufficient — either to be anti-Lord (the majority) or pro-Lord (tenacious apologists of a flawed reputation). In fact, it is hard to be positive about anything; and, as this book may perhaps show, one sometimes has to revise an opinion as one goes along. The matter is rather like a detective story in which a number of important clues have been left out. You cannot say that X did it; you can no more than venture that he might have done it.

Even if the key witness, Captain E.J. Smith, had survived, there might still be some puzzles left. Captain Turner of the *Lusitania* was by no means the only shipmaster to show that such men make poor witnesses in a court of law, and that they are hopeless at pleading their own causes. Smith, of course, could have escaped; as commander of the *Titanic*, he could have stepped into a lifeboat without let or hindrance. But, then again, he could not have escaped. To have lost such a ship and at the cost of so many lives would have been more than his pride could have withstood. Turner of the *Lusitania* did get away with his life and, despite the hounding of Churchill and Fisher, there was no lynching party. But this was wartime: the loss of the Cunarder was the result of enemy action, and, in any case, most people had other things to worry about. Whether or not Smith consciously committed suicide is a matter of no importance. In those cold waters, this elderly gentleman almost certainly died of hypothermia. He did the right thing and the ocean, whilst not entirely removing the tarnish from his reputation, made sure that it suffered less than the unfortunate Lord's.

One of the few people to be accorded heroic status by the *Titanic* affair was Captain Arthur H. Rostron of the *Carpathia*. After twenty-seven years at sea and three months in command of the Cunarder, it was, he agreed, the turning point in his career. Afterwards he rose to become Commodore of the

Cunard Line, master of the *Mauretania*, and, eventually, to receive a knighthood. It was no doubt a coincidence that his second officer, James Bisset, was no less successful. He, too, was to become Cunard's Commodore; he too was knighted; and he became commander of the *Queen Mary* and, later, the *Queen Elizabeth.*

Round about midnight on Sunday 14 April, Captain Rostron prepared to turn in. The *Carpathia* had sailed from New York for Gibraltar and the Mediterranean three days earlier. The weather had been surprisingly clear and, as Saturday had drifted into Sunday, he remarked upon how cold it was. A cold light breeze suggested that there must be ice about to the north — a lot of it, according to his surmise. But his ship was well clear of it, and it gave him no cause for anxiety.

Rostron settled himself for the night, switched off his lamp, and closed his eyes. He was just dropping off to sleep when the door of his cabin, which led into the chart room, was pushed open. His first reaction was one of irritability. As he wrote, 'Who the dickens is this cheeky beggar coming into my cabin without knocking?' There were, in fact, two of them: his first officer and the Marconi operator, Harold Cottam. The first officer made no apologies for the intrusion. Coming at once to the point, he informed Rostron that 'We have just received an urgent distress message from the *Titanic.*' The White Star liner had, he said, struck ice and needed immediate assistance.

Rostron sent him back to the wheelhouse with instructions to turn the ship round. Then he turned to Cottam. 'Are you sure it is the *Titanic?*' he asked. Cottam said, 'Yes, sir'. 'Are you absolutely certain?' Again the reply was 'Yes.' 'All right,' Rostron said, 'tell him we are coming as fast as we can.'

Followed by Cottam, Rostron hurried into the chart room, where the young wireless operator handed him a slip of paper. On it was written the *Titanic*'s reported position: 41°46'N 50°14'W. He marked it on a chart, and worked out a course of N52W. To judge by reports the *Carpathia* had received from other ships, this would probably mean entering the icefield at about 3 a.m. He reckoned it would take about four hours to reach the sinking liner; in fact, it took three and a half hours.

The bosun's mate, who was about to put the watch on duty

to work washing down the decks, was ordered to cancel all routine jobs and to get the boats ready for lowering. It was to be done as quietly as possible. Nobody must become excited: the men were to be told that they were going to a vessel in distress. That was all. No details, such as her identity, were given.

When the chief engineer came to the chart room at Rostron's bidding, he was informed that the casualty was, indeed, the *Titanic* and that he should turn out another watch of stokers to pile on all possible speed. The response was immediate. Many of the men went to work with such urgency that they didn't pause to put on any clothes. The *Carpathia's* normal cruising speed was a sedate 14 knots. Now, confounding even the most optimistic estimates of her builders, she cut a swathe through the ocean at 17 knots.

Fortunately no doubt, the liner's accommodation had been booked to only half its capacity. There were 120 first-class passengers, 50 travelling second class, and 565 — most of them emigrants visiting their countries of origin — in third class. To attend to their health, there were three doctors: one Scottish (a Dr McGee), one Italian, and one Hungarian. McGee looked after the first-class customers: the Italian and the Hungarian cared for the second and third class respectively.

McGee was the next to attend Rostron in the chart room. He, too, was given a brief outline of the situation, and told to assemble his colleagues and their assistants in the various dining rooms. A supply of stimulants and restoratives was to be on hand — and anything else that he might consider necessary.

Sometimes one at a time, sometimes in small groups, Rostron's subordinates were summoned to receive their instructions. The purser, the assistant purser, and the chief steward were detailed to receive survivors at the various gangways. The last of these was instructed to prepare an immediate supply of coffee for the *Carpathia's* crew, and then to apply his staff to brewing more coffee, and tea and soup as well, for the rescued victims of the disaster. He was also to place supplies of blankets near the gangways, in all the public rooms and in some of the boats. Rostron's own cabin was to be made available as accommodation. So were those of his officers and so, too, were the smoking rooms, the libraries and, if it turned out to be necessary, the dining rooms. The *Carpathia*'s third-class passengers were to be herded together to make way for the newcomers (the first- and second-class travellers were not required to make such sacrifices), and they must be urged to remain silent. Discipline, strict discipline, must be observed. The secret of this, Rostron decided, was reassurance. A number of stewards were detailed as reassurers.

The first officer was the last to be briefed, possibly because his list of instructions was the longest. He was told to assemble the entire crew and to make sure they drank plenty of coffee. Once this had been done, he was to see that all the boats were made ready and swung out; that clusters of electric lights were installed at each gangway and over the sides; that a chair with ropes attached was ready at each gangway for hauling up the sick and injured; that canvas bags were placed by the gangways as a means of lifting young children aboard; that pilot ladders and anything else that would serve as such were rigged over the sides; to raise steam on the winches that powered the forward derricks in case it was necessary to load the *Titanic*'s cargo of mail on board; to pour quantities of oil down the lavatories in the forward part of the ship to calm the sea (it was calm enough at the time, but one never knew with the Atlantic); and, finally, from 3 a.m. onwards, he was to supervise the firing of the company's rockets to reassure anyone from the *Titanic* who might be watching.

Apocryphally, perhaps, Julius Caesar has been given credit for the ability to listen to a statement, read a dispatch, write a directive and to issue verbal orders — all at the same time. Whether such a feat was within the competence of Captain Rostron is doubtful. Clearly, however, he was able to turn his agile mind to a great many things apparently simultaneously. While he was deciding what had to be done, and saying how it should be done, he was also navigating his ship through increasingly treacherous waters — and, from time to time, listening to Cottam's accounts of his conversations with the *Titanic* and dictating encouraging replies. When, at 1.30 a.m., Cottam reported a signal saying 'engine-room filling', he realized how grave matters were and that the probability of the *Titanic* sinking had now become a virtual certainty. On board the *Carpathia*, the crew were going about their various tasks quietly and with the apparent ease of men who really knew what they were doing. It was a beautifully fine, clear night, very cold and (Rostron's words) 'every star in the heavens shining bright, the sea calm and no wind. We were racing along splendidly.'

Dr McGee returned to the bridge at 2.35 and reported that all his preparations were complete. 'I was talking to the doctor as to what we might expect,' Rostron recalled, 'and keeping at the same time a sharp look-out, when quite suddenly — and only for a couple of seconds — I saw a green flare about a point on the port bow.' For a few moments he allowed himself to hope that it was evidence that the *Titanic* was still afloat. But, very soon afterwards, a report from Second Officer Bisset, who was stationed on the starboard wing, put an end to any such speculation. Bisset's communication was brief and alarming. He had just spotted the glint of a star upon an iceberg two points on the port bow. The perilous part of the rescue operation had begun.

'I was pretty anxious,' Rostron afterwards admitted, 'thinking of my own passengers and crew and ship.' What had happened to the *Titanic* could just as well occur to the *Carpathia* and nobody pretended or believed that the elderly Cunarder was unsinkable. These were 'rushing, anxious, hours'. The company's rockets began to soar into the sky at the stipulated quarter-hour intervals; and, as the wan green light — which ominously disappeared for minutes at a time, and then thankfully reappeared — as this small token of some-body's survival drew closer, roman candles were added to the *Carpathia*'s firework display.

At 3.30 the purser and the chief steward reported that their arrangements had been made. Five minutes later, Rostron rang down, 'stand by' on the engine-room telegraph. Some mariners — the successful ones certainly — appear to be gifted with a sixth sense that can create an awareness of danger when there is nothing to betray its presence. (During the Second World War, that pastmaster of U-boat destruction, Captain F.J. 'Johnny' Walker RN, was reputed to sense the menace of enemy submarines long before anyone else so much as suspected that they were in the vicinity.) At 4 a.m., Rostron's action suggests that he may have had similar powers. He walked quietly over to the telegraph and pushed the handle to 'stop'. A few minutes later, another berg drifted out of the darkness — dead ahead.

The *Carpathia* crept round the hazard, quickened her pace on the far side and hurried on until the next berg loomed in her path; and the next, and the next ... The green flare still beckoned: as the Cunarder drew closer to it, Rostron could see that it was low in the water. It was not, as he had originally hoped, evidence of the *Titanic*'s survival; but, rather, the desperate appeal of a lifeboat to be noticed. Glimmers of light were now creeping into the sky, and one or two early rising passengers had wandered up on deck. The sunrise, Rostron recalled, was '... beautiful. The whole thing might have been an early morning spectacle improvised for the benefit of the passengers.' Some of the icebergs reminded him of cathedral spires; others (as in the case of the *Titanic*'s quartermaster) of ships in full sail. Some travelled in small convoys of two or three. Others drifted on their various ways unaccompanied.

By now, the boat was very close and he could see that there was a young officer (Fourth Officer Boxhall) in charge of it. There were 25 occupants. Rostron's first intention was to bring his ship round and to pick up the boat on his port side. It would at least provide shelter from the wind that was now stirring itself gradually awake. It was good enough in theory, but a berg had maliciously stationed itself in the way and made the manoeuvre impossible. The starboard side would have to do.

When the boat was within hailing distance, Boxhall called out, 'We have only one seaman and cannot work very well.' Rostron reassured him. It would be unnecessary to come alongside the liner: the liner would come to the boat. Quite apart from the lack of skilled sailors aboard it, he realized that these people must be dreadfully cold, dreadfully tired, and still rather frightened. He instructed Second Officer Bisset to take two of the quartermasters with him, climb down into the lifeboat and take charge. Minutes later, young Mr Boxhall presented himself on the bridge. 'The *Titanic* has gone down, I suppose?' Rostron said. 'Yes,' Boxhall replied, 'she went down at about 2.30.'

There were now 'dozens and dozens' of icebergs, some large, some small, littering the sea. About one-third of a mile

ahead of the *Carpathia*, a growler, between ten and fifteen feet
high and twenty-five feet long, seemed intent upon blocking
the passage — while, two hundred yards away on the starboard
quarter, a larger berg stood sentinel. But there were other
boats, too — all of them within a radius of four or five miles.
'One's imagination,' said Rostron, 'fancied these people shivering for hours during that cold night in that confined space.'

Among those who had been 'shivering for hours' was the
young steward Sidney Daniels and his companions on the
upturned collapsible. 'We were a mixed bunch there,' he
remembered,

> passengers of various nationalities and about four crew,
> including myself. All that night we just sat and waited for
> the dawn to break, hoping to be seen by our other lifeboats.
> Then, as it gradually got lighter [he put the time at about 6
> a.m.], we saw a ship looming up. It was the *Carpathia*, and
> soon one of our lifeboats saw us and took us aboard, which
> really crowded them. Then we began to row towards the
> *Carpathia*, which was lying about a mile away.
>
> When we were taken aboard the *Carpathia*, we were
> given a hot drink. It was the first time in my life that I had
> drunk coffee, for I had disliked the smell of it before. But it
> was very welcome then. We were taken below; our wet
> clothes were taken off; and we were wrapped in blankets
> and put into bunks — some of us two to a bunk, as I was. I
> lay there and shivered for the rest of the day. I expect it was
> shock as well as the cold that made me shiver so much.

Calmly, methodically, the work of rescue continued. By
eight o'clock, all the boats were alongside; and, by 8.20, all the
survivors were on board. At some point during these twenty
minutes, the *Californian* steamed into view. Rostron signalled
her master to take over the search: for his part, he proposed to
depart for New York.

At this point, the *Carpathia* must have been tolerably close
to the spot at which the *Titanic* foundered. There was a
pathetic litter of objects — some deckchairs, fragments of cork,
a lifebuoy here and another there (they reminded Rostron of
debris washed up on the sea shore) — all, indeed, that was left
of the supposedly greatest ship ever built.

Initially, the *Carpathia*'s passengers didn't seem to realize what had happened, nor the scale of the catastrophe that had just occurred. When the survivors came among them, however, they displayed an admirable mixture of sympathy and common sense. They gave up their cabins to them; some of the women took up their needles, cut blankets into suitable pieces, and manufactured clothing for the ill-clad third-class passengers. They encouraged the newcomers to take a little food; and, above all, they listened. There were innumerable sad stories to be told, but one that seemed to affect people most was that of a 'teenaged girl':

A boat had been crammed with women. It was so full that, just as it was about to be lowered, an officer judged it to be unsafe. Somebody would have to give up her place. This youngster immediately got up and prepared to return to the ship. A number of her companions tried to dissuade her, but her mind was made up. 'No', she said, 'you are married and have families. I'm not: it doesn't matter about me.'

Quietly, she went back to the deck and was, one has to assume, drowned. It was a tale that was to haunt those who heard it for the remainder of their lives.

Before taking course for New York, Captain Rostron had assembled most of his passengers and all the available crew members in the first-class lounge, where he conducted a short religious service: offering thanks for those who had survived and expressing mourning those who had died. Later in the day, at four in the afternoon, he buried three bodies that had been taken from the boats and a man who had died not long after being rescued. On this occasion, two forms of ceremony were used: one for the Roman Catholics and one for the Protestants. The latter followed the wording of the Common Prayer Book with one exception. Instead of the committal of the body to the ground, and the words '... earth to earth, ashes to ashes, dust to dust ...' etc., the prayer went: 'We therefore commit his body to the deep, to be turned into corruption, looking for the resurrection of the body when the Sea shall give up her dead' — and so on.

As the *Carpathia* negotiated her way round the ice-pack, the calm weather, which had helped the rescue operation, was elbowed out of the way by a gale, generated somewhere to the north. Early on the Tuesday morning, it was joined by fog which, twenty-four hours later, became very thick (the light vessel off Fire Island was detectable only by the bellow of its fog horn). The bad visibility persisted all the way to the Ambrose light where, at 6 p.m. on the Thursday, the pilot was picked up. Even then, the vile excesses of the weather were not yet done. As she steamed up the Ambrose Channel, it began to blow hard once more, the sky was cut by shafts of lightning and torrential rain poured down. The lightning and the boom of thunder continued until the *Carpathia* arrived off the Cunard pier.

During the voyage back to New York, there had been a curious quietness about the ship. The *Carpathia*'s passengers, who had shown a commendable lack of excitement when the far too few survivors were picked up, seemed to sense the feelings of their new companions. They trod softly and spoke cautiously, aware that what most of them needed was rest — and that, in many cases, the joy of being plucked alive from the Atlantic was marred by bereavement. Those who ventured up on deck could not help noticing that a change had come about in the deployment of lifeboats. Seven suspended from the davits now bore the name TITANIC, and so did another half-dozen on the fo'c'sle head. Before the ship docked, these had to be spirited away and replaced by the *Carpathia*'s own. The work was carried out almost surreptitiously, with an officer and two hands in each. Few, perhaps, noticed them go, for they crept away into the night like intruders that have been sent packing. Once they were gone, at 9.30 p.m., the Cunarder slipped alongside the pier and the bombardment by the anxious and the inquisitive, the official fact-finders and the unofficial newspaper men (who didn't care very much how they got a story, or what the story was, so long as it pleased their editors) began. Keeping the throng at bay, and knowing that firmness had sometimes to be tempered by sympathy (it was not always easy to say who deserved which treatment) was one of Captain Rostron's harder tasks.

Rostron was the man of the hour: the previously little-known master of a not particularly glamorous liner had become a hero on both sides of the Atlantic. Among his rewards was the Congressional Medal of Honour, and special decorations were struck for him and his crew. On one side, the *Carpathia* was depicted steaming through an ocean cluttered with giant bergs rising in sharply pointed pinnacles. On the other were inscribed the words:

> Presented to the Captain, Officers and crew of RMS 'Carpathia' in recognition of gallantry and heroic service from the survivors of the SS 'Titanic'. April 15, 1912.

Meanwhile, Captain Lord, having discovered no survivors in the sea and no reason for self-reproach, had resumed his voyage to Boston. The *canaille* could wait for his blood: for the moment, Bruce Ismay, The Man Who Should Have Drowned, offered more than sufficient target for its wrath. God may have already forgiven him. Others found it harder.

In mid-October 1913 Captain Rostron, still in command of the *Carpathia*, had reached a point about half-way across the Atlantic, when his attention was drawn to a ship drifting at a speed of what he judged to be one knot. Her masts had gone; her tally of lifeboats had been greatly reduced; and her white superstructure was blackened. Smoke was wandering upwards from her decks in lazy coils. There was no sign of any life on board. She was, he thought, 'liable to drift for ever'. Had the *Carpathia* been equipped with a gun, he would have sunk her, for this durable hulk was undoubtedly a hazard to other shipping. As things were, the best he could do was to report her and resume his voyage. Conceivably he made a note to tell his colleague, Captain Barr of the *Carmania*, about the sighting. Barr's seamanship had been greatly tested five days earlier when the SS *Volturno* (for that was the vessel's name) was transformed into a floating furnace. His ship was among the nine that took part in the rescue operation that was, sad to say, only partially successful. (One of the other ships involved was the *Rappahannock*, which, like the *Carpathia*, had played a role in the *Titanic* drama. As the White Star giant was hurrying westwards through water that was still clear, the *Rappahannock* was steering a cautious easterly course through the icefield. At some point, she damaged her rudder. Nevertheless she was able to carry on. At about 10.30 a.m., she passed within sight of the *Titanic* and flashed a warning with her signal lamp. It was acknowledged though there is nothing to suggest that Captain Smith was informed.)

The *Volturno* was a small ship of 3,600 tons that had originally been built for the Canadian National Railway Company at a cost of £80,000. Now she was working for the Royal Line. She was considered seaworthy, reliable, and she carried more than sufficient lifeboats for the crew of 93 and the 564 passengers that departed from Rotterdam on passage to Halifax on 2 October 1913. Most of the latter were emigrants from Eastern Europe; 260 of them were travelling to Alberta and Saskatchewan.

Six days after clearing the mouth of the Maas, she ran into a gale. Next morning, the weather worsened, and she began to roll dangerously. Among the freight in number one hold was a consignment of barium oxide. The violent motion caused one of the containers to be smashed. The action of its contents on the deck started a fire, which was noticed by a male passenger who was on his way to the women's quarters. He raised the alarm and then, becoming panic-stricken, flung himself overboard. The matter was reported to the chief officer who informed the master, Captain Francis Inch. Five minutes later, the flames burned their way through the hatch cover and set alight the deck fittings on the fo'c'sle. Inch ordered a reduction in speed. Turning to the quartermaster, he directed a change of course to bring the wind behind the ship. It would, he considered, give the fire extinguishers a better chance.

By this time, the number of casualties had already risen to more than sixty. The watch below were trapped in their quarters and so were a number of steerage passengers.

The fire, having freed itself from the captivity of the hold, was spreading itself. Tongues of flame began to lick the top of the foremast: an explosion wrecked the saloon and hospital amidships. Another put the compass out of action. Watching its progress, Inch silently gave up hope and, more articulately, instructed his chief officer to provision the lifeboats and have them swung out. The passengers were assembled, tended by the stewards who handed out life-jackets. Meanwhile, in the wireless office, the two Marconi operators, Seddon and Pennington, were transmitting distress signals. When the blaze attacked the bunkers, the engine-room was shut down and the generators packed up. They switched over to the emergency accumulators and carried on until, at about 9 p.m., the aerial was carried away by an explosion. Then they shut the office door for the last time and joined the others, all of them huddled together on the poop.

Seventy-eight miles away, the *Carmania* was fighting her way through the storm on an easterly course. Captain Barr was informed of the *Volturno*'s plight. He immediately ordered his radio officer to relay news of the disaster to other ships. He gave the quartermaster a change of course and told the chief engineer to bring the engines up to maximum power. (The *Carmania* and her sister, the *Caronia*, were the first two Cunarders to be equipped with steam turbines.) Travelling at 20 knots despite a punishing headwind, this fourteen-year-old veteran of the North Atlantic headed for the blazing liner. The first sight of her was a column of smoke on the horizon.

Fortunately, the *Volturno* was on one of the regular steamship routes at 49°12′N 34°51′W, and there was no lack of response to the cries for help. The German vessels *Grosse Kurfürst* and the *Seydlitz*, Furness Withy's *Rappahannock*, the *Tsar* (Russian), the *Kroonland* (American), the French *La Touraine*, the Atlantic Transport Company's *Minneapolis*, the Leyland liner *Devonian*, and the Anglo–American Oil Company's *Narragansett*, were all converging on the stricken ship. The *Carmania* was the first to arrive; the *Narragansett* was the last, which was a pity — she was carrying 3,000 tons of lubricating oil that was badly needed to quieten the unquiet sea. Indeed, when Captain Barr informed other vessels of the *Volturno*'s plight, an oil tanker was at the top of his list of priorities.

The gale was blowing as hard as ever. As the *Carmania* drew closer to the *Volturno*, it could be seen that five of the latter's lifeboats were missing. A number of passengers were clustered together on deck. Among those who watched them from the Cunarder was Arthur Spurgeon, manager of Cassell's publishing house in London, who was returning from a business trip to New York. Afterwards, Mr Spurgeon really let himself go in his account of what happened.

Alas [he wrote], what we expected to be nothing more than an exciting incident developed into a great disaster, which broke down strong men and made women weep ... One will never forget the look of dire despair that settled on the faces of the passengers at the after part of the ship as effort after effort to save them resulted in failure. We knew that only a miracle could save them.

C.F. Hart, a senior executive of the *Daily Mail* who was also travelling in the *Carmania,* was more restrained. Everybody on board the liner, he noted was 'eagerly anxious, but unable to help owing to the mountainous seas. The sight beggars description.' All that he and Mr Spurgeon and the other passengers could do was to wave to the apparently doomed huddle of humanity on the *Volturno*'s poop, and to shout encouraging words that were blown away by the wind.

Things were looking very bad indeed. Late that afternoon, Captain Inch sent this message: 'Position getting desperate. Send rafts' and, just before Messrs Seddon and Pennington abandoned the radio shack at 9 p.m.: 'For God's sake, help us or we perish.' Captain Barr and the masters of the other ships, which, one by one, were assembling, were doing everything they could. But the monstrous seas were making it impossible to cross that relatively small gap that separated the victim from her intended rescuers — just as the monstrous wind was nourishing the blaze as effectively as countless cans of gasoline. Nor was the *Carmania* the ideal ship for such a mission. She was fast: yes. Elegant: certainly. But she did not handle well in conditions like these. Eventually, as darkness fell, the best she could do was to withdraw to the sidelines and illuminate the scene with her searchlights.

She was, however, responsible for the rescue of one survivor. A German named Walter Trintepohl, formerly employed by a firm of merchants in Barcelona and now moving to a better paid job in New York, jumped overboard and, by some miracle, floated across to the *Carmania.* Somebody heard his cry for help and he was hauled on board. The tale he had to tell was disturbing. Whilst the captain and the officers of the *Volturno* were behaving well, the conduct of the ratings (mostly Germans and Belgians, he said) was less praiseworthy. 'People rushed about wildly,' he said, 'and the crew seemed to think they ought to have first place; and, instead of quietening, they made the panic worse.' He alleged that Captain Inch had cut the tackles of a number of boats to make sure nobody tried to lower them and that, on one occasion, he had drawn his revolver in an attempt to drive the firemen back into the boiler room.

Possibly Herr Trintepohl's experience had inflamed his imagination. Whatever the reason, his account was grossly exaggerated. At no time did Captain Inch produce his pistol and, on the whole, the conduct of the *Volturno*'s crew was judged to have been rather good. If anyone had taken panic, it was surely this garrulous German who, by all that was reasonable, should have died in the violence of that furious sea.

Nevertheless, events had not been going at all well on the fire-swept *Volturno*. Some while before the *Carmania* arrived, Inch had rightly decided that the blaze was not to be quenched and that the time had come to abandon ship. The first boat to be lowered was Number Two, with the chief officer, an old Atlantic hand named Miller, in charge. There were several cabin-class passengers on board and a scattering of stewards to attend them. As the boat touched the water, it promptly capsized. Miller and some of the stewards managed to right it and to climb back in. By this time, all the passengers had drowned. Nor did Miller and his men fare better. A wave caught the boat, hurled it away from the ship and sent it scudding into the distance. No traces of it or of its occupants were ever found.

The next two boats were smashed against the *Volturno*'s hull and their human contents spilt into the sea. The fourth seemed at first to be faring better. It actually reached the water, settled in an upright position, but then it went the way of its predecessor, thrust beyond recall to sink somewhere far away. One more attempt was made. The boat in question was Number Seven, situated at the afterpart of the ship. It was, perhaps, the most disastrous of all. Not only was everybody on board lost: its falls fouled the liner's propeller and immobilized her before the blaze's assault on the bunkers put the engines out of action.

By this time, Inch had heard that the *Carmania* was on her

way, and he decided that enough was enough. Earlier on, there
had been some slight panic among the passengers, but they
calmed down until they reached a point at which, Inch said,
'They all seemed ready for their doom, whatever it was.' Now,
seeing the comforting bulk of the Cunarder, their spirits
improved. In reply to Inch's plea for rafts, Barr ordered half a
dozen to be thrown into the sea. Predictably, they all went wide
of the mark. Then Barr attempted to get a boat across with the
second officer, a powerful man named Gardner who had once
survived for twenty-three days adrift in a similar craft, in
charge. The ocean was glad to receive it. As a prelude to its
proposed destruction, it broke (or, in some cases, wrenched
away) five of its eight oars. Without sufficient means of propulsion, it was now useless. This prepared the way for what was
clearly meant to be the next move: picking it up and smashing
it to smithereens against the *Carmania*'s flank. Barr called
down to Gardner, 'Get the crew out and let the boat go.' Three
seamen scaled the rope ladders that had been suspended over
the side, but Mr Gardner was not to be defeated. Somehow, he
and the remaining members of its crew managed to attach the
falls to it; and, with the intrepid officer standing proudly in the
stern, it was hauled upwards and gently repositioned in its
chocks. There was a round of applause from the watching
passengers. The operation had not achieved anything, but at
least the sea had suffered a small defeat.

The object had been to get a line aboard the *Volturno*. Since
this was plainly impossible using a boat, Barr decided to use the
Carmania herself for the task. With great delicacy, he
manoeuvred the hard-to-handle Cunarder to within a hundred
yards of the *Volturno*'s stern. The sorry assembly of possibly
doomed passengers could be seen in greater detail; the fire
appeared to be burning more fiercely than ever. The *Carmania*'s passengers renewed their attempts to encourage,
though the performance of trying to get a rope across did
nothing to support them. One after another, a sorry succession
of attempts ended in failure. Rolling, pitching, flung this way
and that by the huge waves, the *Carmania* turned away.
Captain Barr and his men were reduced to the role of very
worried spectators.

At about 6.30 p.m., the *Grosse Kurfürst* arrived. Just before

midnight, her master thought that the progress of the fire
might be slowing down; that the wind might have moderated,
though only very slightly. At all events, and with the situation
so desperate, he resolved to take a chance. He put double the
normal number of seamen into one of the lifeboats. It was
lowered successfully, but it took two hours to come within
hailing distance of the *Volturno*. The captain had been wrong.
The wind had not lessened one iota. It was impossible to get
sufficiently close to be of any help. The officer in charge
regretfully turned away and applied himself to the problem of
returning to his ship.

One by one the team of aspiring rescuers assembled. At
about the time when the *Grosse Kurfürst*'s men were fighting
their way back to the German liner, the *Minneapolis*'s captain
decided to have a go. An officer was detailed to recruit six
volunteers for the assignment. They, too, came within earshot
of the *Volturno*. The officer called to the very frightened
assembly on the poop: imploring them to jump with the
promise that he would pick them up. But they seemed to be
numbed with shock and nobody moved. It was, perhaps,
understandable. The history of disasters at sea is full of
instances in which the victims have preferred the illusory
security of a fatally damaged ship to the horrors of the sea
below.

The attempts at persuasion might have gone on for longer,
but now the boat was in trouble. A wave had smashed its
rudder, and the odds against returning to the *Minneapolis*
alarmingly lengthened. Fortunately, the *Carmania* picked up
the helpless craft in the beam of one of her searchlights.
Cautiously the Cunarder closed on it and, five hours after the
officer and his six crewmen set off on their fool's errand, they
were swarming up the big liner's side. As the last man
clambered on to the deck, the sea, as if bent on revenge, took
hold of the boat in disgust and flung it at the liner's side.

Few people slept that night. On board the *Carmania* clusters
of wakeful observers formed at the rail to watch the stricken
Volturno. On the latter's poop, Inch, the two Marconi operators, and a number of sailors busied themselves with the
manufacture of small rafts. Some of the women sang hymns;
most of the men were smoking heavily. A group of Jewish

passengers held a prayer meeting that lasted for several hours. One or two people actually managed to doze off for an hour or so.

And the worst was over: the fire had not consumed the after-part of the ship. Just before dawn, the wind became more moderate; and there, at last, was the *Narragansett* steaming out of the murk and ready to pour oil on the very troubled waters. At 5.30 a.m., the *Devonian* managed to get a boat across and soon there was a small flotilla heading for the *Volturno*.

On the whole, the work of transferring the passengers and the surviving members of the crew was an orderly undertaking. A rope had been strung across the burned-out liner's deck, with the men on one side of it and the women and children on the other. No man was to cross it until the last woman and child had departed. Two tried. One threw an infant down into one of the lifeboats and then, despite attempts to stop him, shinned down a rope. The crew in the lifeboat clearly disapproved. According to one eyewitness, 'they gave him a hammering'. Another male bluffed his way into the women and children's reserve by putting on an officer's great coat. Inch spotted him and knocked him down. As a penalty, the captain said, he would be the last to leave. At eight o'clock, when everyone else had gone, he was allowed to make his exit in company with Captain Inch, and those trusty wireless operators Seddon and Pennington. They were taken on board the *Kroonland*.

The survivors were scattered over the ten ships that had taken part in the rescue operation. The *Grosse Kurfürst* received 105, the *Tsar* 102, the *Kroonland* 90, the *Devonian* 59, the *Seydlitz* 46, *La Touraine* 40, *Minneapolis* 30, *Narragansett* 29, the *Rappahannock* 19, and the *Carmania* (if one discounts the crew of the *Minneapolis*'s lifeboat) one — the amazing Herr Trintepohl. Statistically, this works out that 521 of the 657 that set out from Rotterdam in the *Volturno* were rescued. In other words, just over three-quarters. It is in remarkable contrast to the case of the *Titanic*, which occurred no more than eighteen months earlier, and where about one-third of those on board were saved. It could, of course, be argued that the ships involved did not have to steam through an ice-strewn sea, and that the *Volturno* did not sink. Had she gone down, or been utterly consumed by flames within two or three hours of the fire breaking out, the loss of life might have been total. Yet, the weather was about as bad as anything the North Atlantic can conjure up. The truth is that the *Volturno* operation was superbly orchestrated and that, on board the ship and despite Trintepohl's accusations, Captain Inch was in absolute control. But to compare his performance with that of Smith or of Captain Turner of the *Lusitania* is, perhaps, unfair to those masters of the mega-liners. The *Volturno* was a small ship. Small in matters of communication, is undoubtedly beautiful, and communication is essential to control.

Control was something that was in lamentably short supply when, in September 1934, a liner belonging to the New York and Cuba Steam Ship Company (a subsidiary of the Ward Line), the *Morro Castle*, was on her way back to New York after a pleasure cruise to Havana. So far as this book is concerned, the matter of the *Morro Castle* belongs in parenthesis: a footnote, as it were, that is too long to be used as such. Anyone wishing to study the case in more detail would be advised to read Thomas Gallagher's admirable *Fire at Sea*. Here we can consider it only as a macabre example of how not to run a ship.

Little that is good can be said of the *Morro Castle* except that the first-class passenger accommodation was adequately luxurious and that the food was good. As an hotel, albeit one run by a rebellious staff, she might have been satisfactory. As an example of the proposition that a ship is a ship is a ship, she was not. The crew were badly fed, poorly paid, and up to their collective necks in smuggling narcotics and rum. (Cuba was then a clearing house for drugs from Europe on passage to the New World.) The passengers had a tendency to drink too much, which is not remarkable: many of those who travel in cruise liners do it. Unfortunately, the men who should have been gainfully employed in manning the ship were also prone to this small lapse from correctitude.

On the present trip, 455 people were aboard her — including 138 members of the German–American Concordia Singing Society, rich business men from Brooklyn who may have performed well in close harmony, but who badly needed a gargle afterwards. They, and a good many other passengers, were surprised when, on the evening of 7 September, it became known that the master, Captain Robert R. Wilmott, did not propose to dine in public. Instead, he had ordered his meal to be sent to his cabin.

At 7 p.m. Wilmott called the ship's doctor, de Witt van Zile, with the strange request that he should bring him an enema. Van Zile did as he was asked. On entering Wilmott's room, however, he received a rude shock. The master was half in and half out of the bath and wholly dead. The doctor rapidly diagnosed a heart attack and advised the chief officer, William F. Warms, to take over.

Warms's record was by no means unblemished. When serving in a freighter, he had undergone the shame of having his ticket suspended for eighteen months as a punishment for failing to carry out the statutory fire drill. Furthermore, he was the kind of person who will reply to any question so long as he does not have to say anything pertinent such as 'yes' or 'no'. During the hours that were to come, he was, perhaps, almost totally unfitted for command. The crew knew this and those of the passengers who were sober probably suspected it.

The *Morro Castle* was steaming up the United States coastline, when the weather turned bad and she found herself punching a violent headwind. At 2.15 a.m., a passenger named Paul Arneth went looking for the man with whom he shared his cabin and who had unaccountably gone astray. His search led him into the writing room, where he saw smoke seeping through cracks in a cupboard in which were kept 150 spare blankets and, more to the point, a store of highly inflammable liquid used to clean bedding. Since the rear wall backed on to one of the funnels, and since the funnel was apt to become very hot indeed, there could hardly have been a less suitable place for it.

Mr Arneth reported the matter to a steward, who made the first blunder of that awful night: he opened the cupboard door and thereby allowed the flames to go freely about their business. When Warms was informed, he immediately ordered all the fire hydrants to be brought into action at once. It is a simple rule of physics that if you pour water down one pipe, it may gush. But if you pour the same amount through several pipes simultaneously, the result is likely to be a pathetic trickle. Consequently, the blaze spread unchecked, laughing as it were at such sadly ineffectual action.

Up on the bridge, Mr Warms was busy telling anyone who cared to listen to him that he was now Captain Warms. He also discouraged anyone who expressed a wish to visit the late master on the grounds that it was not a pretty sight and that the dead man's face was an ugly shade of blue. What he did not do was to reduce speed from the 18 knots at which the ship was steaming, nor turn from the head wind that was driving the blaze towards the afterpart of the ship.

Meanwhile, the senior radio officer, George W. Rogers, was busy sending out distress signals. Mr Rogers had already served one sentence in jail and he was later to serve another. For the moment, however, he appeared to be on the side of the angels: the one man aboard this loosely run ship who displayed any heroism at all. The United States Coast Guard responded, but there was little it could do. Warms, having misguidedly ensured that the rear end of the liner burned brightly, suddenly changed course in the direction of New Jersey. The wind was now coming from the stern, which enabled the fire to turn its attention to the forward parts of the ship. The main staircases were soon ablaze and many passengers were trapped in their cabins.

At last, the sorry *Morro Castle* dropped anchor about six miles off Atlantic City and Warms gave orders to abandon ship. Like everything else in this tragic business, it was chaotic. The crew more or less ran amok, pushing the passengers out of the way and occupying most of the places in the lifeboats. In one boat, for example, there were thirty-one sailors and one passenger; in another, nineteen members of the crew and, again, one passenger. All told, 133 died but this represented 29 per cent of the passengers and only 15 per cent of the crew. Afterwards, Warms and four other men were charged by the authorities with having neglected their duties. He and two others were each sentenced to a couple of years in jail. The chief engineer, Eban S. Abbot, was given four years (understandably: instead of remaining at his post in the engine room, he telephoned his underlings to stay put and then made haste to a lifeboat). All of them appealed. A higher court listened sympathetically and quashed the verdicts. Nobody paid any penalty for the lives of those 133 people who died, it could be argued, unnecessarily.

The tragedy of the *Morro Castle* might be regarded as the stuff of fiction, and doubtless it has inspired several thrillers. But the strangest twist of all was provided by that industrious reporter, Thomas Gallagher. In *Fire at Sea*, he asserts that Rogers, the wireless officer who had been acclaimed a hero, was, in fact, the villain. According to Mr Gallagher, he murdered Captain Wilmott by poison and then deliberately set fire to the vessel. It may seem improbable, but Gallagher, with an armoury of telling facts, manages to convince us.

One good thing, however, came out of the official investigation into the *Morro Castle*: the United States authorities introduced a rigorous set of regulations designed to avert the possibility of fire at sea. One was that the use of wood must be confined to the absolute minimum in the construction of new tonnage. For instance when, in 1950, the *United States* was laid down, she was made almost entirely from steel and aluminium. Wood was forbidden — even for the oars of the lifeboats. The only exceptions were the Steinway pianos. The original idea had been that they should be made from aluminium, but Steinway refused — and won. Possibly somebody remembered that pile of 150 extra blankets which had set the *Morro Castle* ablaze: at all events, the bedding in the *United States* was manufactured from a fireproof material based on glass fibre.

Fire and iceberg, storm and tempest, sometimes mechanical failure — these have always been the hazards of crossing oceans. Since the 1960s, a new menace has crept out of the shadows: the terrorist. Hotels, aeroplanes, cars, even trains, have been targets for attacks — so why not a liner? In May 1972, it seemed probable that what had been regarded as a possibility might become a reality. To judge by telephone calls received by Cunard's New York office, bombs would explode aboard the *Queen Elizabeth 2* (*QE2*) as she reached a point in mid-Atlantic on her eastbound crossing. They would be detonated by a fanatic who was prepared to sacrifice his life for some undefined cause. The only way of avoiding the disaster was to hand over $350,000 (about £134,500 at the current exchange rate) by way of ransom.

The first half of 1972 had not been a fortunate period for the *QE2*. On 23 April, she arrived at Southampton thirty-six hours late after fighting her way through a 100 mph hurricane. Glass and cutlery to the value of £2,500 were smashed. Eight windows were broken; two grand pianos and one upright were destroyed. Hundreds of people were horribly seasick and three of the crew suffered broken bones. On the eve of docking, the master, Captain Mortimer Hehir, gave a champagne party at which everyone was presented with a 'storm certificate'. It was inscribed with the words 'I commend all passengers for sharing my unique experience with great cheerfulness and calm.' As Captain Hehir said, 'It was the worst storm in duration I have ever experienced. I have never known a wind of that velocity to last so long.' Each of the women passengers was given a bouquet which, they agreed, was very nice of the company.

Meanwhile, another storm, an economic one, was brewing up. In the previous year, Cunard had been acquired by Trafalgar House Investments in return for £26.5 million. Estimates by the firm's accountants suggested that, in 1972, the *QE2* would incur a loss of £1.7 million, rising to £4.4 million in 1975. The winter months in particular were disastrous, and there was talk of laying up the great liner. But then the owners thought again and did one of those U-turns that are the privilege of big business and prime ministers. The ship was not to be taken out of service after all. Instead, she was to be treated to a lavish refit that would provide more first-class cabins, better restaurant facilities, and so on.

But the *QE2* was still not out of danger. Every month seemed to produce its problem and the one for May (from the ocean rather than the board room) was icebergs. She was on a westbound crossing this time with 1,450 passengers on board and Captain William Law in command. Heavy gales compelled Captain Law to reduce the ship's speed from 28 knots to 21, and then, from the United States Coast Guard, came an ice warning. It seemed that the bergs had drifted farther south of Newfoundland than at any other time within the previous thirty years. What with the high winds and now this new menace, the liner was eight hours late when, at last, she docked in New York.

The telephone call threatening to explode six bombs, which were said to have been planted on board the ship, was taken by Charles Dixon, Cunard's American vice-president in charge of finance and operations. The original intention, Mr Dixon was told, had been to demand $1 million. But 'we are reasonable people' and 'we' (no identity was given) had decided to settle for less. Mr Dixon was to take the money to a telephone kiosk two hours' drive away from Manhattan on Route 299, where he would receive more instructions. He was to be unarmed and would, he was warned, 'be watched from three directions'. The alarm was passed on to London, where it was taken very seriously. As Victor Matthews (later Lord Matthews), chairman of Cunard, said afterwards, 'We realized it could be a great big confidence trick, but we could not take risks with the lives of our passengers.' Mr Matthews informed the security authorities. There were 1,438 passengers and a crew of 900 in the ship, which was now hove-to a thousand miles from New York *en route* for Europe. Captain William Law was, once again, in command.

An RAF Nimrod was detailed to take up station over the liner and to act as a communications centre. Sergeant Clifford Oliver of the 22nd SAS, Lieutenant Richard Clifford and Corporal Thomas Jones (both of the Royal Marine's Special Boat Squadron) were warned to be ready for take-off in a Hercules transport that would fly them to the liner and from which they would drop by parachute. It remained to find an officer to put in charge of the operation: somebody, that is to say, with experience of bomb disposal.

The action now moved to a place in the country that is the secret headquarters of the British Army's Land Service Ammunition. To be more precise, it erupted on the desk of Lieutenant-Colonel George Styles, GC, the officer in charge of the Explosive Ordnance Disposal. Colonel Styles had not only to select the man; he had also, so far as such a thing is possible, to direct much of the work from an office half an ocean away.

As he saw things, there were three questions: was it possible to drop a man by parachute on to a ship? Was this still possible if that ship was in mid-Atlantic? And could such a feat be achieved on that very same day? There could be no doubt about the answer. In every case, it had to be 'yes'. It might have seemed a daunting business to many people, but never mind. Colonel Styles had to make it feasible.

He picked up his telephone and asked for an officer in the

personnel branch. Between them, they short-listed half a dozen potential candidates. Eventually, Captain Robert Williams was selected. 'I did this because I knew him,' the Colonel said. 'I knew his father: I knew his capacity and capabilities. He had, I think, done one parachute jump in his life, and he was interested in freefall parachuting and goodness knows what. At the time, he was at the Army School of Ammunition.'

Meanwhile, Styles's colleagues had been busy attending to other matters. Since Captain Williams would have to take a lot of equipment with him, the Special Boat Squadron's support would be needed when he came down into the ocean. This had to be arranged, just as the equipment itself had to be assembled and suitably packed.

Once Williams had been briefed about his assignment, Styles was able to take a break for lunch. As he was eating a hurried meal, he could hear the sound of a helicopter's engines as it flew over the mess. Inside the machine was Williams *en route* for the RAF's parachute training centre at Abingdon. He was due to receive some unusually rapid instruction about how best to land (if such a word is permissible under the circumstances) on water. Once he was deemed to be adequately proficient, he was taken on the next leg of his journey — to RAF Lyneham, where the equipment and the rest of his team were waiting. They embarked in the Hercules; at about 3 p.m., the aircraft took off.

Nearly all the miracles of modern communication should have been at the disposal of Styles that afternoon. But, to begin with, they seemed to be less than adequate. With Williams and his companions airborne, it was of paramount importance to talk to the *QE2*. An RAF Nimrod had already taken up station over the ship as a flying communications centre. This was the logical way of approaching the matter; but, said Colonel Styles, 'I was told that the Nimrod was so inundated with calls that I would have to wait.' Under such circumstances, this was clearly nonsensical. He returned to the telephone and, this time, went through to the Admiralty. He is nothing if not direct in his approach, and his summing up of the situation *vis-à-vis* the Nimrod was suitably crisp. 'How, then,' he asked, '*do* I get in contact with the *QE2* in mid-Atlantic?' The response became more helpful. He was given a civilian telephone number (British Telecom's) at Portishead in Somerset.

'When I got through to them,' he recalled, 'they said, "We're sorry, sir, but the *QE2* is not accepting any calls."' At this point one begins to marvel at the Colonel's patience. Here was Britain's pride of the North Atlantic in apparent danger, and nobody seemed able to provide communications for the one man that was arranging some positive action. He must have made this sufficiently clear, for the operator's next statement was: 'Hang on — I'll connect you.' The call was taken by Captain Law, who promptly handed matters over to the chief engineer. Much of their conversation had to do with the problem of how best to blow up such a ship. Once that had been settled, it was possible to draw up a plan for making a search. Throughout the afternoon, there were many similar conversations, with the 'Chief' reporting his progress (they had discovered three or four suspicious objects) and Styles offering advice. It was only after Williams had arrived with his equipment intact, that Styles felt it safe to relax.

Robert Williams and his three companions dropped in two sticks at a height of 800 feet. Each was wearing a rubber frogman's suit and they came down in the water about 300 feet from the liner's bow. The fall was made the more difficult by the low cloud base. Later, a flight lieutenant in the Nimrod's crew remarked, 'I could not have jumped myself — even for the money!' The worst that Williams experienced was a bad attack of seasickness; but then, as Colonel Styles said, 'It was pretty rough. If you're a fairly inexperienced parachutist and your first drop for real is into the ocean, and then you're picked up by these frogmen with their little rubber boats and things, I think *you'd* be seasick. I would be, too.'

By the time Williams came on board, the engine-room staff had completed their search. He cautiously examined the objects that had looked as if they might be dangerous and pronounced them harmless. Then, under less pressure, he was able to make sure that nothing had been missed. No fresh uncertainties came to light; of bombs there was no trace whatsoever. The whole thing had been a hoax. Nevertheless, lessons had been learned. From Colonel Styles: 'The best person to search a ship is a sailor. All that was needed from me was my assessment of how that ship could be blown up, and if I told you, and you published it in your book, every terrorist in the world would know how to do it. A ship can be a very real target. If we wanted to, we could blow one up on her next voyage, you and I.'

So far, thankfully, nobody has yet tried.

Meanwhile, Mr Dixon did as he had been told to do. Packing the money (used $10 and $20 notes) into a dark blue canvas bag, he drove to the telephone box beside Route 299, which turned out to be near Beacon — a smallish town on the Hudson River to the north of New York. No doubt somebody watched him arrive for, within a few moments, the telephone rang. The speaker gave him an uncomfortable reminder of how the old *Queen Elizabeth*, renamed *Seawise University*, had ended her life in flames when berthed in Hong Kong harbour the previous January. Then he gave instructions to take the cash to the wash-room of a nearby motel. Again Mr Dixon obeyed, but nobody collected the blue canvas bag or removed its contents.

Not long afterwards, however, agents of the FBI did come to collect a Beacon shoe-shop owner named Joseph Landisi. Forty-nine-year-old Landisi was charged with demanding money with menaces from Cunard and also with threatening to demolish buildings and aircraft belonging to American Airlines (his asking price in this instance was $301,600 — about £116,000). A jury found him guilty of both offences, and he was sentenced to twenty years in jail and a fine of $10,400 (£4,000). Cunard expressed its gratitude for the work of Captain Williams and his colleagues by making tolerably generous contributions to Soldiers', Sailors' and Airmen's Families Association.

Throughout the drama of the non-existent bomb, Captain Law reassured his passengers with frequent announcements over the public address system. Ignorance, after all, is the ally of fear. Even if there had been some sort of deadly device on board, it seemed questionable whether it could have done very much damage. The ship was, after all, divided into fifteen watertight compartments which, at the press of a button, could be sealed off by the closing of fifty-eight electro-hydraulically operated doors. She was as stormproof, fireproof, and bomb-proof as shipbuilding technology could make her. Nevertheless, there can never be a return to the kind of complacency that killed the *Titanic*.

Evidence of this was provided with tragic conviction on 23 June 1985. An Air India Boeing 747, *en route* from Montreal to Bombay via London, vanished from radar screens 120 miles to the west of Ireland. Whatever happened occurred so suddenly that the captain was unable to send out a mayday alarm. All of the 329 people on board were killed. Suspicion was immediately directed at Sikh extremist groups in Canada: indeed two of them actually alleged that they were responsible. However, when the bodies were recovered, they revealed no traces of an explosion, and nor did the voice and flight recorders that, three weeks later, were recovered from the ocean bed. But these pieces of equipment depend upon the aircraft's electricity. Once this has been put out of action, they become useless.

If terrorism had not been the cause, what alternatives were there? The Boeing 747 is not only a tough aeroplane; it is also very forgiving. As an aviation expert told me:

It is terribly difficult for a captain to lose complete control of an aircraft of this kind without being able at least to say something over the radio. Furthermore, the 747 is highly aerodynamic. Not long ago, one of them plunged from about 41,000 feet to about 20,000 feet over Los Angeles before the pilot regained control. This was entirely due to the aircrew climbing the aircraft to an altitude where, fully loaded, it became unstable — that's to say that the difference in speed between flying and stalling was only about 10 knots. This aeroplane had a flame-out on one engine — due, it seems, to injudicious fuel adjustment by the crew — and it went into a roll after stalling. The captain, for some reason, had left it on the automatic pilot, and the crew then tried every desperate remedy — such as lowering the undercarriage, putting on flaps, and all sorts of other panic measures. Because of the G-strain, they resulted in undercarriage tyres flying off and doors getting opened.

None of this altered the fact that, by the time the Boeing had come down to 20,000 feet, its aerodynamic qualities had re-asserted themselves, and it virtually flew itself back on to an even keel. The crew were then able to take over and fly normally. When all these jolly japes occurred, the aeroplane was in cloud, and it is quite clear that the crew became disorientated and didn't believe their instruments. This has really nothing to do with Air India, but it does show that the 747 is quite capable of flying itself out of trouble — even when the crew does its best to screw things up.

Structural failure was, of course, a possibility, though there was an obvious reluctance to accept this. There are, after all, more than 600 of these aircraft in service. To ground the lot would play havoc with airline schedules and finances. As time went by, it began to seem as if, far from fearing that the disaster was caused by a bomb, there were some who hoped that it might have been. The alternative seemed to be even more fearful. One newspaper (the *Daily Mail*) even printed the hypothesis that the Air India plane had been hit by debris from a Soviet space craft that had not completely burned up while re-entering the atmosphere. This was quickly denied. Re-entry had taken place on the previous day, and the scene of the episode was not the North Atlantic, but somewhere in Brazil.

At the time of writing, the investigation continues. Conceivably the matter will never be solved. Nevertheless, the very fact that terrorism was originally assumed to be the cause is an uncomfortable reminder that aircraft are more vulnerable than ships, and that aircraft carry the overwhelming majority of passengers between Europe and North America.*

How very different things were in 1912. In *The Power House*, written by John Buchan in 1913 (though not published in book form until 1916), the villain observes that 'Modern life is the silent compact of comfortable folk to keep up pretences. And it will succeed till the day comes when there is another compact to strip them bare.' Some sixty years later, there were several such: the PLO, the Baader Meinhof gang, the Red Brigades, Black September, the IRA, and so on. The last of these, as Seinn Fein, already existed at the time of the *Titanic*, though its members certainly did not have the technical exper-

---

* Shortly before the proofs of this book went to press, a short newspaper item, on 14 March 1986, announced that a judicial panel in New Delhi had decided that a bomb was to blame.

tise to threaten a ship such as this. Nor would they have wished to. Many of its steerage passengers were Irish emigrants on their way to America: victims of a condition that provided a breeding ground for such underground organizations. As for the rest (again to quote Buchan), 'A few illiterate bandits in a Paris slum defy the world, and in a week they are in jail. Half a dozen crazy Russian *intellectuels* in Geneva conspire to upset the Romanovs, and they are hunted down by the police of Europe.'

No: terrorism could not have been taken seriously as a threat, and a not especially efficient confidence trickster such as Landisi would never have thought it worth trying to ransom the pride of the White Star Line.

It was, no doubt, as well. Deliverance could not have been dropped from the sky: even communications would have been a problem. And, after all, the toll of lives was great enough in all conscience when, so to say, the infernal device was as unsophisticated as an iceberg: one of countless calved in the Davis Strait, and drifting unheedingly on a collision course with a liner driven by a captain intent upon getting to New York on time.

The Coast Guard's Story

On 15 April 1924, a dozen years exactly after the death of the *Titanic*, the United States Coast Guard cutter *Modoc* steamed to the point in the North Atlantic where the great liner sank. The United States ensign fluttered at her stern, surmounted by the flag of the Red Cross. Her complement lowered their heads in prayer as a chaplain conducted a memorial service. This may be unremarkable: it was one of many held for the dead of that dark (in all senses) April night of 1912. Nor did it have the thought-provoking qualities of those moments on 12 June 1967, when the Cunarder *Scotia*, eastbound for England, hove-to at the same place. Towards the end of his life, Joseph Grove Boxhall, one-time fourth officer of the *Titanic*, expressed a wish to join his comrades who had perished with the ship. Mr Boxhall had recently died and here, at the scene of what must have been his most unhappy memory, his ashes were committed to the deep.

A more interesting matter than the service conducted on board the *Modoc* is the photograph of it. A few cables from the stern of the ship, a tolerably large iceberg is loitering. Sharply rising to a tall peak in the middle, it might seem to resemble a church with its spire in the centre. Alternatively, and less fancifully, it could be regarded as a small island rising to a climactic pinnacle. Its likeness to the berg photographed all those years ago by a passenger in the German liner *Prinz Adalbert* is amazing. There is, of course, no strip of red paint (assumed to have rubbed off from the *Titanic*) running along the waterline, and there are small differences in matters of detail. But these could be explained by the angle from which the shot was taken, or else by erosion.

Were it not for the fact that the authenticity of both pictures has been attested by those whose integrity is impeccable, one might suspect foul play. For even a moderately able re-toucher, it would not have been difficult to add or subtract the red line and to modify slightly the berg's appearance. But one cannot presume to question the good faith of the United States Coast Guard, which issued what we might, perhaps, refer to as Picture A. Similarly, any attempt to cast doubts upon the veracity of Picture B, which appears in Walter Lord's *A Night to Remember* (possibly *the* book about the *Titanic*) might understandably result in a libel action initiated by Mr Lord.

Even so, the coincidence is singular: so singular that it is tempting to invest it with the supernatural. This, of course, one cannot do. Supernatural explanations are the last resort of the researcher who cannot find any plausible reason. The most one can do is to draw it to your attention, and to report that the best of several versions of Picture A appears in Harold Waters's *Adventure Unlimited* (reproduced here).

Harold Waters served for many years in the United States Coast Guard. He enlisted in 1922 and his first ship was the same *Modoc* — a cutter 240 feet long and manned by a crew of eighty. Among them was an official ice observer, Lieutenant Edward H. Smith USCG (commonly known as 'Iceberg' Smith and, later, to become Rear-Admiral Smith). To fit himself for his task, Lieutenant Smith had studied oceanography and meteorology at Harvard, at the Geophysical Institute in Bergen and at the British Meteorological Office. The International Ice Patrol had only been in existence for a matter of ten years, but it was clearly taking its responsibilities extremely seriously. Indeed, it had already experimented with methods of demolishing bergs, but all of them — and they included the application of chemicals, gunfire, and mines and other explosives — had failed. They had not even reduced the sizes of these floating hazards. The most that any patrol could do was to

report their dimensions, their apparent course, and their rate
of drift. Their demolition would ultimately be effected by
nature — once they had passed south of the line (known as the
'Cold Wall') that is the meeting place of the Labrador Current
and the Gulf Stream.

On one patrol, the *Modoc* encountered a massive berg,
which the crew appropriately dubbed 'Big Boy'. It was 305 feet
tall, 820 feet long, and 'Iceberg' Smith judged its weight to be
about two million tons. The cutter dutifully tagged along
behind it. As it made its way farther into the waters of the Gulf
Stream, the process of disintegration began. Almost as if it was
determined to ensure the survival of its species, its first act was
to calve and thereby produce growlers that presently floated
away into the distance.

The death of a large berg, if we are to believe Mr Waters, is
dauntingly impressive: Armageddon on a small scale, an erup-
tion of rage by nature, call it what you will.

... at noon of the fourth day [he writes] ... a mighty convul-
sion, preceded by ear-splitting salvoes, brought thousands of
tons of ice hurtling down from aloft to make the sea boil
with their splashes. The tumult gave no sign of ceasing as
Big Boy groaned at the cracking that was rending him apart.
The huge dome split and plummeted into the sea with a
splash that set a miniature tidal wave in motion.

Big Boy, his stability irreparably disturbed, began rolling
slowly, causing more thousands of tons of ice to break away.
The calving continued until Big Boy, losing equilibrium,
rolled completely over, threshing and heaving like a mortally
stricken giant as he lashed the sea into a welter of white-
foaming frenzy.

Big Boy had passed his cup.

The spectacle of one of these potential killers seemingly
dying in agony might be pleasing to those seeking revenge for
the *Titanic*'s loss. But a berg, one sometimes has to remind
oneself, is an inanimate object, the debris of a glacier that has
snapped off into the sea. The berg did not run into the *Titanic*;
the *Titanic* ran into the berg.

An official of Her Majesty's Coastguard in Britain has

described its United States counterpart as 'the seventh largest navy in the world'. Its responsibilities include search-and-rescue, countering oil pollution, fishery protection, foiling illegal attempts to immigrate, the combat of smuggling, and the defence of the United States coastline in times of war. Unlike similar authorities in other parts of the world, it is completely self-sufficient, with its own aircraft as well as its own ships. Comparing it with the British Coastguard, my informant said:

> Be careful of quoting the UK's system of doing things: it is fairly unique. It's like so many other things in this dear old country of ours, it has evolved over centuries. It is not a pattern that other nations tend to follow. If the UK was a newly independent country, and you had a bagful of money and you wished to set yourself up with an organization, you'd probably go for a microcosm of the American system. You want to scale down the American Coast Guard by about one hundred, and you're getting somewhere near what you want. In fact, we recommend anyone who comes to us for advice not to use our system. Apart from its number of roles and its enormous size, the thing about the United States Coast Guard is that it has all its own resources. It has a navy. It has helicopters. It has patrol aircraft. It has Coast Guard cutters. It has the lot. As I said, it is entirely self-sufficient.

Because it did not exist in its present form, the United States Coast Guard played no part in the *Titanic* incident. But, even if all those resources had been available, its contribution would have been limited. As the British Coastguard representative explained:

> So far as rescuing people from large passenger ships in the middle of the Atlantic is concerned, only two things have changed in principle from 1912. One is that, unlike the *Titanic*, every passenger-carrying ship has more lifeboat and life-raft capacity than there are souls on board — which the *Titanic* certainly didn't. The other point is that, although radio existed in 1912, the advance in modern communications gives you an infinitely better chance of getting the

information to the shore authorities who are going to organize the rescue — and getting it there very much more quickly. What has not changed is that, out at that range — although you might be able to get an aircraft out in pretty short order for co-ordination — an aircraft cannot land on the sea. It cannot rescue anybody physically. You're still going to have to muster merchant ships from wherever to pick up the survivors. There's nothing else you can do. There are still no short cuts to recovery at sea.

Just so: but had it been possible to co-ordinate the ships in the vicinity of the *Titanic* that night, the story might have had a very much happier ending, despite the shortage of lifeboats. It was, after all, something of a fluke that the *Carpathia*'s wireless operator happened to pick up the distress signal — and an accident of mismanagement that the *Californian*'s did not. Had the *Carpathia* not chanced to hear the call for help, it seems doubtful whether there would have been any survivors at all. Nowadays, things are very much better organized and so, you might say, they need to be. Whilst communications have gone far beyond the dreams of people like Marconi, the North Atlantic's itinerant population has diminished considerably. Compared with nowadays, the North Atlantic was thronged with ships on the night of 14-15 April 1912. So long as the ice allows it, the *Stefan Batory* plods across from Europe to Montreal — just (for her days are numbered) as her successor will. The *QE2* makes about a dozen round trips a year, which can hardly be described as a regular service. And that disposes of the passenger ships. There are, of course, freighters. But, just as Brunel realized well over a century ago, larger ships are more economical than small ones. That lesson has sunk in, with the result that today's vessels are bigger and fewer. The trade routes of the North Atlantic are no longer well-trod highways, but rather lonely places — even though they are used by more merchantmen than, say, those across the Pacific, or the South Atlantic, or any other ocean you may think of. Indeed, HM Coastguard's representative went so far as to say that 'If you are anywhere near one of the main routes between Europe and North America, you have a reasonable expectation that there'll be somebody around. If you are somewhere off-beat like the southern point of Greenland, or get into trouble in the Iceland–Faroe gap, that might be more exciting for you.'

As the survival of the *Bermuda Sky Queen*'s occupants in 1947 so successfully demonstrated, a flying-boat might be preferred to a land-based aircraft for the search-and-rescue business. Given reasonable conditions, it seems logical to suppose, it could carry out both functions: find the casualty from the more revealing vantage point of the sky and, having done so, land on the water and pick up survivors. But flying-boats are no longer manufactured, and a fundamental about such operations is that conditions very seldom are 'reasonable'. High winds and steep waves would almost certainly make landings and take-offs impossible. In this respect, the *Bermuda Sky Queen*'s safe arrival on the very disturbed sea by Ocean Station 'Charlie' was something that makes one inclined to consider the possibility of miracles. Nevertheless, a flying-boat is something that, by its very nature, has been designed to float. A land-based aeroplane has not. When, during the between-war years, the heavyweight boxing champion Max Baer flew the Atlantic, he stuffed the wings of his aircraft with ping-pong balls — thinking that they would increase its powers of flotation. Happily, the idea was not put to the test. However, in October 1956, a Pan American clipper thumped down with a large splash in the sea not far from Ocean Station 'November' (then occupied by the cutter *Ponchartrain.*) Against all laws of probability, the thirty-one people on board were rescued. One's speculation about miracles intensifies.

In fact, to return (if briefly) to the point, the United States Coast Guard did use HU-16 Albatross flying-boats for nearly thirty-two years — not to mention other species of this amphibious breed. Referring to them affectionately as the 'Goat', the Coast Guard invested in 464 of these machines, which, between them, put in a total of half a million flying hours and gave a very good account of themselves. But these were essentially medium-range aircraft that would have had no business to stray into the mid-Atlantic. Their rescue capability was shown particularly well when they hauled fleeing Cubans from the Straits of Florida in the great exodus of the 1960s and, later, in the early part of the present decade. (The ability

of an escaping Cuban to distinguish between what might be
seaworthy, and what all too apparently was not, appears to
have been slight.) Significantly, five members of the Albatross
tribe have since been converted to carry twenty-eight passengers apiece, and are now employed on an inter-island
service in the Bahamas and over the Caribbean.

So, in the very deep sea, the agent of deliverance must be a
ship.

Closer inshore, from an aerial point of view, the mechanical
functionaries of search-and-rescue are helicopters. The United
States Coast Guard has its own — just as it has everything else
(HH-3F Sikorsky Pelicans for medium-range work, and HH-
65A Dolphins for short range). The Canadian Coast Guard
lifts off from the ground with assistance from the Federal
Department of Defense (though it is self-sufficient in terms of
cutters, icebreakers, and so on), and HM Coastguard in Britain
has one — a Sikorsky S61 chartered from Bristow Helicopters
Ltd. It is stationed at Sumburgh on Shetland; the crews are
provided by Bristows.

But this is by no means the sum of these machines at the
Coastguard's disposal. The others are provided by the RAF
and the Royal Navy. They are stationed at twelve aerodromes
sited at reasonably regular intervals around the coasts of
England, Wales and Scotland. During the daytime, they are on
fifteen minutes' standby, though they invariably become
airborne in less time (between three and five minutes for a
Wessex; five and seven minutes for a Sea King). At night, it
takes longer, though it is normally within one hour.

The Westland Sea King can carry twenty survivors and can
fly for six hours (about 600 miles) without refuelling. But this
— and it applies to all helicopters, whatever the type — can be
extended by a kind of aviation opportunism. For example, a
while back, a Sea King recovered a casualty 450 miles from its
base, making a total distance of 900 miles. The scene of the
disaster was a point well to the west of Ireland. 'Refuelling at
intermediate points — such as forward fuel dumps, oil and gas
rigs, and forward airfields whether at home or in other
countries — can take one quite a long way', said a representative of the Ministry of Defence, Air. 'In this case, the helicopter picked up fuel in the Irish Republic and from a gas rig

off the south-west coast of Ireland. It did this on its way out to the incident, and on the flight back. On another occasion, a single-engined Whirlwind, which has a normal endurance of two and a half hours, managed a seven-hour sortie in the North Sea by "rig-hopping".'

As this may suggest, the matter of search-and-rescue at sea is one in which nations really do co-operate. The same member of the Ministry of Defence cited a case in which a ferry almost went aground off the coast of Northern Ireland in 1983.

Because of the number of passengers involved, several helicopters were employed from the UK mainland. The Dutch, the Danes, and other Continental countries heard that this was going on, and said: 'If you've got problems on your east coast, we will detach forces to cover for you.' They were prepared to come into our territory — our airspace — and to take over our responsibility, to help us out.

The same officer pointed out that, with their limited range and capacity, helicopters are only a panacea.

In the case of a large shipping catastrophe, the remedy has got to be other ships. Within their range, helicopters are ideal for evacuating seriously injured people in reasonably small numbers, or for bringing out specialized fire-fighting equipment. They are rather like British Rail's Red Star parcel service: if you want something urgently and can't get it quickly by other methods, a helicopter will do the job for you. But if you want to get a thousand people out of a burning passenger ship, don't ask helicopters to do it. They can't. You'd have to get them out of the sea by some other means.

Nevertheless, there was an instance in October 1980 when helicopters, working with US Coast Guard cutters, saved the lives of 500 people. The Dutch cruise liner *Prinsendam* caught fire in stormy seas two hundred miles off Sitka in the Gulf of Alaska. Most of the passengers were elderly, but they and the crew were lifted off by a fleet of four United States Coast Guard helicopters, one contributed by the US Navy and two from Canada. They were deposited on the US Coast Guard cutter *Boutwell* and on the tanker *Williamsburgh.* No lives were lost. The *Prinsendam* sank seven days later.

A successful operation such as this clearly owes much to the discipline of those who are rescued, and the senior citizens on board the *Prinsendam* must have conducted themselves well. As the man from HM Coastguard said:

> Whether your passengers will panic is something you just do not know. It is assumed that the ship's officers will be able to control panic and that they will get the survivors to safety, but you can't prove it. One of the problems is that, if you have any form of accident to the ship that involves a list, you may jam the high-side lifeboats in their davits, and you may not be able to get anybody aboard the low-side lifeboats because they are swinging several feet away from the ship. So, yes: there is a problem of evacuating the ship in an orderly manner. No matter how well you prepare for it, you'll only find out whether it works on the day.

The case of the *Andrea Doria* is possibly the best example of its working; that of the *Morro Castle*, of its failure. In the first instance, the conduct of the liner's crew was admirable; in the second, deplorable. Similarly, and years earlier than both cases, the loss of the Lamport and Holt liner *Vestris* (10,494 tons) might have produced fewer deaths had the master, Captain W.J. Carey, exercised more control over his men. But, then, Captain Carey made a lot of mistakes on 12 November 1928.

Built in 1912, the *Vestris* was beginning to show her age. There is evidence to suggest that her hull was leaking and that, on this voyage from New York that should have ended at Buenos Aires, she was overloaded (to mention only one thing, she was carrying 80 tons of coal in addition to the standard 2,769 tons). However, she carried eight lifeboats with a total capacity of 800, which was more than sufficient to accommodate the crew and the 128 passengers on board.

She was 350 miles off Chesapeake Bay, when she ran into bad weather and the coal shifted. By the following morning, the wind had moderated, but the liner had now developed a 32° list to starboard. By ten o'clock, it had become even more pronounced and at last Carey decided to abandon ship. Previously, he had been busy reassuring people that 'there is nothing to worry about'. Indeed, it was not until 9.15 that he instructed the radio officer to send out a distress signal.

The US Coast Guard ship *Tucker* (a veteran four-funnelled destroyer left over from the First World War) was three hundred miles away, but there were other vessels closer to hand: the German liner *Berlin*, the French oil tanker *Myriam*, the freighter *American Shipper*, and the United States battle-ship *Wyoming*. Had there been an orderly evacuation, there seems to have been no reason why the majority of those on board the *Vestris* should not have survived — in spite of the fact that the boats on the port side had been smashed against the hull.

But there was nothing orderly about the leaving of the *Vestris*. The crew rushed the boats on the starboard side and few of the male passengers seemed reluctant to follow them. As a result, only eight women and no children came out of it alive. Captain Carey, seemingly bemused by the awfulness of the situation and in combat with his conscience, remarked to a stoker, 'My God, my God, I am not to blame for this', and then walked into the sea. He was not, the stoker observed, wearing a life-jacket. But then, quite possibly, it might not have been of any avail. The liner had scarcely settled, when a crowd of sharks swam on to the scene and applied themselves to a meal such as few sharks enjoy.

The *Berlin* picked up 23 survivors, the *Myriam* 53, the *Wyoming* 9. By the time the *Tucker* reached the spot, there were only the dead to be recovered — and not many of them. The Coast Guards plucked ten bodies from the sea by using grappling irons.

So far as search-and-rescue are concerned, the North Atlantic is divided up into zones of responsibility. Whilst they do not overlap, the rescue agency of one nation often enters another's to help out. On the western side, it is shared by Canada and the United States. In mid-ocean, either the USA, Canada, or the UK is involved — depending upon where the casualty is; and, on the European side, Norway, Britain, Ireland, France and Spain shoulder the task. The British zone extends westwards to a line running from 61°N 30°W to 45°N 30°W — in other words along the 30° longitude beginning at a point to the south-west of Iceland and coming to an end many miles to the west of and just to the north of Spain's northern coast. However, a chunk is removed from this pattern by France's responsibility for the Bay of Biscay.

From the representative of HM Coastguard:

> Within a search-and-rescue region, if the matter is a marine casualty, the government concerned is obliged by international convention to mount an efficient rescue operation. How it is done is entirely up to that government. Our own is a signatory to the convention and we supply a service. The co-ordination for marine incidents is provided by Her Majesty's Coastguard — all of them civil servants belonging to the Department of Transport. In the case of aircraft, the Ministry of Defence has the entire responsibility for rescuing aviators from the sea. Similarly, the Coastguard has entire responsibility for rescuing mariners from the sea.

To create the equivalent of the US Coast Guard, the British Department of Transport would require contributions from the Royal Navy, the Royal Air Force, HM Customs and Excise, as well as from Trinity House (like HM Coastguard, it comes under the Marine Branch of the Department of Trade: it is responsible for lights around the coast of the UK and for pilotage), and the Royal National Lifeboat Institution. It would also — as it does now — have to exercise its own powers to enforce legislation concerning the safety of ships and those who sail in them.

Since the US Coast Guard is so self-sufficient, it is tempting to see it as something that was designed in one piece. This would be wrong. It, too, evolved as one responsibility was placed upon another. With its role of protecting the revenue against smugglers dating back to 1790, it can rejoice in whatever glory there is to be had from being the first of anything — in this instance, the first sea-going arm of the United States government (the US Navy was not created until later). In 1849, the US Life-Saving Service was established. After the search for icebergs had been added to the quest for contraband-runners in 1914, the two services were amalgamated as the United States Coast Guard in 1915.

But this, perhaps, is to oversimplify the matter. According to an official history, the service is an amalgamation of five federal agencies: the individual states (which assumed responsibility for warning lights as long ago as 1716), the Justice Department (which became perturbed by the number of lives lost by boilers exploding in the early steamboats and, in 1838, decided to institute a system of inspection), the Department of Commerce (at one time in charge of the Bureau of Navigation), the Treasury Department (which created the Life-Saving Service in 1841 but kept it separate from the Revenue Cutter Service until 1915), the Department of Transport, and the Navy (which took over the Coast Guard in the two world wars). Nowadays, the service is answerable to the US Treasury — except when the safety of the nation is in jeopardy, or that of some other nation (such as South Vietnam).

To anyone weaned, as I was, on the late and very much lamented *Blackwood's Magazine*, it is impossible not to digress when writing about the United States and Canadian Coast Guard services. Their histories are packed with what used to be called 'good yarns'. In the case of the former, for instance, the perils confronting lighthouse keepers were not entirely confined to those created by the sea — though that, in all conscience, was hazard enough. To quote from *Coast Guard History*, 'Tens of lighthouses have been crushed and washed away. This was a common occurrence in the southern United States during the 19th century, where construction preceded technology.' Red Indians may seem to be a less probable source of danger: if one is to judge by motion pictures, they seem to have lived inland — mostly on rough, scrubby, ground with an obligatory range of mountains in the distance. But this is obviously misleading as John W.B. Thompson found to his cost on 23 July 1836.

Mr Thompson was keeper of the light on Cape Florida. At four o'clock that afternoon, he was walking towards his living quarters when he noticed a large body of Indians about twenty yards from him. They seemed to be hostile: the house was some distance away, and he could see that the wisest thing was to turn round and retreat into the lighthouse. He broke into a run. 'At that moment,' he recalled, 'they discharged a volley of rifle balls, which cut my clothes and hat and perforated the door.' By good fortune, they did not perforate Mr Thompson

— though, as the warriors crowded closer, he had some difficulty in forcing his way inside.

By expending a good many rounds of ammunition, he managed to keep them away until nightfall, but their determination to do away with Mr Thompson and his light was far from exhausted. Under cover of darkness, they set fire to the door and an adjacent window. Then they fired bullets into the tanks containing 225 gallons of oil, which promptly unburdened themselves of their contents. His bedding was drenched and so was his clothing ('In fact, everything I had was soaked in oil'). He retreated to the top of the tower with small hope of survival.

> At last [he wrote] the awful moment arrived, the crackling flames burst around me. The savages at the same time began their hellish yells ... The lantern was now full of flame, the lamps and glasses bursting and flying in all directions, my clothes on fire, and to move from the place where I was, would be met by instant death from their rifles. My flesh was roasting, and to put an end to my horrible suffering I got up and threw the keg of gunpowder down the scuttle. Instantly, it exploded and shook the tower from top to bottom. It had not the desired effect of blowing me to eternity.

But the fire presently died down; and the Indians, believing that Thompson was dead, had no further business to transact. They departed. Next day, a rescue party arrived.

John W.B. Thompson's experience, unpleasant though it was, seemed to suggest that, if one had to be in some sort of jeopardy, the hostile forces of humanity were less harmful than those of nature. He did at least survive and so (though rather charred and battered) did the light. During 1893, three lighthouses in the area of Chesapeake Bay did not. They were removed without trace by ice. In 1906, no fewer than twenty-three lighthouses on the shores of the Gulf of Mexico were erased by a hurricane which, while it was about it, removed Sand Island from the map as well. In that same year, California's Point Arena lighthouse was dismantled by an earthquake, but this was worth hardly a paragraph of print compared to the immensity of the disaster that was taking place along the coast at San Francisco.

The most accident-prone lighthouse in United Kingdom waters is, beyond doubt, the Eddystone, fourteen miles south-south-west of Plymouth. The original Eddystone, elaborately elegant in appearance, was the work of a civil engineer and engraver named Henry Winstanley. Mr Winstanley seems to have been almost as prone to misfortune as his creation. For instance, one day in June 1697 — a year after construction had begun — the warship normally supplied by the Admiralty to patrol the area failed to turn up. Taking advantage of this lapse, a French privateer sailed on to the scene, fired a few shots at the emerging structure (which was enough to reduce it to a pile of smouldering timber), took Winstanley prisoner, and darted back to France. The architect of Eddystone was detained there for two weeks, and then released on the orders of Louis XIV.

Once you have settled on an idea, it may be as well to stick to it. The devastation of the privateer's guns had compelled Winstanley and his builders to begin all over again. But the lapse of time had given the engineer pause for thought. Was, he wondered, his original concept sufficiently high? In 1699, he came to the bold conclusion that it was not. Throwing caution to the winds, he extended it to a prodigious one hundred feet. The idea was ambitious, but it overlooked whatever the laws are governing stress and suchlike. No doubt the extension enabled the light to be seen from farther away, but it also reduced the structure's stability. This became gruesomely clear in 1703, when a tempest wrought havoc in much of southern England. Winstanley probably welcomed it at first, for he had boasted that he would like to be out there in 'the greatest storm that ever was'. Well: it had arrived at last. At first the bad weather made it impossible for him to visit his creation and he fretted impatiently at Plymouth. At last, on the afternoon of 26 November, the wind seemed to be abating. Despite warnings from local mariners that the trip he had in mind would be foolish, he set off for the rock with a boatload of workmen and some supplies. There seems little doubt that he got there safely; but, just after midnight, the Eddystone light went out. Next morning, all that remained of Winstanley's masterpiece were a few twisted iron girders. Of the man himself, the workmen, and the keepers, there was no trace.

In 1709, another lighthouse was built to warn mariners of the perils of Eddystone rock. The architect this time was a man named John Rudyerd. It survived until 1755, when something went grievously wrong with the lanterns. They set fire to the tower which blazed for a while and then collapsed in ashes.

John Smeaton, who was responsible for what we might call Eddystone Mark IV, was more successful. He produced his design in 1759 and, to his eternal credit, it endured for 120 years. When, at last, it was judged to be unsafe, it was carefully taken to pieces, leaving only the stump behind. The rest was re-erected on Plymouth Hoe as a memorial to Smeaton. Work on the final version (for the time being, at any rate) was begun on another part of the rock in 1878 and completed in 1882. By no means the least of its virtues was a massive foundation, enabling its light to flash its warning (two white flashes at ten-second intervals) from a height of 135 feet above mean high water and, in clear weather, giving it range of nearly eighteen miles.

To include a mention of lighthouses in matters relating to the *Titanic* and the perils of the North Atlantic may seem to be a digression. But an ocean, like most questions, has two sides of it. The coastlines, indeed, are usually the most dangerous places of all. In 1837 the United States Congress authorized the President 'to cause public vessels to cruise upon the coast in the severe portion of the season to afford such aid to distressed navigators as their circumstances and necessities may require; and such public vessels shall go to sea prepared fully to render such assistance.' Since, during the days of wooden hulls and sails, most disasters occurred close inshore, it might, perhaps, be regarded as the beginning of search-and-rescue. Certainly during the mid-nineteenth century, when the emigration industry from Europe was at its height, such prudence paid off. Many of the overcrowded ships approaching New York were at the mercy of the strong north-easterly winds that seemed dedicated to the destruction of these vessels by sweeping them on to the New Jersey shore. It was, indeed, the extent of this maritime carnage that brought about the genesis of the federal life-saving service in 1848. This, in its turn, led to the building of lifeboats — although, in Britain, they had been in operation for well over fifty years and the Royal National Lifeboat Institution had been established in 1824. The tales of the doughty little vessels are many and various, and they have been more than adequately told elsewhere. It would, however, be a shame to omit the story of that January night in 1899, when a ship found itself in difficulties in Porlock Bay, Somerset. Not least, it illustrates the proposition that, in order to go down to the sea in ships and occupy one's business in great waters, it is first of all necessary to get there.

Lynmouth lifeboat had the responsibility for dealing with the casualty, but a westerly gale was blowing: high seas were lashing the front of this tiny port and creating havoc in the harbour. It was impossible for the boat to put out from its base, so what alternative was there? Eventually somebody came up with the apparently impossible idea that it should be transported overland and launched from Porlock — a distance of more than ten miles, and the task made harder by having to climb from sea level to a clifftop several hundred feet high and then descending from it. In places, the gradient was one in four and a half. Banks had to be removed to make the path wide enough, trees felled and gateposts pulled out of the ground. The only illumination was by oil lamps. Nevertheless, the crew, aided by a band of voluntary helpers, accomplished the journey in ten and a quarter hours. They paused neither to eat nor to rest and when, at last, their craft was afloat, they were dreadfully tired. But they reached their target minutes before she sank, removed the crew to safety and brought them ashore.

Eight years earlier, on 18 January 1881, a brig named the *Visitor* had been driven ashore in Robin Hood's Bay, Yorkshire. A violent storm was raging and there were heavy falls of snow. The local lifeboat was unable to get off the beach, and after several attempts, it was decided that the Whitby boat — six miles away, but tolerably snug in the shelter of a harbour — might fare better. However (and this is a contradiction) it nonetheless seemed best to make the greater part of the journey overland. The distance, admittedly shorter than that of the Lynmouth epic, was made harder by thick snow, drifting to seven feet in places. Nor did the fact that it entailed ascending 500 feet to a clifftop help. Two hundred men and eighteen horses were involved; but, two hours later, the small vessel was ready for launching, and on the second attempt, she was floated off. The crew of the *Visitor* were rescued. The successful operation may have made some amends for a disaster that had occurred on the previous Saturday. On this occasion, the intrepid Whitby lifeboat crew and their helpers made a rather shorter trip by land — one and a half miles. The victim was the brig *Lumley*, which had been thrust on to Upgang rocks north-west of the town. By the time the rescuers arrived, all traces of the *Lumley* and her complement had been erased by the sea.

The Canadian Coast Guard can trace its origins back to a rescue station on Sable Island, where provisions and stores were kept ready for shipwrecked mariners. Sable Island, in case you are not familiar with it, lies two hundred miles eastwards from Halifax and might be described as the only member of the perfidious Newfoundland Grand Banks community that dare show its head above water. According to *The Nova Scotia Pilot*, it is 'formed of two nearly parallel ridges of sand, shaped by the wind into sandhills, which frequently change their positions; many of these sandhills terminate in steep cliffs, while others are fronted by grass, and terminate in broad beaches.' Apart from fishermen intent upon diminishing the island's population of walrus and seal, the people of Sable Island were mostly shipwrecked seamen who, having arrived there against their will, were unable to get away from the place.

In January 1798 the Governor of Nova Scotia detailed the schooner *Black Snake* to sail to the island, pick up its collection of castaways, and to leave behind a small party responsible for life-saving duties during the rest of the winter. One year later, or thereabouts, Sable Island suddenly found itself in the news — and the story was to have a weird sequel.

HRH Edward Augustus, Duke of Kent — the youngest son of George III and eventually to become father of Queen Victoria — arrived in Canada in 1799 to take up his duties as Commander-in-Chief of British North America. By some mismanagement, the Duke's departure preceded that of his staff and his possessions, which eventually set out across the Atlantic in a ship named the *Francis*. The *Francis* never reached her destination. By 1801, Sable Island had become invested with a bad reputation as base for pirates and wreckers. Clearly some rather more positive form of administration was needed, and the Nova Scotian authorities appointed a commission to consider the matter. As a result of its members' deliberations, a superintendent and four men, equipped with a portable house and a whaleboat, were ordered to take up residence. One of their first discoveries was that the *Francis* had gone aground on the shore: that everybody on board had died and that the Duke's treasures had been removed from the wreck.

Sable Island was not only treacherous to those who, heading for the mainland, wished to avoid it: it also endangered the schemes of those who actually wanted to land on it. When it was discovered that the superintendent and his gang of four had not entirely put an end to the islanders' misdeeds, a Captain Torrens was detached from the garrison at Halifax and sent out to investigate. The Torrens story has never been completely authenticated, but it seems that, instead of making a more conventional landing, his ship was wrecked on the sands. There is no record of what happened to the crew, but presently we find the army officer and his dog sheltering in a hut constructed from flotsam found on the beach. One night (or so the legend has it) he was visited by a woman dressed in white. Her hair was in a mess and she held out a hand draped with seaweed. The dog — as dogs are supposed to do when confronted by the supernatural — showed every sign of fear. Torrens, looking more closely at his strange visitor, noticed that one of her fingers had been cut off, and that blood was pouring from the wound. He opened a first aid pack that he had taken from the wreck and was about to apply a bandage when, as suddenly as she had come, the lady vanished. He searched the vicinity of the hut, but there was no sign of her.

On his return to Nova Scotia, Torrens conceived the idea that some survivors from the *Francis* had managed to get ashore, taking pieces of jewellery with them. Eventually, pursuing the investigation, he discovered a family that had been evicted from Sable Island. The men were away in the fishing grounds off Labrador, but the women were in residence when Torrens visited the house. Artfully, he drew their

attention to the ring on one of his fingers and invited them to
admire it. The daughter of the family chipped in smartly by
saying that it was not one-half so good as the one that her
father had found on a woman's hand on Sable Island. Dogged
in his search for the truth, Torrens managed to discover that it
had been pledged to a Halifax watchmaker in return for a loan
of 20 shillings. Sure enough, when he called on the trader, the
ring was there, and Torrens bought it. He told the man that, if
any member of the former Sable Island family should wish to
buy it back, he must insist that they 'bring back the finger that
was cut off to get it'. The pawnbroker (for such he was) should
then report the matter to the garrison.

Nobody ever came to claim the ring, but a lady of the
garrison immediately recognized it. It had belonged, she said,
to a Mrs Copeland — the wife of an army surgeon who was in
charge of the Duke of Kent's servants on board the *Francis.*

Rather more germane to the theme of this book is the story
of the 2,300-ton Marseilles-registered *Douala* — a motor vessel
that found herself in trouble on 20 December 1963. She was
shipping water through a damaged hatch and, in the opinion of
her master, was in danger of sinking. According to his
reckoning, her position was about thirty miles south of Ramae,
an island off the southern coast of Newfoundland.

The weather conditions were appalling. The wind was
gusting to hurricane force, the sea was officially recorded as
'phenomenal', and frozen spray and flurries of snow were
cutting visibility to less than half a mile. Forty minutes after
the distress signal had been received, the Canadian Coast
Guard Service ship *Sir Humphrey Gilbert* (a diesel-driven
icebreaker that was also used to supply lighthouses) was
assigned to search for the French vessel.

At 5.50 on the following morning, the *Sir Humphrey Gilbert*
was herself in trouble. A barge carried on the foredeck broke
loose, slid across the hatch and crashed into the port bulwark.
There was minor damage to both the barge and the ship and,
with heavy icing, it took four hours before the craft was
secured and the Coast Guard vessel was able to get under way
again. By this time, the *Douala*'s captain had radioed that
matters had become critical indeed. At 11.52 a.m. he
announced that he was about to abandon ship.

Other vessels had also been looking for the casualty, but the given position was clearly inaccurate and the fact that the aerial had been damaged made her difficult to pin down by radio. Whenever the weather conditions allowed it, aircraft from three Royal Canadian Air Force bases joined in the search, and this was increased on the 22nd. At three o'clock that afternoon, one of them sighted a lifeboat. Fortunately, the *Sir Humphrey Gilbert* was not too far away. Her commander, Captain G.S. Burdock, reached the scene in thirty minutes; he took on board sixteen survivors, but failed to recover three bodies. Three hours later, a RCAF CP-107 Argus (a four-engined aeroplane then used for marine patrol and anti-submarine operations) located a second lifeboat. In this case, a fishing vessel named the *Rodrique* rescued three of the *Douala*'s crew. The master and seven other men were killed when trying to leave the fatally injured ship. One more died aboard the *Sir Humphrey Gilbert.*

The Coast Guard vessel landed the survivors at Port aux Basques, Newfoundland, at 4.30 that afternoon. Later, she sailed for the lighthouse on St Jacques Island, but the horror of those fearful December days was not yet over. When she arrived on the following morning, it was to discover that the store had been demolished by the wind, the two lightkeepers had been drowned, and the light was unattended.

The RCAF's Argus, which was descended from the Britannia turbo-prop airliner, has since been replaced by the CP140 Aurora, a version of the Lockheed P3. This, if aeroplanes can be likened to families, has a lineage that goes back to the Lockheed Electra. The Electra, unlike its offspring, was a civilian aircraft. As the Nimrod, which the RAF uses for long-distance search-and-rescue, its main purpose is anti-submarine warfare: or, to put it another way, it is essentially a military aircraft that can, in peacetime at any rate, be diverted to a more humane purpose.

As one writer very aptly entitled a novel, 'the rich are different'. The United States Coast Guard can afford to have its own aircraft for long-range search-and-rescue, and the task of combating submarines from the air is left to the United States Navy. For this purpose, the Coast Guard uses the HC-

130 Lockheed Hercules — possibly the most versatile flying machine ever to come off a drawing board. In most instances, however, it is employed as a military transport rather than as a warplane. With a cruising speed of 300 knots, it can remain in the sky for ten hours at a stretch and, in the case of the Coast Guard, carry 35,000 pounds of emergency equipment. For similar assignments beyond the range of shore-based helicopters, the British Coastguard relies on RAF Nimrods based at St Mawgan in Cornwall and at Kinross in Scotland.

The ancestry of the Nimrod can be traced back to the Comet civilian airliner, though it is not easy to see any resemblance. In *Combat Aircraft*, Bill Gunston observes that it 'surpasses all other aircraft in use for ocean patrol in speed, quietness, flight performance, reliability and all-round mission efficiency'. In theory, its economical cruising speed and its endurance of over nine hours mean that it can operate at long range: indeed, its range can be extended by using air-to-air refuelling. There have actually been instances in which a Nimrod has remained airborne for as long as eighteen hours. Its primary purpose is anti-submarine warfare; but, said the representative of the Ministry of Defence, Air:

> There is always a Nimrod available for search-and-rescue. If there is an incident out in the Atlantic, it's possible that there might be a Nimrod out there already, doing its other work. In which case, it could be diverted to the higher priority search-and-rescue task.
>
> Nimrod is very useful, because it has got long endurance; it can go fairly quickly out to any area; and it has lots of very good navigational equipment, radar, and other gear on board. Consequently, it can go to an accurate position and then search for a boat or whatever. It can do it at night, in fog, or at any other time, and it's got a huge communications system. Its crew can talk to the UK from anywhere, and update the co-ordinator of the rescue about what is going on.

In the case of the *QE2* bomb hoax, the conversation took place through the international radio telephone network — coming, so to speak, ashore at British Telecom's long-range station at Portishead in Somerset.

One Nimrod is always on one hour's stand-by for search-and-rescue duties. In practice, it is normally airborne well within the hour, and a back-up aircraft can be ready within six hours. In whatever case, its bomb bay is loaded with life-saving equipment — including food, medical supplies, rubber dinghies, and so on. Every item is colour-coded according to international convention. Consequently, the survivors down below know exactly what they are fishing out of the sea. They will, of course, owe their eventual survival to a ship, but this is not to underrate the Nimrod's importance. Quite apart from the fact that the supplies it drops may make all the difference between life and death, its presence means that, once found, the casualty will not be lost. Furthermore, by acting as an airborne communications centre, it can ensure that the rescue is properly co-ordinated.

For the commander of a ship, whether it is a merchantman or a man-of-war, there is nothing optional about going to the assistance of a vessel in difficulties. As the representative of HM Coastguard said:

All vessels are under an international obligation to respond to a distress call on international frequencies if they think they can assist. Once they've committed themselves, they cannot leave until they are dismissed by the rescue co-ordinating authority. So once you've acknowledged the signal; once you've said, 'I'm (say) forty miles away and I'm proceeding towards you', you have automatically committed yourself until the shore authority of whatever country is involved says, 'Thank you very much indeed. No more for you. Carry on.'

The headquarters of HM Coastguard are in the Marine Directorate of the Department of Transport in London. The work of search-and-rescue at sea is carried out by six regions (sub-divided into twenty-five districts) covering the whole of the United Kingdom. Each has a Marine Rescue Co-ordination Centre (MRCC) or sub-centre containing an operations room permanently manned by three duty officers, plus an emergency planning room, facilities for the press, and so on. The organization is responsible for keeping a radio watch on 156.8MHz Channel 16 — a VHF frequency for vessels within thirty miles, although the range can be greater depending on the height of the aerial. British Telecom attends to the other frequencies for ships in distress: 500KHz — usually for those of more than 1,600 gross tons carrying trained radio officers — and 2182KHz, for vessels without radio officers. All distress communications via satellite are handled at MRCC Falmouth. The signals actually arrive at the neighbouring UK Coast Earth Station on Goonhilly Down.

From HM Coastguard's representative:

MRCC Falmouth has the entire international system of satellite communications at its disposal, and anything at very long range automatically goes there. Anything else within 200 miles of the coast will be handled by the rescue centre nearest to it. The Royal Air Force has two Rescue Co-ordination Centres (RCCs): one northern and one southern, and our centres apply to whichever is appropriate. Our people up north call up Edinburgh; down south, Plymouth. The dividing line is 52°30′N. We cannot call out an aircraft independently; nor can an aircraft itself have the complete picture. For example, a man with appendicitis on a fishing boat doesn't necessarily have the same priority as a Jumbo jet crashed somewhere off the west coast, or a military fighter that has come down in the North Sea.

In any search-and-rescue operation, the first thing is to locate the casualty, which is not always easy. Not the least of the problems is that the master of the ship in distress may not know exactly where he is, as the Coastguard's representative described:

Sometimes you go to the reported position of a casualty and he isn't there. If the ship had anything quite as expensive as the navigational equipment on the *Royal Princess*, there'd be no difficulty. Unless there was an instant and total failure of all communication systems, you'd get an extremely good satellite position out of her — to within a couple of hundred feet. But if you have some old merchant ship that hasn't taken a star sight for four days, and hasn't got a satellite navigation system, you're back where you were in the days of the *Titanic*. You've got a better chance of getting a good position nowadays because of modern technology, but there's no guarantee that you'll get what you expect.

One system that has done much to improve the situation is known as AMVER (Automated Mutual Vessel Rescue System). It is run by the United States Coast Guard from a centre on Governor's Island in New York harbour. The gist of it is that any captain setting out across the Atlantic files the details of his trip — rather in the way a pilot files a flight plan. Thereafter, he reports any changes of course or speed. Using methods based on dead reckoning, a computer calculates the vessel's positions throughout the voyage — to which it can add other pertinent information, such as the radio watch schedule or whether there is a doctor on board.

From this mass of information, a recognized search centre of any nation can receive a computer-predicted print-out of all the ships in the vicinity of a casualty, and details of their capabilities. 'Suppose,' said the Coastguard representative,

Falmouth receives a message saying 'I've hit an iceberg and I'm sinking in Position X', one of the first things Falmouth will do will be to get in touch with the United States Coast Guard, asking 'What have you got on AMVER about merchant shipping in the area?' They may report back that they've got fifty ships within one hundred miles, each of them travelling on such-and-such a course, and at such-and-such a speed. This is no substitute for an all-stations alert, which you would have anyway. But the rescue co-ordination centre will have a very much better idea of what is likely to be able to assist — instead of just blind chance, not knowing who's where on the North Atlantic.

Smaller ships sometimes vanish without trace; large ones seldom do. Their world disintegrates; but it is hoped that, among the vestiges remaining on the surface, there are lifeboats and life-rafts carrying people. Tracing them is obviously harder than finding the ship herself. 'It depends on how accurate the position was initially, and how long the life-rafts have been in the water,' explained the representative of the Ministry of Defence,

The action of wind and water on these small craft is very

complex, and a considerable mathematical effort has to go into working out where any given one of them would have gone in a certain sea state over a period of time. And, of course, it doesn't drift in a straight line. This gives you a rapidly expanding area to search. It isn't just a question of flying out to Point X and finding it. It isn't as simple as that: you could search for days looking for a life-raft or a lifeboat that was reported as being in a certain position at a certain time.

Nowadays, lifeboats are painted in distinctive colours that show up better against the surface of the ocean — unlike white, which used to be the custom in most cases, and which could easily be mistaken for a wave cap. Pigeons, it seems, have a particular aptitude for spotting them. In the May–June 1983 issue of *Naval Aviation News*, a report was published of a project code-named SEA HUNT that was carried out by the United States Coast Guard Office of Research and Development. Studies had revealed that these birds had a search-rate ability superior to that of man, and that they could process a much larger proportion of the visual field in the same amount of time. It had also transpired that they could be taught to respond to the colours red, yellow and orange (the regulations insist that boats and rafts are painted in 'some highly visible colour'. Orange, generally, is preferred). But this was not the end of their education. A special pod, large enough to contain three of the birds was attached to the underside of an H-52 helicopter. The 'observers' were placed inside it with overlapping fields of vision: one facing roughly at ten o'clock, another at two o'clock, and the third at six o'clock. Whenever one or another of them sighted a red, yellow or orange object, it was schooled to peck at a key, which closed a switch and turned on an indicating light in the cockpit. The pigeons detected the targets in eighty out of eight-nine cases. The flight crew, on the other hand, scored only thirty-four out of eighty-nine. For good measure, the birds spotted the target before their human colleagues in sixty-seven out of eighty cases.

In the early sixties, they shot a satellite into the air, and it didn't fall to earth. Instead, it went into orbit and, so far as I know, it is still there. Since then, the ironmongery of space has proliferated. Some of it is useful; some, perhaps, less so (this is not the proper place to debate the question of cable TV and whether Third World communities' concept of The World Beyond should be based on *Dallas*). What is certain is that this technological achievement has already shown a great potential for the protection of life on the great waters.

The media, it often seems, has an insatiable appetite for bad news. The fact that the governments of the United States and the Soviet Union are in conflict about the use of outer space as a battleground receives more than enough publicity. Very much less, on the other hand, is heard about a system in which East and West work together in perfect harmony — to the benefit of mariners and aviators in distress. It is known as SARSAT/COSPAS. SARSAT stands for 'Search and Rescue Satellite-Aided Tracking'. COSPAS says more or less the same thing in Russian. Work on the former began in 1976 as a joint venture between the US and Canada — joined, in the following year, by France. To judge by the timing of subsequent events, Soviet technicians were already thinking along similar lines. In 1980, the East and West set up a joint project team.

On 30 June 1982, COSPAS I was launched, and, six weeks later, it became operational. During the early part of 1983, SARSAT I made its journey into space as part of the US National Oceanic and Atmospheric Administration (NOAA)'s programme. COSPAS II and SARSAT II followed within a few months, and the coverage of the globe was complete. In its early days, SARSAT was a project involving the United States and Canada as partners. The latter nation was chiefly interested in its application to crashed aircraft; as a document issued by the Canadian Coast Guard's Search and Rescue Headquarters pointed out:

A study performed by the US Interagency Committee for search and rescue shows a 60 per cent survival chance for aircraft survivors if recovery is within eight hours. After forty-eight hours, the chance of survival is only 10 per cent. During one four-year period in Canada, twenty-nine aircraft were never located after being overdue. In Canada's cold marine environment, detection and location time are even more critical since survival time is a matter of a few hours at most. In these cases, it is hoped SARSAT will be of great benefit in reducing detection, location, and mission time.

What is good for the victims of an air disaster is no less beneficial for those of a ship in distress. Norway and the UK are both associate members of SARSAT. A local user terminal has now been established in Britain, though it is not yet complete. At present it can operate on only one of three frequencies — 406 MHz. By early 1987, it will have been upgraded to handle calls on 121.5 MHz and 243 MHz (which is linked in only to SARSAT). However, even in its present form, it is sufficiently effective. Frequency 406MHz, unlike the other two, provides worldwide coverage. Furthermore, it has been accepted by the International Maritime Organization as that on which a life-saving gadget known as EPIRB will work. This, to all intents and purposes, is a buoy fitted with radio beacons that is automatically flung overboard when a ship sinks. By transmitting signals without any human assistance, it helps to pinpoint the wreck, and thus make the task of search and rescue easier.

The principle is that ships and aeroplanes should be fitted with radio beacons tuned to transmit on the emergency frequency of 121.5MHz. The signal goes up to the satellite, which relays it to a so-called 'local user terminal' on earth. In the case of Britain, and assuming it is a maritime distress call, it is passed on to the Maritime Rescue Co-ordination Centre at Falmouth via the RAF's RCC at Plymouth. 'If,' said the Coast-guard spokesman, 'you can transmit on this frequency, the satellite — either SARSAT or COSPAS — will be able to pick you up within two hours of your transmission beginning, and, with luck, pinpoint you to within about twenty miles. Usually it is a lot more accurate than that. But if you've narrowed it down to twenty miles, you can send the long-range patrol aircraft, or ships — and, of course, if it's within their range, the helicopters can go out.'

But, to quote him again, 'the main thrust of the International Maritime Organization into the 1990s will be FGMDSS (Future Global Maritime Distress and Safety System).' In this case, not only a ship, but also its lifeboats, can be equipped to emit distress signals transmitted on high-frequency radio. 'Your ship out in the middle of nowhere, a *Titanic*, has a major disaster,' he said. 'An automatic emergency transmission will be initiated. It can be picked up by INMARSAT (or by COSPAS/SARSAT) — and there are many ships that are going to be fitted with INMARSAT terminals. There are also shore stations all round the world. We have ours at Goonhilly Down in Cornwall right next to the Naval Air Station, and near the Maritime Rescue Centre at Falmouth. Thus Falmouth will be able to take immediate action to deal with the distress.'

And, from an International Maritime Organization spokesman:

> The basic concept of the FGMDSS systems is that shore search and rescue authorities, as well as shipping in the vicinity of a distress, will be rapidly alerted and be capable of being involved in a co-ordinated rescue operation. The concept applies to all cargo ships and passenger ships on international voyages regardless of their geographical location. Additionally, the system will provide for urgency and safety communications, as well as the dissemination of navigational and meteorological information to ships.

It required a disaster of the immensity of the *Titanic* to awaken the slumbering authorities to the need for improved methods of protecting life at sea. During the decades since then, the advances have been considerable, and high tech is now involved. There is a limit, however, to what all this can achieve. Other ships can be alerted and sent to assist in a way that would have astounded Captain Lord of the *Californian*. The position of the vessel in distress can be narrowed down to a matter of yards. Even, with the advent of FGMDSS, properly equipped lifeboats and, possibly, life-rafts, will be discernible. Nevertheless, in a high wind and a rough sea, none of these things will save any lives. That can only be accomplished by the disciplined behaviour of those on board the casualty, and by good seamanship on the part of the crews of rescue ships.

The tragedy of the *Titanic* is that, apart from adequate provision of boats, none of these developments would have been necessary to have reduced enormously the score of victims. Given two hours on a calm ocean, with another vessel no more than nineteen miles away (let us discount the *Samson*), there was no reason why every survivor of the impact with the berg should not have been rescued. If anyone imagines that the colossal investment in technology reduces by one fragment the burden of human involvement, the ocean will remain as dangerous as it was in 1912. Perhaps there should be a perspex model of an iceberg in the chart room of every ship, and on the desk of every shipowner. It would be symbolic of the fact that, in the endless war between the sea and those who use it as a highway, the former always has a trump card to play when it realizes that its opponent is less than alert. There is, not to stretch fancy too far, an iceberg in all our lives — biding its time, awaiting the unguarded moment when we shall strike it.

The End of the Story

The *Titanic*'s wireless operators, though less than five hundred miles away, could communicate with the station at Cape Race only by night. Had it been possible to transmit the passengers' messages during the daytime, Jack Phillips and his colleague, Harold Bride, might have been more receptive to the flow of signals pouring in from other ships and to the warnings of the ice hazard ahead. And yet the *Titanic* was fitted with the most powerful equipment available at the time.

Wireless was something *new*. Not many more than a dozen years had passed since Marconi carried out his early experiments in the villa at Bologna. This, surely, was progress enough and yet, only thirty-three years after the *Titanic* disaster, a writer of science fiction was predicting the possibility of a system that seemed to have more in common with the stories he wrote than with anything in direct descent from the originators of radio. It did, admittedly, require another twenty years before his prophesy became a reality, but the words of Arthur C. Clarke came to pass.

Writing in the October 1945 issue of *Wireless World*, he put the proposition that it would be possible to place a satellite at a fixed point above the equator. Provided that it was at the correct height, and that its speed matched that of the earth's rotation, Mr Clarke asserted that it would, as it were, remain stationary. Furthermore, once in position, it could be used to relay telephone calls and (surely even more impressive for something conceived in 1945) television programmes.

Seventeen years later — and just half a century after the loss of the great liner — it looked as if Mr Clarke's dream might materialize. A satellite, 'Telstar', was launched into space. There were others, too, ascending to heights of 200-300 miles (320-480 kilometres). Unfortunately, once in orbit, they proved to be in rather too much of a hurry. In *A Midsummer Night's Dream*, you may recall, Puck promised to put a girdle round about the earth in forty minutes. The satellites were almost as quick: they completed the celestial circuits in a couple of hours or even less. Consequently, none of them was ever above the horizon for more than thirty minutes at a time. Not surprisingly, the aerials down below were unable to keep up with them.

By June 1965 they had got it right and there, poised over the Atlantic, was a masterpiece of literally high technology named 'Early Bird'. The world's first commercial satellite service was in business. Two years later, another became fixed in space over the Pacific and, in July 1969, the Indian Ocean followed. The coverage of the globe was complete. Although it did not come about until 1982, the system now known as INMARSAT was feasible. Appropriately, the service was inaugurated by the Marchesa Maria Cristina Marconi — widow of the maestro himself, who had died in 1937. A paltry seventy years separated the rudimentary devices used by men such as Phillips and Bride and an age in which you can dial-a-liner simply by picking up your telephone.

Anything that improves the science of communication is to be welcomed: lack of it turns a mishap into a disaster. Not only was this true of the *Titanic* herself: it was also a factor in the events that followed the sinking. For far too long, people — and they included the President of the United States and the senior management of the White Star Line — did not know whether the ship was alive or dead, let alone the fate of those who had sailed in her. When the first reports of an incident reached New York, International Mercantile Marine's Vice-President, P.A.S. Franklin, resorted to the usual rubbish about the *Titanic*'s unsinkability. In fact, it was not until 6.15 p.m. on the 15th that he knew what had actually happened, and not until 7 p.m. on that day that he made it known to the public. By this time, he had chartered a special train to take the friends and relatives of survivors to Halifax where, in common with many other people, he assumed they would be put ashore. It got as far as Boston and then turned back. Apparently the survivors were coming to New York after all. Mr Franklin had no idea of how many (or how few) there would be.

The newspapers that came out on the evening of the 15th and on the morning of the 16th did little to clarify matters: indeed, with the exception of the *New York Times*, they added to the confusion — kindling hope in many minds that should have been conditioning themselves to accept sorrow. The truth of the matter is that, like Franklin, their editors had no reliable evidence to work on.

Carr Van Anda of the *Times* was no more fortunate than the others: he was, perhaps, a better detective. They all knew that the liner had struck a berg — there was no secret about that. The truth about what happened afterwards was known only to those on board the *Carpathia*, and the *Carpathia* was strangely silent. Van Anda alone drew the conclusion that, since the *Titanic*'s wireless was no longer transmitting, the ship must have sunk. This assumption not only enabled him to print a reasonably accurate story on his front page; it also gave him time in which to plan how best to acquire a first-hand account of the disaster.

Why was the *Carpathia* not more communicative? There were several reasons. Captain Rostron was a practical man, anxious to get on with what he judged to be the first priority: bringing the survivors to New York and making it known who they were. Not the least of his problems was Bruce Ismay, now lodged in Dr McGee's cabin and obviously in a state of shock. He refused food and, mentally paralysed by the scale and awfulness of the disaster (worried, too, perhaps by his sin of having survived it), showed a reluctance to communicate. Eventually, Rostron managed to convince him that he really ought to say something. Doubtless with assistance from the captain, he dictated the following message: 'Deeply regret advise you *Titanic* sank this morning after collision iceberg, resulting serious loss of life. Full particulars later. Bruce Ismay.'

But was this sufficient? He asked Rostron's opinion, who replied tersely that it was and returned to his duties on the bridge. Later in the day, however, Ismay sent another signal — instructing the White Star office in New York to delay the impending departure of the *Cedric* and signing it YAMSI, the code-name he reserved for private communications (on second thoughts, it hardly deserves the word 'code' — as anybody can see, YAMSI is ISMAY spelt backwards). The message was dispatched at the request of the *Titanic*'s surviving officers, who preferred the idea of returning to Britain in a White Star ship.

Rostron himself probably had other reasons for saying as little as possible. Until the courts of inquiry had deliberated and announced their findings, the matter of the *Titanic* was so to speak *sub judice*. There may also have been a sense of loyalty to the reputation of that former Grand Old Man of the Atlantic, Captain Smith. Some while before the *Titanic*'s collision with the berg, Rostron had assumed that Smith would change course to avoid the icefield, and proceed more cautiously. This he judged to be the correct procedure. Smith had not done this and he had made a terrible mistake. But every man, in death as well as in life, is entitled to a fair trial. The official inquiries would assess the late master's conduct. It was not for Rostron to prejudge the matter — or to say anything that might inadvertently give a clue to his opinion.

In the *Carpathia*'s wireless office, Harold Cottam had gone without sleep for far too long and he was nearly exhausted. There was now another Marconi operator on board, Harold 'Judy' Bride, but Bride was in the ship's hospital suffering from severe frostbite. Cottam's task, apart from transmitting the brief utterances of Ismay, was to send a summary of the situation and the names of survivors to the *Olympic*, which would relay the information to Cape Race. His condition can best be gathered from remarks that crept into his messages. For example: 'I can't do everything at once. Patience, please,' and 'Please excuse sending but am half asleep.' Clearly he needed help and the only person that could assist was 'Judy' Bride. Courageously, for he must have been in considerable pain, young Mr Bride allowed himself to be carried from the hospital to the wireless shack, where he assisted the grossly fatigued Cottam.

As the Cunarder approached New York, she was met by the US navy's fast scout cruisers *Salem* and *Chester*. They had been dispatched on the instructions of the President, William Howard Taft. It would be nice to think that Mr Taft's prime concern was to gather intelligence that might allay the fears of the crowds waiting anxiously in New York for news of relatives who might or might not be still alive. In fact, his purpose seems to have been to discover the fate of one Major Archie Butt, a personal friend and a White House aide, who had been travelling in the *Titanic* (Major Butt was one of the victims). The names of some third-class survivors were, to be sure, received by the *Salem*, but the exchange of signals was not a success. According to Bride, the US Navy men were 'wretched operators', which may not have been entirely fair. Bride and Cottam were using the European version of Morse, whilst the *Salem* and *Chester* were accustomed to the American version. They were not, you might say, speaking the same language; in any case, the appalling weather was doing nothing to help the transmissions.

Throughout her voyage back to New York, the *Carpathia* was inundated with requests for information by the press. None of them were acknowledged — let alone answered. Carr Van Anda had done well to form his own conclusion and to abide by it despite the actions of his competitors. The *Times*'s banner headline on 16 April was: TITANIC SINKS FOUR HOURS AFTER HITTING ICEBERG; 866 RESCUED BY CARPATHIA, PROBABLY 1250 PERISH; ISMAY SAFE, MRS ASTOR MAYBE, NOTED NAMES MISSING. It was not entirely accurate, though the report was no more than ten minutes out in its timing of the sinking and, in general, it gave a very fair account of what had occurred.

By contrast, *The Evening Sun* led off with: ALL SAVED FROM TITANIC AFTER COLLISION and went on to allege RESCUE BY CARPATHIA AND PARISIAN; LINER IS BEING TOWED TO HALIFAX AFTER SMASHING INTO AN ICEBERG. The *Wall Street Journal* told its readers: 'The gravity of the damage to the *Titanic* is apparent, but the important point is that she did not sink. Her watertight bulkheads were really watertight.' The Boston *Globe* dispatched a reporter in the departing Cunarder *Franconia* and did rather better. At least, with assistance from the liner's Marconi operator, he managed to contact the *Carpathia* and get the number of survivors correct. He also established that they were all in their right minds (some accounts alleged that they had been driven insane by the ordeal). But this took longer.

On the far side of the Atlantic, the press were equally wild in their stories. The London *Daily Sketch*, for example, described the Allan liner *Virginian* as first on the scene, closely followed by the *Carpathia* and the *Parisian.* All the passengers, it seemed, had been taken off in lifeboats and put on board the last two ships in this trio. Meanwhile, the *Virginian* had been busy taking the *Titanic* in tow, and was last seen heading towards Halifax with her stricken charge. One of the few items of sense on a page of errors was the statement of a ship's officer in Manchester. As this mariner pointed out, 'Rocks and islands we have charted, and know their whereabouts to a nicety, but when a big iceberg comes drifting into your path in the darkness, or in a fog, there is an element of fortune as well as careful seamanship if you avoid trouble.'

Why, then were so many mistakes made? Basil Cardew, once motoring correspondent of the *Daily Express*, is reputed to have remarked in one of his more flippant moods, 'Why spoil a good story for the sake of a few facts!' Those editors of 1912 may have subscribed to this view. Here was one of the biggest disasters that had ever happened: no doubt *the* biggest to occur on the high seas and yet, in view of the *Carpathia*'s reticence, there was very little to go on. What Captain Rostron did not provide (or was it Messrs Cottam and Bride?), the imagination would have to make good. The myth of the unsinkable was fresh in their minds. Consequently it followed that, even if her hull had been rather modified by an impact with an iceberg, the *Titanic* would remain afloat. And, under these circumstances, there seemed to be no reason why another ship of suitable power should not have taken her in tow. As for all the passengers being taken off in boats, the White Star publicity material had obviously not pointed out how inadequate this line of escape was. Indeed, the American editors may well have assumed that there was enough room for everyone: in an American ship, there probably would have been. (Which does not excuse the *Daily Sketch*: it ought to have known better. But, then, everyone was so dazzled by the splendour of the new liner that such unglamorous issues as survival were apt to escape attention.)

However, before too much criticism is heaped upon the heads of these uninvestigative journals, it is necessary to consider two things: the question of the Associated Press telegram and the Marconi Connection.

To disentangle the jumble of errors behind the former is impossible at this distance, but the essentials are clear enough. Wireless was still a novelty which, unhappily, was not exclusively the province of professionals. There were already scores of amateurs listening in and, to anyone within receiving distance of Cape Race, the *Titanic* incident was a matter for considerable excitement. Whatever skills may have been required to overhear the messages do not appear to have been matched by the ability to interpret them. We go back to Holmes and his admonition that 'It is a capital mistake to theorize before one has data.' 'Data' in this instance should be qualified by the adjectives 'correct' and 'complete'. What happened was that some ham radio enthusiast picked up two signals and, omitting parts of each, blended them into one. Thus 'Is the *Titanic* safe?' And '*Asian* 300 miles west of *Titanic* and towing oil tanker to Halifax' became '*Titanic* safe — towing to Halifax'. Ironically, the tanker in question was almost certainly the helpless German ship that the liner *Baltic* had mentioned in her ice warning at 1.40 p.m. on the day that preceded the disaster.

Somehow, the Associated Press had picked it up, rashly decided that it was likely to be true, and issued it as a news flash. The *Virginian*'s role as the vessel with the *Titanic* in tow was the product, no doubt, of a similar confusion between what ought to have been the truth and what was true. Some days later, *The Times* of London condemned it as fiction 'of a very cruel and heartless kind'. The rebuke was certainly justified: facts are for checking and had a man such as the late Harold Ross, the only begetter of the *New Yorker*, been employed by Associated Press, the 'cruel and heartless' mistake would not have been committed. (Ross, it may be remembered, was the stickler for accuracy, who was apt to pencil 'who he?' in the margins of manuscripts on occasions when a particular character had not been sufficiently identified — see any one of several biographies featuring Ross, or *Who He?* by Jonathan Goodman.)

In fact, on the day following the disaster, *The Times* seems to have hedged its bets. In one edition, you could have taken your choice between a tolerably accurate account of the disaster and a hotch-potch of the *Virginian* and other works of the imagination.

The *New York Times* was a model of near-accuracy — if one overlooks the fact that it increased the number of survivors by 154. But then, this newspaper had reporters at Cape Race and Boston, and seems to have been privy to the messages from the *Olympic*. This, of course, was later to cause its editor and Marconi to be accused of collusion in what were the dawn days of chequebook journalism. There may even have been something in it. When the *Carpathia* docked at New York, one of the very few people permitted on board was Guglielmo Marconi — accompanied by ace *Times* writer Jim Speers. In return for $1,000, 'Judy' Bride described his experiences in considerable detail, and that was another scoop. The Boston *American* did reasonably well after the *Californian* was alongside her berth and the donkeyman Ernest Gill took considerable trouble to demolish the assertions made by his master, the unfortunate Captain Lord. In London, *The Times* fared rather better than any other paper in the matter of follow-up stories. Among the surviving second-class passengers was a young schoolmaster named Lawrence Beesley. Mr Beesley had scarcely set foot board the *Carpathia* than he took up his pen and set down everything he could remember about the disaster. On landing, he dispatched his account in the form of a letter to *The Times*. Later, he expanded it into a book.

William Randolph Hearst's organization was less successful. To satisfy the requirements of its readers, it chartered a large tug named the *Mary Scully* to meet the incoming *Carpathia*. Jack Binns, the hero of the *Republic*'s collision, was put in charge of the wireless; and, as a fail-safe device in case he was unable to make contact, a semaphore signalman was stationed on deck.

Fog obscured the latter, and the Cottam–Bride duo were too busy transmitting the names of survivors to heed Mr Binns's signals. The *Mary Scully* returned to port newsless.

Considering the state of radio communications in 1912, and Captain Rostron's reticence, it is, perhaps, surprising that *any* more or less accurate report of the catastrophe was printed. Nowadays, aircraft, satellites, and an abundance of press officers have opened Pandora's box: the truth, and all the evils that attend it, is exposed and no secrets are hid. Indeed, if a ship such as the *Titanic* had the decency to sink in daylight, television viewers would no doubt be able to watch death, as they say, 'live'.

As always after a disaster at sea, there was a spate of letters from the public, urging reforms or the adoption of innovations intended to ensure that such a catastrophe should not occur again. One that found its way into *The Times* (of London) was from the Hon. John Scott-Montagu who, probably more than anyone else, introduced King Edward VII to the delights of motoring. (Scott-Montagu later became the second Lord Montagu of Beaulieu; his son, the third Baron, inherited his father's love of motoring and founded the National Motor Museum.) As became an enthusiast of the horseless carriage, he suggested that ships should be fitted with headlamps, enabling their look-outs the better to detect any hazards (such as icebergs) that lay in their paths.

It seems unlikely that Scott-Montagu's letter influenced Albert Ballin, Chairman of the Hamburg–Amerika line. Nevertheless, three giants that were under construction in German shipyards were fitted with searchlights on their foremasts. There is no evidence to suggest that they were ever used to illuminate oncoming icebergs, but perhaps the passengers found them reassuring. More importantly, the lesson of the *Titanic*'s structural weakness had clearly been assimilated. The first of the three, the *Imperator* should have been launched by the Kaiser in mid-April, thus reflecting Wilhelm's determination that the *Titanic*'s reign as the largest ship in the world would be a short one. In fact, the ceremony was delayed until 25 May to allow the builders to insert an inner skin that extended to a point well above the waterline. It was tested by hoisting the pride of the Hamburg fire brigade's fire engines on board and using it to pump water from the pier-side mains into the five-foot-wide space in between. But, then, as the Battle of Jutland so convincingly demonstrated (and the operations against *Bismarck* and the *Scharnhorst* in the Second World War), the Germans had a genius for building strong ships. To take an example, at Jutland, the battle-cruiser *Lutzow* sustained twenty-four hits by heavy shells, was flooded by something like 10,000 tons of water, and yet was able to remain afloat for quite some time before having to be abandoned. The *Seydlitz*, a marginally older vessel, shipped 5,000 tons of water after fearful punishment and nevertheless managed to limp home to Wilhelmshaven in battered dignity.

Writing in the Chicago *Record-Herald*, Ben Hecht had this to say of Ismay:

> To hold your place in the ghastly face
> Of death on the sea of night
> Is a seaman's job, but to flee with the mob
> Is an owner's noble right.

Others didn't put it so eloquently, but their meaning was the same. Once free from the shackles of the courts of inquiry, the hapless head of White Star retreated to Ireland where he went to ground on his estate and remained there for the rest of his life. The dream of three super-ships that he and Pirrie had conceived that night in Belgrave Square was in a sorry state. The *Olympic*, to be sure, was soldiering on, but the *Titanic* was dead. The third, the *Britannic*, was not due to be launched until the following year. She was completed too late to serve on the Atlantic mail route. From Harland & Wolff, she sailed for the Mediterranean. She was used for bringing home casualties from the Dardanelles. On her sixth voyage, she struck a mine in the Aegean. Fortunately, there were no wounded on board; and, of her 1,100 crew, only 28 were killed. One of the survivors was Violet Jessop — a nurse who, four years earlier, had come alive out of the *Titanic* disaster.

When the White Star liner *Adriatic* was about to sail for New York, the passengers refused to go aboard until the captain had assured them that he would take a more southerly course than was usual. At Southampton, the *Olympic*'s stokers went on strike. Upon no account, their ringleader insisted, would they return to work unless they could be sure of more lifeboats. In fact, both points were soon to be taken care of by the authorities. The summer track across the Atlantic was moved sixty miles to the south, and ships would never again sail without sufficient lifeboats.

But this was not the end of the matter. The *Olympic* was almost identical in design to the *Titanic*, and if one was sinkable, so, too, must the other be. When the year was done, she was taken to Belfast where, for six months, workers toiled on her hull. When their task was completed, the watertight bulkheads reached up as far as the promenade deck. The double bottom no longer came to an end when it reached the bilges: it curved and then ascended. Afterwards, White Star announced in its advertisements:

The White Star Line's
New "Olympic"
Fitted with
DOUBLE SIDES
and additional
WATERTIGHT BULKHEADS
Extending from the
BOTTOM to the TOP
of the vessel
Will sail from New York
APRIL 12–MAY 3
and Regularly Thereafter

It was all a far cry from the myth of less than a year ago. But it was not very much more than a cosmetic job. The double sides did not go up sufficiently high, and there is room for doubt about whether, had she struck a berg under conditions similar to those of her sister, she would have remained afloat. There had never been an unsinkable ship; nor, unless some very remarkable discovery is made, will there ever be.

Cunard's directors may have told themselves that White Star need no longer be taken too seriously as a competitor. The *Lusitania* and the *Mauretania* were running a fast and reliable service between Southampton and New York, and a new ship,

the *Aquitania*, had been laid down. She would come into
service in 1914. However, they had no reason to congratulate
themselves on their good fortune. Just as the Royal Navy's
supremacy was under threat from the Kaiser's determination
to build dreadnoughts, so was Cunard's commercial supremacy
endangered by the Kaiser's insistence that Germany must have
the largest, most luxurious, liners that ever crossed the Western
Ocean. The *Imperator* and her sisters, the *Vaterland* and the
Bismarck, would provide this expression of Teutonic might.

Albert Ballin, who realized the dream, and Wilhelm II were
strange allies. The latter, as has become more and more
apparent, was anti-Semitic, and yet Ballin was a Jew. The
Kaiser was cantankerous and vain: a man who regarded
himself as second only to God — and sometimes seemed to
doubt whether, in this relationship, he really was the junior
partner. Ballin was charming, patient, and endowed with the
diplomacy that his master so noticeably lacked. Indeed, during
the years that led up to the First World War, it was he who,
whatever might happen on the Continent, tried to ensure that
there would be peace with England. Above everything, he had
style.

Three individuals played major parts in manufacturing the
ultimate in luxury for wealthy people on the move. George
Nagelmackers created the great trains — such as the Orient
Express and The Blue Train — and then built superb hotels to
ensure that arrival at the destination would not be a descent
into the second rate. A young Swiss named César Ritz, who
began his career as a waiter in Paris, perfected the concept of
hotel luxury. And Ballin made the liners. To this élite of
caterers for the élite can be added Charles Mewes, who was
responsible for the decor at posh places, and Auguste Escoffier,
perhaps the greatest chef that ever composed a menu. Ballin
was to enlist the services of Ritz, Mewes, and Escoffier.

They were not particularly pretty ships, these enormous
newcomers to the North Atlantic scene. They had none of the
grace of liners such as the *Olympic* or the *Mauretania*. Nor
were they built to break speed records. Indeed, when the
Imperator came into service, she turned out to be top heavy; the
height of her three funnels had to be reduced and extra ballast
was added. Certainly, her appearance was not helped by the

construction of a thirty-foot-long bronze version of the Imperial eagle on her bow, with the words *Mein Feld ist die Welt* engraved upon it. There is even evidence to suggest that the huge wings obstructed the views of the look-outs. Happily, nature showed its distaste for man's vulgarity. Heavy seas off Cherbourg removed the wings: on her return to Cuxhaven, the rest of this misguided adventure into heraldry was removed.

Ballin's masterpieces were not to serve the Hamburg–Amerika line for long. In spite of his efforts as a peacemaker, war erupted. Initially he opposed the torpedoing of ships with women and children on board, and air-raids on civilian targets. But, later on, his attitude hardened. Five months after the armistice, he was heard to say, 'We know our goal, our rifles cocked and traitors to the wall.' The ultimate treachery came when his fine ships were handed over to the Allies as part of the reparation process. The *Imperator* was given to Cunard and became the *Berengaria*, the *Vaterland* went to the United States Line and reappeared as the *Leviathan*; and the *Bismarck*, now called the *Majestic*, became the property of White Star (and thereby restored the situation that the loss of the *Titanic* had demolished: the ownership of the largest liner in the world). All this was too much for poor Ballin, who retired to his bed and took an overdose of sleeping tablets. If it is possible to receive compensation after death, he may have been glad to know that, when the Hamburg–Amerika line resumed business in the early twenties with very much smaller ships, the first of the new generation was named *Albert Ballin*. But she registered only 20,000 tons compared with the *Bismarck*'s 56,000 tons.

The loss of the *Titanic* has so often been described as the end of an epoch, though nobody has properly explained what that epoch was. It was certainly not the end of the moneyed traveller: during the years between the wars, there were more than enough of them to go round. It was not the end of the giant luxury liner: larger and even more luxurious ones were yet to be built. It was by no means the end of 'the old order', whatever that was. War did far more to redress the social balance than the sinking of a single ship — no matter how large the liner's casualty list. The only epoch it can take any credit for ending is that of gross negligence to do with matters concerning safety at sea; and that, surely, is not to be mourned.

During the years that separated the First from the Second World War, the old rivalries returned to the ocean. North German Lloyd re-established German might on the North Atlantic with the *Bremen* and the *Europa*. The French Line (Compagnie Générale Transatlantique) produced such fine liners as the *Ile de France* and, later, the superb *Normandie* (which died in flames at her berth in New York harbour during the Second World War); Cunard built the *Queen Mary* despite desperate financial problems, and then followed up the triumph by starting work on the *Queen Elizabeth*. In the spring and early summer, the icebergs continued to drift south from their birthplaces in western Greenland, but they found no substantial targets, and neither did storm and tempest. Smaller ships found themselves in trouble, and some of them sank. But the giants plied the ocean with impunity and the only serious casualty was a commercial one. The White Star Line eventually had to give up the economic struggle and amalgamate with Cunard, which for a while became Cunard–White Star until it discreetly dropped the second barrel of its now double-barrelled name.

The *Queen Mary*, the *Queen Elizabeth*, the *Ile de France*, and the *Europa*: they all survived the Second World War. The *Normandie* did not. The fire was the result of human negligence; but, by then, she had been taken over by the US government and renamed the USS *Lafayette*. The *Bremen* was destroyed by RAF bombs in her home port of Bremerhaven. Her sister, when the hostilities were over, was presented to the Compagnie Générale Transatlantique. The name *Europa* was erased and replaced by *Liberté*, and she became the flagship of her new owners' fleet.

After the war, the naval architects busied themselves at their drawing boards to produce a new generation of Atlantic liners. In 1950, as a response to the United States Line's appetite for power on the North Atlantic (presumably whetted by the ownership of the *Leviathan*) the *United States* was laid down. She was completed two years later. Designed for almost instant conversion into a troopship in time of war and built at a cost of $77 million, she was the fastest liner afloat (she is said to have done 40 knots on her trials) and, probably, the safest. Her hull was sub-divided into compartments like those of a warship and she was as nearly fireproof as anything that floats can be. Almost instantly, there was criticism of such extravagance. In what war, people were apt to ask, would a trooper the size of the *United States* be of any use? Hadn't the Second World War already shown that big ships were easy prey for submarines and aircraft? Perhaps it had, if you are discussing battleships. But the *Queen Mary* and the *Queen Elizabeth* had managed to survive. What is more, wars come in all sorts of sizes and where, it might be asked today, would Britain have been without the *QE2* and the *Canberra* during the Falklands Campaign? But this is academic talk: the *United States* was never required to serve as a trooper, and she never will.

In 1962, the French Line's *France* set off on her maiden voyage: and, in 1969, the *Queen Elizabeth 2* came into service (after a good deal of dithering — not least over her name. For some while when she was under construction, she was known as *Q4*, which begs all sorts of questions). But, even before the *France* had been completed, a statistic had been produced that really did mark the end of an epoch — or else foresee that the end was nigh. In 1957, the number of passengers crossing the North Atlantic in both directions by air was more than one million. For the first time, it exceeded the total of those who travelled by sea. *Punch*, as so often, could see what was coming. In one of its drawings, the *United States* was depicted in the foreground — with, overhead, an aircraft clearly marked with the name COMET on the side of its fuselage. In its wake, a vapour trail spelt out CONGRATULATIONS, SISTER. The irony of this perky comment was not to be missed.

All wars are bad, but to add nothing of benefit to the peace that follows is to compound the evil. The First World War's contribution to the wealth of nations was the development of air transport. In 1919, the newspaper tycoon Lord Northcliffe offered a prize of £10,000 to the first aviator to cross the North Atlantic non-stop. In May of that year, three United States Navy flying boats took off for the Azores. Two were lost: one got there and flew on to Lisbon. It was a commendable effort, but it did not qualify for the award. Stopping at islands such as the Azores resulted in disqualification.

On 14 June of that year, two Royal Air Force officers — John Alcock and Arthur Whitten Brown — hefted a modified Vickers Vimy bomber into the sky from a field in Newfoundland. Sixteen hours later, after experiencing some of the worse nastinesses of the North Atlantic weather, they landed on an Irish bog. It may have been a poor conclusion compared to the rapturous reception Lindbergh received when he did it solo in 1927, and when all Paris (or so it seemed) turned out to greet him. But the adulation came later, and so did £10,000 and two knighthoods. Afterwards, Brown wrote, '... sooner or later, a London–New York service of aircraft is certain to be established. Its advantages are too tremendous to be ignored for long.' (He may not have realized it, but he had just pronounced the death sentence at the very start of the *belle époque* of Atlantic liners.) To achieve it would require 'organization, capitalization, Government support, the charting of air currents, the establishment of directional wireless stations, research after improvements in the available material'.

Aeroplanes of whatever kind would, he wrote, be 'impracticable as a means of non-stop flight, because they have definite and scientific limitations of size, and consequently of lift'. Thus, on a flight of 2,500 miles, an aeroplane would have capacity for neither passengers nor freight. The answer, he concluded, had to be an airship — in which a voyage could 'be made directly from London to New York, and far beyond it, without a halt'.

Proof of this seemed to be supplied just over a fortnight after his and Alcock's flight, when the R34 (owned by the Royal Navy) flew from a base near Edinburgh to Long Island in four days, and then flew back to a field in Norfolk rather more quickly. If this difference in journey times had been more carefully observed, it might have saved quite a few lives and several heartbreaks. The truth about the North Atlantic, as any sailor knew, is that the winds storm across it in an easterly direction. To fly from America to Europe was, if not easy, at least within the scope of contemporary aviation. Attempt it from Europe to America, and you were punching strong headwinds all the way.

Britain and the United States tried airships and, with a few exceptions (such as the R100, which crossed the Atlantic to Canada and back in 1930) they ended in disaster — more often than not accompanied by the flames of blazing hydrogen. Germany was more fortunate; but, then, Germany, as personified by Count Ferdinand von Zeppelin, had more or less invented the airship.

In 1929, the *Graf Zeppelin* made her inaugural flight to New York. There was only one setback: when a rain squall ripped some of the fabric from the horizontal fin on the port side. The damage threatened to jam the elevator, which would have made the airship unmanoeuvrable. Dr Hugo Eckener — who was designer, captain and, after von Zeppelin's death in 1917, head of the company — cut back the speed and ordered a gang of riggers, led by his son, to repair the fault. That was one of the beauties of these lighter-than-air machines: you could rectify mishaps while they were in the sky. Returning from an air raid over England during the First World War, a Zeppelin engineer actually changed a piston in one of the engines when still not far from the target.

The *Graf Zeppelin* went on to run a successful service between Germany and South America. There was trouble on only one occasion, and that was not the airship's fault. A revolution was taking place down below: bullets were zipping across the airfield and it seemed injudicious to land.

Such success inspired the creation of something even larger, a monster 811 feet long intended for the Frankfurt–New York service. She was called the *Hindenburg* — though Hitler, who had recently come to power, would have preferred his own name to have been used. In this instance, as in so many others, the Nazi leader was (indirectly, at any rate) responsible for the disaster that followed. The original idea had been to use helium for buoyancy: a gas that provides less lift than hydrogen, but which is non-inflammable. Unfortunately, it cannot be obtained just anywhere. There is some in Russia, none in Europe, and plenty in Texas. When the Zeppelin company approached the United States for supplies, the US government considered the Nazi philosophy, noted its undoubtedly war-like intentions, and turned the request down. Hydrogen, no matter what its dangers might be (and the *Graf Zeppelin* had no reason to complain of them), would have to suffice.

The *Hindenburg* went into service in 1936 and performed well during her first season. In early May 1937, she set off on her first flight of the year. She encountered strong headwinds all the way: was late in arriving off the coast of New Jersey and then was delayed for another hour by a passing thunderstorm. A sudden gust of wind slammed her off-course as she approached the mooring tower, and the helmsman's rapid correction may have caused a bracing wire to snap and puncture a gas bag. In any case, minutes from the end of her journey, the *Hindenburg* unaccountably burst into flames. Within thirty-two seconds, she had been consumed by the blaze. Thirteen passengers and 22 members of the crew died; 61 people survived, which is remarkable.

Hitler dismissed the fate of the *Hindenburg* as 'an act of God' (divine disapproval for choosing the wrong name?); other theories ranged from sabotage to a discharge of electricity in the atmosphere igniting a leaking gas bag. The one certain thing is that the age of the airship died in the flames of the *Hindenburg*.

On 5 July 1937, Pan American World Airways' flying-boat *Clipper III* took off from Botwood, Newfoundland, on course for Foynes, Ireland. At the same time, Imperial Airway's flying-boat *Caledonia* flew from Southampton to Foynes, refuelled, and then set off across the North Atlantic *en route* for Botwood and thence to Montreal and New York. Captain A. Wilcockson, pilot of the *Caledonia* recalled:

> The flight was quite a thing at the time. We took about 15½ hours to get across and we had enough petrol for nineteen hours. That first trip was a bit difficult, because it was blowing half a gale at Foynes when I left, and raining as well. I had these conditions for the first 1,200 miles: the bad weather lay right along the course. It wasn't until quite early on the following morning that I was able to go up above 1,200 feet and get a starsight. I couldn't go up during the bad weather, because of the headwind — I hadn't got the range. With Grey [the pilot of the Pan Am boat] it was easier. He went up to 10,000 feet and had a marvellous crossing.

During the last two years of peace, there were several experimental flights across the Atlantic, notably by the Imperial Airway's boats *Cabot* and *Caribou*. In 1939, they made eight crossings; no passengers were carried. Pan Am was also making progress. Throughout the war, it ran a regular 'Clipper' service to Lisbon. Anyone wishing to travel on to London then had to embark in a DC3 run by KLM in exile and manned by air crews who had escaped from German-occupied Holland. Mostly, the Luftwaffe allowed the aircraft to proceed unmolested, though KLM Flight 2L272 was shot down over the Bay of Biscay on 1 June 1943. Among the victims was the actor Leslie Howard, who was returning from a tour of Spain and Portugal sponsored by the British Council.

More significant to the future of transatlantic aviation were the operations that were taking place farther north. Here, land-based aircraft were now making the crossing regularly and in large numbers. It seemed stupid to entrust the transport of Hudson and Liberator bombers from United States factories to the uncertain safety of ships on an ocean thronged with U-boats. They were, after all, perfectly capable of flying across. Thus an organization named the Air Ferry Service came into being. Having delivered their charges, the ferry pilots had to return to North America for more. Since the Battle of the Atlantic was taking place at the time, a journey by sea was highly dangerous and the authorities were unwilling to jeopardize such valuable lives. Moreover, an ocean passage took up a good deal of time. The solution was the formation of the Return Ferry Service — begun by aircrews from Imperial Airways and then, after the take-over on 1 April 1940, from BOAC (now British Airways).

The aircraft were uncomfortable and abominably cold. One passenger succumbed to frostbite, and lost all the fingers of one hand. Nevertheless, it was reliable. The eight Liberators assigned to the service gave little trouble and they also provided a means of transport for those less than very important persons whose duties took them to the USA or Canada.

Having amassed so much experience, it followed that regular air services across the North Atlantic would become a feature of post-war life. Nor was it long in coming. On 1 July 1946, an 094 Lockheed Constellation (derived from a United

States Navy transport aeroplane) left London for New York with fare-paying passengers on board. Three years later, the Boeing Stratocruiser was introduced, which was a civilian version of the B29 Superfortress (most of these immediately post-war carriers had military antecedents). It could accomplish the crossing in fourteen hours with about sixty people on board. One of its attractions was a bar that could be reached by descending a narrow staircase leading to the lower deck. In this respect, it foreshadowed the Jumbo Jet — except that, in the latter case, you have to go upstairs.

The air route across the Atlantic turned out to be remarkably safe. It was as if the sky (or was it the sea?) had assuaged its anger by consuming early pioneers who departed, usually from the European side, and never arrived. There have, of course, been exceptions. On 27 January 1948 the Avro Tudor *Star Tiger* took off from Heathrow bound for Bermuda. It was scheduled to call at Lisbon and the Azores. It carried a crew of six and twenty-nine passengers (among them Air Marshal Sir Arthur Coningham, who had commanded the 2nd Tactical Air Force during the Normandy landings in 1944). At 3.15 a.m. on the morning of the 29th, having stopped at Santa Maria for a while to refuel, the captain radioed his position as 34°35′N, 51°40′W. He expected to touch down at Bermuda in two hours' time. Owing to strong headwinds, he had been compelled to fly at a comparatively low altitude. That was the last that anyone heard of him, or of anyone else on board the aircraft, or of *Star Tiger*.

Almost exactly a year later, a second Avro Tudor, *Star Ariel*, went missing on a flight that should have ended at Santiago. The pilot landed at Bermuda on 17 January to refuel and, at 7.45 a.m., took off on the next leg — a comparatively short hop to Jamaica. Again, the disappearance was total. Twenty people died. Thereafter, Avro Tudors were withdrawn from passenger service.

Inevitably the inventive Mr Berlitz included the Avro Tudor mysteries in his collection of cases concerning the Bermuda Triangle — an expanse of water that does not stand up to serious geographical examination. Nor, come to that, are the instances quoted by Mr Berlitz entirely credible. Had any vestiges of the missing airliners been discovered, their loss would no doubt have been explained.

Star Tiger and *Star Ariel* were by no means the only aircraft to vanish from the sky into, presumably, the sea. On 1 August 1948, a six-engined French flying-boat was lost on a flight from Martinique to French West Africa. Fifty-three people died. On 23 March 1957, a USAF Douglas Globemaster disappeared. Again, the death toll was fifty-three.

On 14 August 1958, a KLM Super Constellation crashed into the sea 110 miles to the north-north-west of Ireland. Every one of the 91 people on board was killed. To those of a macabre imagination, it may be tempting to seek a parallel between this disaster and the Air India Boeing 747 that made its death plunge in June 1985. To be sure, there are common factors. In neither case was the captain able to transmit a mayday. In both cases, bodies and aircraft debris were retrieved; and, also in both, the media was quick to suggest the possibility of sabotage. Some might even try to find it more than a coincidence that both aircraft fell from the sky just over 100 miles from the Irish coast. But at this point any such speculation must cease. The Super Constellation ran into trouble many miles to the north of the Air India tragedy, and any attempt to create an 'Irish Triangle' in the manner of Mr Berlitz and his Bermuda version is doomed to failure. The inquiry that handled the KLM incident did indeed consider the possibility of a bomb, just as it speculated upon whether the aircraft might have been struck by lightning. In neither case was there any conclusive evidence. In the end, it decided that there was a strong probability that an outboard propeller had over-speeded due to oil pollution. Had the air crew been able to react sufficiently quickly, the situation might have been brought under control. The fact that they failed was not to their discredit: it was indicative of the rate at which events had occurred. Afterwards, Lockheed — manufacturers of the Constellation — re-designed certain components, and no such malfunction ever occurred again (assuming that it had happened in the first place).

The total number of lives lost in major aircraft disasters over the North Atlantic since civil flights began in 1946 is about 1,000: a figure exceeded in some instances by the destruction of just one, not necessarily very large, ship. With the exception of the Air India Boeing in 1985, there have been no mid-ocean casualties among the big jets, though the early versions of the DH Comet produced tragedy enough elsewhere. A year after the Comet I's inaugural flight to South Africa in 1952, one of them crashed near Calcutta and forty-five people died. The conditions had been particularly turbulent, and an Indian court of inquiry blamed the weather. Even so, de Havillands carried out severe tests, but no evidence of any fault in the design came to light.

On 10 January of the following year, a Comet took off from Rome Airport bound for Heathrow. Shortly afterwards, a radio message from the captain was cut short in the middle. Then, from a height of 27,000 feet, the aircraft was seen to fall from the sky at a point near Elba. One eyewitness described it as 'a blazing torch'. Thirty-five people died. The Comet fleet was grounded and more tests were carried out. Again, they revealed nothing.

A fortnight after the aircraft had come back into service, yet another disaster occurred. Again, Rome had been the point of departure; the intended destination was Cairo. At 7.05 p.m., the captain radioed his estimated time of arrival. After that, all contact with the aeroplane was lost. The toll, this time, was twenty-one. The Comets were grounded again and, four days later, the Air Registration board withdrew the Certificate of Airworthiness.

By a stroke of good fortune, a substantial part of the Comet that had crashed into the sea near Elba was recovered. At last there was some evidence to work on. It transpired that the cabin structure had failed, and that the failure had begun in the corner of a window. Having discovered the weakness, it was possible to put it right, and the career of the Comet (afterwards very successful) was resumed.

Nevertheless, it had given travellers, who were looking forward to the arrival of jets over the Atlantic, pause for thought. In fact, with a range of 3,800 miles, Comet I could never have been used on the New York service. As a British Airways spokesman told me, 'It would probably have got there in the end, but only under very favourable circumstances and with not too many passengers on board.'

Comet IV was quite another matter, and it was one of these

aeroplanes that, on 4 October 1958, took off from Heathrow and seven hours later, after a non-stop flight, landed at New York. The return trip (thirteen hours in a piston-engined aircraft) took only six hours and forty-five minutes. The Boeing 707 came on to the North Atlantic route soon afterwards. The era of the great transatlantic liner may not yet have been over, but the end was in sight.

In port, a Royal Mail liner looked as if she were just taking a brief rest. At sea, she seemed so purposeful: in a hurry to go about her business and then to return home and begin all over again (perhaps the *Titanic* had been in too much of a hurry). Brunel had been right when he envisaged Bristol as one stop on a long railway journey: the place where passengers exchanged the express train for the express ship. The same applied to Liverpool and, later, Southampton. Nowadays, trains all look very much alike; then, depending upon who owned them and the type of locomotive, you could tell one from another. Similarly, the appearances of aircraft differ only according to their types. One Boeing 747, for instance, cannot be distinguished from another — at any rate by an inexperienced eye. No doubt numbers are painted on them that convey some message; but, even if they are near enough to be seen, they have little meaning to the layman.

No two passenger liners were identical. Even given the same specifications, the behaviour of Ship A differed from that of Ship B. Some were reputed to be 'lucky'; others had a reputation for misfortune. The *Olympic* could be discerned as similar but not the same as the *Titanic*. The *Mauretania*, one of the most famous liners ever to ply the North Atlantic, held the record for the fastest crossing (and, therefore, the Blue Riband) for longer than any other ship, and was loved by pretty well everyone who sailed in her. Her career lasted from 1907 until 1935 — when she died, so to speak, in her bed. By contrast, her sister, the *Lusitania*, was mortally wounded after eight years in service. The one, perhaps, was indulged by fortune; the other certainly was not.

Nowadays, passenger ships still differ one from another — although they share a less exacting trade, and their appearances reflect the fact. The more recently built ones, designed expressly for cruising, have been created with an eye for economical fuel consumption and with the idea of keeping their lodgers amused. They look like floating holiday hotels, belonging to the age of Conrad Hilton rather than César Ritz; and, no matter how lavish the cuisine, it suggests the entrepreneurial skill of Sir Charles Forte rather than the artistry of Auguste Escoffier. Some do not look as if they *belong* in the ocean: a number actually give the impression of being top-heavy — doubtless the result of a determination to give as many rooms as possible (they don't seem to call them 'cabins' any more) a view of the sea, or the land, or whatever. They must, of course be seaworthy; there are more than enough regulations to ensure that they are — though some nations are more scrupulous in their attention to them than others. But, in most cases, they travel in calm waters and never mind that nonsense about the Bermuda Triangle — the Caribbean is crowded with cruise liners enjoying the elsewhere elusive sun. Rewarding as the myth may have been to its creator, it has had no effect upon tourism. But, then, Mr Berlitz probably never intended it to be a warning. Trips to such places as Alaska or Spitzbergen are the last resorts for those who have seen everything else.

There is, of course, nothing new about cruising. Before the war, most travellers, given the choice by circumstances, preferred to cross the Atlantic in summer. During winter months, trade declined and many of the big ships wandered off into more moderate climates with tourists on board. But, even so, the expresses had to keep running, maintaining a link that was essential and for which there was no substitute.

Laurens van der Post, in *Yet Being Someone Other*, wrote (of Cape Town harbour):

But what makes the scene so haunting is that the regular passenger ships which called at the Cape for some centuries and made the harbour a place of beauty, grace and colour every single day of the year, including Christmas and Sundays, have gone forever ... The passenger liner, bound on a distant mission and performing a regular service of great cultural value in a world scattered, separated and far-flung over seven seas, has ceased to exist ...

Cape Town harbour is, of course, by no means the only loser. Every great port is the poorer. With the passing of these elegant visitors, a glorious — if transient — architectural feature disappeared. Nothing replaced it and you have only to visit, say, Southampton to see how an area that was once romantic has degenerated into drabness.

What has happened to the survivors of this great breed of ships? The *France* despite a sit-in strike by her French crew, was sold to Norwegian owners, who renamed her *Norway* and sent her cruising. The *Queen Elizabeth* was (you might almost say) cremated in Hong Kong harbour — a fate, possibly, more dignified than that of her partner, the *Queen Mary*, which spends her declining years as a tourist attraction at Long Beach, California (surely the nearest an ocean liner can come to being confined in an old people's home?). The *United States* is, as they say, in 'mothballs' at Norfolk, Virginia. If she is to ever sail again, she will have to be given new engines — something that would cost millions of dollars. Whether such an outlay could ever be recouped seems doubtful. Even the American market for these pleasure trips, vastly bigger than any other, carries only $1\frac{1}{2}$ million passengers a year, and there are some sixty-five or seventy ships already competing for the trade. The *QE2* is, admittedly, a kind of part-timer on the North Atlantic; but she, too, has problems. Her hull is sound enough, but there are many things that require attention — not least her engines. The cost of taking her out of service and replacing them would work out at something like £50 million.*

The only regular on the Atlantic — and she too, must go cruising when the ice blocks the Saint Lawrence — is the *Stefan Batory*. It may seem strange that the flagship of a Polish owned company should be named after a king who died valiantly in combat against the Russians, but there are several anomalies. Outside Poland, for example, it is in order for the organiz-

---

*Since this was written, plans have been announced to remove the liner's present steam turbines and replace them with a diesel-electric installation. The work is to be carried out at Bremerhaven and will mean that the great Cunarder will be withdrawn from service for the better part of a year. However, it should give the ship another twenty years of life.

ation's agents to call themselves Gdynia America Shipping Lines. Inside, one has to assume, the word 'America' is looked upon with less favour, and 'Polish Ocean Lines' is used. In any case, if you want to split hairs, she does not go to America at all, but to Canada.

Built in 1952 for the Holland–America Line, the *Stefan Batory* was originally named the *Maasdam.* She was neither very large nor at all fast, but she was economical. Some years later, Polish Ocean Lines proposed to build a 20,000-ton liner to be called the *Polonia.* The project never came about: instead, in the autumn of 1968, they bought the *Maasdam.* She is still a fine ship, which runs at a profit and has a devoted following — not least among those (and there still are such people) who have a fear of flying. But she, too, is quite near to the end of her days, and it appears doubtful whether she will outlive 1986. It seems that whatever replaces her will probably travel to New York rather than to Montreal. If she is built in Poland (which is unlikely), she will be called *Polonia.* If she is purchased second-hand, she will continue to bear the proud name of *Batory.* (The *Mardi Gras* belonging to the Carnival Cruise Line Inc. — but originally Canadian Pacific's *Empress of Canada*, an 18,261-tonner built in 1961 — is one likely candidate.)

Precautions intended to produce safety at sea have improved beyond measure since the loss of the *Titanic.* They affect the construction of ships, communications, aids to navigation, and the conduct and capability of crews. In many cases, however, the implementation of the regulations depends upon what flag a vessel is flying. Some countries of registration — and Poland, in this respect, is on the side of the angels — are entirely scrupulous; others are very much less so. On 30 June 1984 the cruise liner *Sundancer* belonging to the Seattle firm Sundance Cruises Inc. was proceeding from Vancouver to Alaska. Even though she was under the guidance of a pilot, she went aground on a rock and her hull became partially flooded. Seventy passengers had to be treated for minor injuries, but all 787 aboard her were able to step ashore at Duncan Bay on Vancouver Island. A Canadian Coast Guard cutter was in attendance, and a United States Coast Guard helicopter from

Astoria, Oregon, helped to pump out the water. After a gash ten metres long in the hull had been sealed, she was taken into dry dock. Later, her owners declared her a total loss — not because the damage was irreparable, but because the bill for repairs would have exceeded the insurance value.

In July of that year, the cruise ship *Columbus C,* under charter to an Italian firm, hit a breakwater and ran aground when entering Cadiz. The engine-room was flooded, and, the vessel developed a 25° list. Nobody was hurt and, as maritime disasters go, both the *Sundancer* and the *Columbus C* have to be considered rather minor. Of more concern nowadays are oil tankers manned by incompetent, only partly trained, crews that seem hell-bent on self-destruction. Not only do they harm themselves and their ships: the oil spillages that are a conse-quence of their ineptitude put part of the environment at risk — despite the most praiseworthy attempts by coast guards and other authorities to clean up the mess. Not the least of the tragedies is that, although these vessels are equipped with aids such as radar, those responsible do not know how to use them properly. What is more, some countries — such as the Cayman Islands, Malta, Cyprus and the Bahamas — allow foreign shipowners to register under their flags. The object is to dodge legislation and taxation, but, by becoming 'flags of conveni-ence', the nations shoulder a responsibility they are unable to fulfil. They have no regard for such essentials as the inspection of ships, the checking of officers' qualifications, and for casualty investigations. Speaking to a writer from *Reader's Digest,* a former Greek master admitted that 'In five ships, I had only one second mate who was certificated, and I myself took command with only a chief officer's ticket.'

The first intimation that very large tankers, manned by incompetent personnel, might be a source of danger occurred on 18 March 1967, when the *Torrey Canyon,* carrying 120,000 tons of crude oil, crashed on to Pollard Rock — a member of the Seven Stones, which are situated some miles to the north-west of the Scillies (ironically, they are not marked on charts of the North Atlantic, but they do appear on a road atlas published by the Ordnance Survey). The weather was perfect; the ship was travelling at 17 knots, which was not excessive. There were, after all, three lighthouses within sight, plus the

Seven Stones light vessel. Any reasonable navigator should
have had no difficulty in taking the vessel safely to her destination at Milford Haven. But the Italian captain was dog-tired
and he was wildly out in his calculations. He had intended to
pass west of the Scillies; but found himself to the east of them
when his radar picked them out, and then disastrously changed
his plan. Nobody on the bridge appears to have been aware of
the reef — in spite of all its warnings. As John Fowles observes
in *Shipwreck*, 'The tragedy began with a landfall error
more characteristic of the eighteenth than the twentieth
century.'

Pollution, clearly, was now a major problem, and the United
States suffered a particularly bad attack of it in 1976, when the
Liberian-registered *Argo Merchant* ran on to the Nantucket
Shoals off Massachusetts. The tanker's back was broken and
seven million gallons of crude were discharged into the sea.
Since then, members of the United States Coast Guard have
gone aboard and examined all visiting vessels.

Running on to a shoal, or on to a rock, however, has not
been the only hazard. The 292,660-ton Greek-registered
tanker *Atlantic Express* was off the coast of Tobago in the West
Indies when, on 19 July 1979, she collided with the 210,257-
ton Liberian ship *Aegean Captain*. In the explosion that
followed, twenty-six people died. And so it goes on. Compared
to blunders on this scale, Captain Smith's strange conduct on
the night of 14 April 1912 seems the merest peccadillo.

To its credit, the International Maritime Organization has
made considerable efforts to improve matters. To quote from
one of its documents: 'The subdivision of passenger ships into
watertight compartments must be such that, after assumed
damage to the ship's hull, the vessel will remain afloat in a
stable position.' The quest for unsinkability is obviously
continuing. The IMO is also trying to establish an internationally acceptable minimum standard for the proficiency of crews.
Whether it will succeed is quite another matter. The difficulty,
as with so many other measures devised by the organization, is
to enforce them. Nor does there seem too be any great sense of
urgency among some of its member nations. An improvement
that is agreed at one of its Conventions takes years to ratify. It
is impossible to escape the conclusion that the attitude which

was really responsible for the *Titanic* disaster still exists in some quarters.

Further evidence of this was suggested on 16 February 1986, when the Russian cruise liner *Mikhail Lermontov* hit rocks and foundered off New Zealand's South Island. The cause of the accident was obviously an error of navigation; the miracle, perhaps, was that, of the 470 passengers and 330 crew aboard the 19,872-ton ship (built in 1972), there was only one casualty. The master was reluctant to ask for assistance; rain, fog and darkness did their best to frustrate the work of searchers; and yet — with the exception of this solitary man (an engineer) — everyone on board was rescued. The success was undoubtedly achieved by the promptness of other vessels in the vicinity and the fact that the accident occurred quite close to the shore. Perhaps Captain Vladislav Vorobyov remembered the *Titanic* story; at all events, the ship's orchestra played on almost to the end.

That a liner steaming off a well-charted coast and with a pilot on board should be lost in 110 feet of water may be sufficiently disturbing. However, if the *Daily Telegraph* is to be believed, there was another worrying feature. The *Mikhail Lermontov* was equipped with sufficient lifeboats — of that there can be no question. The matter at issue concerns the condition of them. In the *Telegraph*'s account, a naval officer was said to have observed that 'many of the lifeboats ... were so rotten that survivors holed the hulls with their feet'. Several of the inflatable rafts had refused to open; a number of engines in the boats were unserviceable; and the lights on several life-jackets found in the water were out of action. Nor had the instructions on pieces of recovered rescue equipment been translated into English. The inevitable conclusion must be that, if there had not been other ships close to hand, there would have been a quite considerable toll of casualties. Put another way, it is useless to have adequate lifeboat accommodation if it is not properly maintained.

One hazard, however, does appear to have been overcome: ice. In the spring and in summer, the bergs migrate from their calving grounds in western Greenland and wander south. But never again is one likely to find a prey such as the *Titanic*. People travel in smaller parcels, such as aeroplanes; the big ships steam towards a brighter sun — coming alive in the very waters where the bergs die. Nevertheless, the symbol offered by the great liner's killer has never melted away. As latter-day calamities show so well, the ocean is always waiting to catch the unwary: the cost of negligence is disaster.

Fourteen years before the *Titanic* sank, a writer named Morgan Robertson wrote a book entitled *Futility*. It gave a fictional account of a liner named the *Titan* (4,000 tons larger than her near-namesake) which was considered to be unsinkable. After running down a sailing ship and making no effort to pick up survivors, the *Titan* receives her come-uppance when she strikes an iceberg and sinks. There is plenty of adventure and romance; but, stripped to its essentials, and leaving out the bit about the sailing ship, there is an uncanny similarity between the fiction and the fact. Indeed, there are many who prefer the true story, which is certainly more moving.

Were Mr Robertson alive today, he might consider writing another tale, borrowing a few ideas from Herman Melville. In this, Captain Smith would survive the sinking, leave White Star, and purchase a second-hand gunboat with his savings. He would then devote the rest of his life to searching for a particular iceberg with a line of red paint on one side of its base. Discovering it at last, he would pepper it with shot — to no avail. The conclusion, perhaps, would be his death from disappointment: his realization that (having read *Moby Dick*, let us say) an iceberg is even harder to destroy than a great white whale. As in most things to do with the ocean, nature will have the final say-so. The berg's life will end — in its own good time. But that end will be as spectacular as anything a novelist could invent.

Afterword

It says somewhere that the Atlantic assumed an approximation of its present size and shape about 43 million years ago — and then after many upheavals and revisions. Man has been using it as a highway for less than five hundred years. Thus, in the case of humanity versus the ocean, the latter must be accounted the more experienced opponent. It is, however, handicapped by the fact that its methods do not change. It relies on storm and tempest, fog, dangerous shores on either side, and a litter of icebergs. Mankind, whilst sometimes committing the most appalling mistakes, nevertheless manages to devise the means to make the crossing of this unquiet immensity progressively safer.

To estimate the number of lives lost to the North Atlantic's anger — even during the past 150 years — is impossible. Between 1840 and 1893, 7,523 people perished in 125 steamship disasters. Add to this the casualties of the *Titanic* and *Volturno*, and the figure falls not far short of 10,000. This does not include those who died of fever in the plague ships that carried nineteenth-century emigrants — the ocean, after all, was not to blame for them. And it does not take into account the 1,024 who perished when the *Empress of Ireland* sank in the St Lawrence on 29 May 1914. The forces of nature had nothing to do with that.

Whether it is fair to include the 129 who were lost on 10 April 1963, when the nuclear submarine USS *Thresher* failed to surface after a test dive 220 miles east of Cape Cod, seems unlikely. It was surely due to a mechanical failure. War and the

271

instruments of war do not indeed have any place in this narrative. Thus, in this scoreboard of disaster, we should not include the *Lusitania*'s 1,198 victims, or (worse still) the 4,000 or so who died when HM Troopship *Lancastria* was sunk by enemy action off St Nazaire on 17 June 1940. They simply serve to show that, as an agent of death, man himself is superior to the ocean.

This book has been based upon the *Titanic* — a subject that, some critics will probably protest, has already been more than sufficiently covered. Perhaps: but still its grim fascination endures. When, quite recently, a troupe of strolling players enacted the drama on a site in London's dockland, they played to capacity audiences. The inability to escape its thrall may become more understandable when one considers the scale of things. The awful coincidence of the liner and the iceberg being in the same place at the same time put an end to 1,490 lives. This represents not quite half, but certainly one quarter of what we may perhaps call the North Atlantic's personal victims.

When, in 1985, the mortal remains of the liner were discovered, the excitement was considerable. At least one survivor pleaded that the dead should be allowed to remain in peace and so should their tomb. Dr Ballard, the expedition's leader, was in accord with this attitude. Nevertheless, the bounty hunters were alerted. Exactly how much bounty there is to be hunted is still unknown. Early reports had it that de Beer diamonds to the value of £5 million were in her safe. Then this sum increased to £120 million — possibly taking into account the declining value of the pound between 1912 and 1985. However, this line of speculation was concluded by an announcement by de Beer that, in fact, there were no diamonds at all. No one was certain about to whom the wreck belonged, either. The Commercial Union insurance group made vague noises about owning the wreck, and then had second thoughts. When, under government pressure, Cunard took over the White Star Line in 1934 was the *Titanic* included in the latter's assets? It seems unlikely, but nobody could say for sure. And then, of course, there were the personal possessions of the passengers: to whom did they now belong? In this context, the question was important. For want of de Beer diamonds, they appeared to be the most valuable items capable of recovery. Again, there was no clear-cut answer.

Such small problems did little to deter the lunatic fringe of the salvage business. Selling fragments of the ship herself could turn out to be a prosperous, if rather nasty, industry. One scheme, using flotation bags, was considered promising — on the doubtful grounds that it had been employed successfully to raise a converted trawler (the Greenpeace Movement's flag-ship, *Rainbow Warrior*) from Auckland harbour some weeks previously. The fact that the water here is rather less than two and a half miles deep, and that the size of a trawler is not to be compared with that of the *Titanic,* seemed to be irrelevant. Another notion was to enclose the ship within a shell of ice (for reasons that I do not understand, nitrogen was to be the freezing agent); and yet another had something to do with the use of molten wax (again the reader's indulgence is asked for lack of explanation). The more sober end of the salvage business clearly regarded all such projects as ridiculous. This, plainly, was a very sick wreck, and the probability of its ascending intact through more than 13,000 feet (let alone what might happen when it received its first exposure to fresh air for seventy-three years) was too remote to be worth consideration.

Of all the projects, the most worthy of note strikes me as that involving ice — not because it conjures up the notion of a bold and innovative approach (though it does), and not because there is a pleasant logic that the devil of destruction should be changed into the angel of deliverance, but because it is the most romantic. If one read a report in the London *Standard* correctly, the idea was inspired by the behaviour of a can of beer and some ice in a bath. The can sank, but the ice floated. This gave the prospective beer drinker, a Welsh gentleman named John Pierce, cause for thought. If he succeeded, he decided, the *Titanic* in her second incarnation should be towed back to her builders' yard at Belfast. She would then be completely restored — in the manner of the Orient Express — and dispatched from Southampton on the date of her original departure. With a bit of luck, she would reach New York and thus conclude the voyage that was so rudely interrupted. Mr Pierce is clearly an above-average dreamer.

However: to the point. One man does seem to have benefited from the publicity attending the discovery of the wreck — Captain Smith; or, rather, his memory. A statue of this unfortunate mariner had been intended for display outside the town hall of his birthplace, Hanley in Staffordshire. But the city fathers, judging his performance on that disastrous voyage to have been less than excellent, rejected it. Consequently, and inexplicably, it was exiled to a park in Lichfield, thirty-five miles away. Quite how the finding of the long-lost liner's remains can have redeemed Smith's reputation is by no means obvious. But Hanley was quick to claim what it believed to be its own, while Lichfield, having afforded sanctuary for so long, was adamant in its refusal to give it up.

Finally, to suggest that raising the *Titanic* would be a victory for man versus the ocean is rubbish. That battle has already been lost (or won, if you view it from the latter's point of view). Several other ships passed without hindrance through the icefield during that April night in 1912. The North Atlantic, with a nice sense of discernment, chose the greatest prize. No matter what may happen in the future, nothing can deny it and its agent, the iceberg, that awful triumph.

APPENDIX A

Satellites and Systems

METEOSAT: a meteorological satellite controlled by the European Space Agency that has its headquarters at Darmstadt in West Germany. Stationed at a height of 36,000 kilometres (roughly 22,320 miles), its orbit coincides with the speed of the earth's rotation. Thus it is positioned permanently at a point above the equator.

NOAA7 and NOAA8: United States meteorological satellites that pass over the north and south poles at heights varying from 700 kilometres to 1,500 kilometres — or, roughly, 435 to 932 miles (they are closest to earth when travelling over the poles). NOAA stands for 'US National Oceanic and Atmospheric Administration'.

INMARSAT: The International Maritime Satellite Organization (hence INMARSAT) took over from MARISAT in February 1982. It enables radio signals to be transmitted to a satellite and thence relayed to a station on earth — thus overcoming the problems of the ionosphere and static, and relieving the congestion on more conventional radio facilities. By no means all ships are equipped to use it.

SARSAT: Search and Rescue Satellite-Aided Tracking, to give it its full name, began as a joint venture with the USA and Canada in partnership — soon afterwards joined by France — and with Norway and the UK as associates. Ships and aeroplanes are fitted with radio beacons transmitting on 121.5MHz. The distress signal goes up to the satellite, which relays it to a 'local user terminal' on earth. It is then passed on to a Maritime Rescue Co-ordination Centre. SARSAT provides an accurate position of the casualty, and thus speeds up the rescue operation.

COSPAS: The Russian equivalent of SARSAT. The two systems were developed jointly and operate together.

AMVER: Automated Mutual Vessel Rescue System. It is run by the United States Coast Guard from a centre on Governor's Island in New York harbour. Before setting out, a captain files details of his trip and any other relevant information — such as the radio watch schedule and whether he has a doctor on board. Thereafter, he reports any changes of course or speed. Using methods based on dead reckoning, a computer on Governor's Island can trace the ship's location throughout its voyage. This information is at the disposal of any recognized search centre of any nation — taking the form of a computer-predicted print-out listing all the vessels in the vicinity of a casualty, and giving details of their rescue capabilities.

FGMDSS: Future Global Maritime Distress and Safety System. As its name implies, this is for the future. A vessel equipped to use it will, if in distress, automatically transmit a signal that will be picked up by INMARSAT or SARSAT/COSPAS and relayed to the appropriate Maritime Rescue Co-ordination Centre. Lifeboats and life-rafts will also be equipped to use it. In addition, it will disseminate navigational and meteorological information.

APPENDIX B

The Disasters

The disasters listed here are only those mentioned in this book. With the exception of the *Lusitania*, they do not include wartime losses — nor do they take into account the victims of aircraft crashes. Thus they are no more than a fraction of the price exacted by the North Atlantic for its so-called 'conquest'. They are merely intended as a guide for the reader.

1854 On 27 September the Collins liner *Arctic* collided with the French steamer *Vesta* 65 miles south-west of Cape Race, Newfoundland. 322 were killed.

1856 The *Arctic*'s sister, *Pacific*, disappeared on 23 January when on passage to New York. The presumed cause was collision with an iceberg. 186 died.

1859 The *Royal Charter* was wrecked off the Anglesey coast during a severe storm on 25 October. 438 were killed; 18 survived.

1873 On 1 April the White Star liner *Atlantic* ran on to rocks off Meagher Island near Halifax, Nova Scotia. 637 died; among the 414 survivors, there were no women and only one child.

1875 The *Schiller* ran aground on a reef near the Scilly Islands on 7 May. Only 43 of the 372 on board survived.
   On 6 December the German liner *Deutschland* grounded on the Kentish Knock in the North Sea. 157 were drowned; 155 rescued.

1879 The *Arizona* hit an iceberg head-on; but the collision bulkhead withstood the impact, and the liner was able to steam stern-first to St John's, Newfoundland.

1886 On 11 March the liner *Oregon* collided with a schooner off Fire Island when approaching New York. The *Oregon* was lost but there were no human casualties.

1898 The liner *Bourgogne* collided with the British sailing ship *Cromartyshire* 60 miles off Sable Island and sank within a few minutes. Of the 600 on board, 571 died.

1907 The *Suevic* ran ashore on the Lizard, Cornwall, and the *Jebba* smashed on to the rocks at the foot of Bolt Tail, Devon. Both events occurred on 17 March. In neither were there any casualties, and the *Suevic* (or most of her) actually lived to sail again.

1909 The liner *Republic* collided with the *Florida* on 23 January in the vicinity of the Ambrose light vessel. The *Republic* sank, but there were only four casualties on each ship. Currently there are plans to salvage the liner.

1910 The Cunarder *Slavonia* ran on to rocks two miles south of Flores in the Azores. There were no casualties, but the *Slavonia* was a write-off.

1912 On 14 April, the *Titanic* hit an iceberg when nearing the Grand Banks. 712 were rescued; 1,490 died.

1913 The *Volturno* was destroyed by fire in mid-Atlantic on 9 October. 521 of the 657 on board were rescued.

1914 The CPR liner *Empress of Ireland* was rammed on 29 March by the Norwegian collier *Storstad* in the St Lawrence. 1,024 died; 458 were rescued.

1915 On 7 May the Cunarder *Lusitania* was torpedoed by the U-20 ten miles south of the Old Head of Kinsale, Ireland. Of the 1,198 casualties, 124 were American citizens.

On 7 September, the former White Star liner (now serving

with the Royal Navy) *Oceanic* ran aground of the Shaalds of Foula, Shetland. There were no casualties, but the ship was a total loss.

1928 The *Vestris*, one day out from New York on passage to Buenos Aires, foundered in rough seas on 12 November. 110 were drowned. Of the 85 who were rescued, only eight were women and there were no children among them.

1934 The cruise liner *Morro Castle* was destroyed by fire off the coast of New Jersey on 8 September. 133 of the 455 on board were killed.

1956 The Italian liner *Andrea Doria* collided with the *Stockholm* off Nantucket Island on 25 July. 52 of the 1,706 on board were killed.

1959 On 29 January the Danish ferry *Hans Hedtoft* was lost after hitting an iceberg in stormy seas 37 miles off Cape Farewell, Greenland. All 93 passengers and crew were drowned.

1963 3 August: the Yugoslav freighter *Kastela* was lost with all hands after hitting a berg in the Hudson Strait.

19 December: the Greek cruise liner *Lakonia* was destroyed by fire to the north of Madeira. 128 died (95 passengers and 33 crew).

20 December: the Marseille-registered freighter *Douala* foundered in heavy seas off Newfoundland. Eight lives were lost.

Index